Capitalism and Class in the Middle East

Theories of Social Change and Economic Development

By the same author
Weber and Islam
Marx and the End of Orientalism
The Dominant Ideology Thesis (with N. Abercrombie and S. Hill)
For Weber
Confession (with M. Hepworth)
Religion and Social Theory

Capitalism and Class in the Middle East

Theories of Social Change and Economic Development

Bryan S. Turner
Flinders University of South Australia

Heinemann Educational Books · London
Humanities Press · New Jersey

Heinemann Educational Books Ltd
22 Bedford Square, London WC1B 3HH
LONDON EDINBURGH MELBOURNE AUCKLAND
HONG KONG SINGAPORE KUALA LUMPUR NEW DELHI
IBADAN NAIROBI JOHANNESBURG
EXETER (NH) KINGSTON PORT OF SPAIN

ISBN 0 435 82893 2

First published 1984

ISBN 0-391-03055-8 (Humanities Press)

Printed in Great Britain

Contents

Acknowledgements

Chapter 2 appeared originally in *Science and Society*, vol. 38, 1974. Chapter 3 was first published in the *British Journal of Sociology*, vol. 25, 1974. Chapter 4 is taken from *Arab Studies Quarterly*, vol. 1, 1979. Chapter 5 was published in *Social Compass*, vol. 25, 1978. Chapter 6 is based on sections from *Marx and the End of Orientalism*, London, 1978. Chapter 7 first appeared in *Science and Society*, vol. 40, 1976. Chapter 8 is based on Elizabeth Miller's thesis (in progress) 'Jewish–Christian relations in modern Israel', University of Aberdeen. Chapter 9 was originally published in Georg Stauth (ed.) *Iran: Precapitalism, Capitalism and Revolution*, Saarbrucken, 1980. Chapter 10 draws substantially on Dr Bazlul Chowdhury's doctoral thesis 'A sociological study of the development of social classes and social structure of Bangladesh' (University of Aberdeen, 1982). I am particularly grateful to David Hill for his editorial assistance in bringing these articles together to form a coherent perspective on the Middle East.

1 Social Statics and Dynamics

> Immutability is the most striking characteristic of the East; from the ancient strife of Cain and Abel, to the present struggle between the Crescent and the Cross, its people remain in their habits of thought and action less changed than the countries they inhabit.
>
> Eliot Warburton, *The Crescent and the Cross* (1844)

> The moment of the rose and the moment of the yew-tree
> Are of equal duration. A people without history
> Is not redeemed from time, for history is a pattern
> Of timeless moments.
>
> T. S. Eliot, *Four Quarters* (1944)

In nineteenth-century sociology, it was generally agreed that the analysis of social phenomena involved two separate activities. The first was social statics, by which sociology would develop typologies of social systems in terms of their necessary conditions of existence and the interdependency of their parts. Social dynamics concerned the analysis of the historical development of social systems in order to arrive at general laws of social evolution. In social dynamics, evolution came to be defined in terms of increasing structural differentiation and higher levels of social integration by which social systems adapted to their environments. Both the distinction between statics and dynamics, and the conception of evolution as differentiation clearly indicate the impact of social Darwinism on social theory. The use of biological analogies, the adoption of a scientific terminology from physics and the confidence in positivism also point to the centrality of 'progress' in nineteenth-century social thought.[1] In classifying social progress, it was common either to see history in terms of stages or to think in terms of some decisive social transition. In the thought of Herbert Spencer,[2] the critical shift in human history was from 'militancy' to 'industrialism', which involved a transition from societies based on egoism and conflict to ones organised in terms of altruism and co-operation. In the thought of Emile Durkheim,[3] this transition was from mechanical solidarity (based on shared belief systems and common rituals) to organic solidarity (based on social reciprocity developing out of a complex division of labour). Similar nineteenth-century theoretical dichotomies (status/contract, sacred/profane, traditional/rational) point to an underlying confidence in historical progress and social teleology.[4]

Although these evolutionary theories were in principle relevant to the history of all human societies, social theory tended to make a sharp distinction between the dynamic character of Occidental societies and the stationary nature of Oriental societies. It was very widely assumed that the social and economic structure of Asiatic societies was different from that of western societies; it was argued that Asiatic societies lacked the institution of private property, a middle class and progressive religious views. As a result, economic stagnation was typically combined with political despotism. This theory, which was prominent in British utilitarianism, can be traced back to French debates about royal absolutism in the seventeenth century. However, an interest in the nature of 'Oriental Despotism' was particularly important in the nineteenth century because the expansion of European colonialism on a global scale served to sharpen the contrast between the industrial societies of the West and the apparently stagnant civilisation of the East. Since what characterised the Orient was, in the words of the romantic Eliot Warburton, its 'immutability', the causes of social change in Oriental societies would have to be exogenous. Western science and technology were the only means by which the East could be revolutionised, since its endogenous culture was either corrupt or imitative. Colonial control over these societies was not only inevitable, but morally desirable. Colonialism was not so much an act of political oppression, but a civilising mission.[5] The contrast between economic growth and stagnation, between parliamentary democracy and Oriental Despotism was also a contrast between rationality and irrationality. The Oriental mind was sensuous, exotic, childish and imaginative, but incapable of rigorous and rational thought. Ernest Renan, who is credited with the invention of philology and anti-semitism, in 1883 referred in a lecture at the Sorbonne to the fact that anybody familiar with Islamic societies would recognise the 'inferiority of Mohammedan countries, the decadence of states governed by Islam, and the intellectual nullity of the races that hold, from that religion alone, their culture and their education'.[6] Islam was an 'iron circle' around the head of believers that ruled out creative thought and scientific advancement. Secularism and industrialism were necessary conditions for Oriental development; both ingredients were supplied by European colonialism.

Although these positivistic aspects of early theories of social change have been seriously challenged by contemporary sociologists,[7] it can be argued that structural functionalism, which dominated sociology in the 1960s, embraced most of the fundamental assumptions of Spencerian evolutionism. The original distinction between statics and dynamics became a basic feature of functionalist typologies of systemic reciprocity and analyses of structural differentiation. Functionalism often explicitly adopts an evolutionary perspective on social change and recognises the importance of biological functionalism for the development of sociological theory.[8] The general characteristic of social change from a functionalist perspective is the increasing social differentiation of social systems,[9] as a result of which the system is said to adapt to its environment. Within the sociology of development, this functionalist perspective on social change became closely identified with theories of modernisation, which analysed development in terms of a dichotomy between tradition and modernity. The modernisation process itself was unilinear and the end product was a secular, pluralistic, urban and literate democracy. Modernisation may be blocked periodically by the stubborn resistance of traditional institutions and values, but the global march of modernity is inexorable. Societies undergoing the painful process of development may get out of step and the contradictions between their modern and traditional sectors create both social and psychological conflicts.[10]

Functionalism in general and the modernisation thesis in particular have been subject to massive criticism. Critics claimed that functionalism was poorly equipped theoretically to offer convincing explanations of social change (especially revolutionary conflict) because of its concentration on questions relating to social equilibrium.[11] Functionalism explains social change as immanent within the social system and consequently neglects exogenous sources of change. Modernisation theory was specifically criticised because it could not adequately explain the social backwardness of certain peripheral societies despite (or because of) the application of modernisation policies and reforms. The teleological assumptions of modernisation arguments were also noted,[12] which in fact equated modernisation with westernisation. Finally, it was criticised as a white-wash which obscured the brutal facts of western exploitation; the real cause of Third World underdevelopment was located, not in the backward mentality of peasants, but in the unequal exchange that exists within the global pattern of production and trade.[13]

In recent years, therefore, the sociology of development and, more broadly, the analysis of social change have been increasingly influenced by contemporary Marxist thought. The paradox of this influence is, however, that these theories are self-consciously neo-Marxist rather than Marxist; they involve fundamental departures and revisions of the explanations of change offered by Marx and Engels. Contemporary attempts to apply Marx's theory to the analysis of peripheral social formations and Third World underdevelopment have exposed certain problems and ambiguities in Marx's explanation of social change in terms of transitions between modes of production. Two issues can be mentioned here. The first is that Marx and Engels, in the concept of the Asiatic mode of production, treated the Orient as static.[14] The absence of private property in land and the self-sufficiency of the village economy in the Orient meant that class divisions did not develop and hence the motor of history was absent in Asia, where the state held the population in a condition of general slavery. Marx and Engels inherited and embraced many of the assumptions that typify Orientalism.[15] Secondly, in so far as Marx regarded socialism as an inevitable outcome of the historical development of human society, then Marx's theory of social change is teleological and evolutionary.[16] This critical probing into Marx's account of social change has in fact opened up a number of more general theoretical difficulties in conventional Marxism. One issue is that between explanations of the general character of a social formation by reference to the predominant form of class conflict and explanations of the transition of modes of production in terms of systemic contradictions between relations and forces of production. The analysis of modes of production suggests a far more deterministic and evolutionary account of history than the analysis of class conflict at a particular conjuncture. This difficulty is particularly acute in Althusserian Marxism, which has had a significant effect on recent attempts to formulate a 'scientific' theory of change.

TURNER

Although this collection of articles is overtly about the nature of social change and social structure of Middle East societies under the impact of capitalism, they raise covertly a number of basic issues in the theoretical analysis of societies. These theoretical issues emerge in relation to two questions which inform the articles in this collection. The first concerns the analytical relationship between Marx and Weber. In general, I argue that there is little to choose between Marxist and Weberian approaches to precapitalist societies, in particular to Islamic precapitalism. It is true that Marx approached the stationariness of Islamic society in terms of economic relations of production by stressing the peculiarities of property ownership in the Middle East and Asia; Weber emphasised, by contrast, the importance of military and political organisation. Despite these differences, their perspectives converged on the notion of social stagnation as the essential feature of Islamic history. Furthermore, their analysis of Asia provided a theoretical pretext for the analysis of western social development. These essays are thus opposed to any sharp separation between Marxist and Weberian sociology, a separation which has provided the context for much sterile debate. The second theoretical issue concerns the problem of explaining social change from a structuralist perspective. Although the structuralist analysis of modes of production was developed partly as a response to the persistent teleology of conventional Marxism and partly as a response to reductionism, structuralism often appears far too abstract to give any account of actual changes in the political and social organisation of modern societies. These essays are thus addressed to the problem of reconciling two Marxist approaches to social change, in which change is either brought about contingently by class conflict or structurally by the contradictions within the mode of production. Although this contrast is often regarded as a modern development in Marxism, especially in the work of Louis Althusser, it is in fact endemic in Marx's own approach to history.

In *German Marxism and Russian Communism*, John Plamenatz outlined a series of philosophical difficulties in Marx's historical materialism and, although his analysis has been superseded in many respects by recent evaluations of Marxist theory, many of his critical comments are still pertinent to contemporary issues in Marxist analysis. For example, Plamenatz suggested that it is possible to interpret Marx as claiming either that social revolutions are the consequences of contradictions between the forces and relations of production or that the revolutionary restructuring of society is caused by class struggles. In the first version of historical materialism, social classes are effects of economic changes; as Plamenatz expressed it, materialism 'explains class conflicts as effects of something more "fundamental" than themselves'.[17] In the second version, classes are not effects but causes of social change; it is class conflicts 'which both cause the contradictions between the "forces" and "relations of production" and resolve them'.[18] This apparent contradiction between treating social classes as either effects of changes in the economic structure of society (relations/forces of production) or causes of changes in modes of production is closely associated with the precise nature of determinism in Marxist theory, that is with the general answer offered by Marxism to the place of human agency and intention in social change. In this introductory chapter, I shall attempt to show how this theoretical problem is reproduced in the work of contemporary 'structuralist' Marxism, particularly in the theories of Nicos Poulantzas, and to argue that the solutions offered by 'structuralists' are inadequate. This theoretical dilemma, which has profound political implications, can be characterised as a conflict between the explanation of revolution via social-class analysis and the explanation of structural crises via mode of production analysis.

The early work of Poulantzas, especially *Political Power and Social Classes*,[19] appears to offer an explicit deterministic theory of modes of production in which social classes are the effects of three structures or 'instances' (political, ideological, economic). Although modes of production are treated as 'articulated combinations' of the three levels, the economic level is still invested with a certain primacy in that it determines which of the three levels will be dominant. For example, in feudalism the economic determines that ideology (in its religious form) will be dominant. Poulantzas thereby attempts to provide a theoretical scheme by which certain problems in Marxist theory (base and superstructure, determination by the economic in the last instance, economically determined classes) can be resolved. Poulantzas's treatment of modes, social formations and classes does not, however, represent any abandonment of determinism; the theory is not multi-causal, multi-factorial or causally indeterminate. It might be said that the theory offers an elaboration and specification of the conventional notion that 'the base determines the superstructure'; complex determinism replaces simple determinism. Poulantzas's commitment to deterministic science in *Political Power and Social Classes* is closely connected with the emphasis on the *structure* of social formations, rather than on the characteristics of *individuals* – their intentions, attitudes and beliefs. This feature of his theory was underlined in the debate with Ralph Miliband, whose account of the state was held to exhibit the analytical weakness of the 'problematic of the subject'. Miliband treated classes and political structures as ultimately reducible to interpersonal relations between members of social groups. By contrast, Poulantzas claims that his theory regards the state and classes as 'objective structures' in a 'system of regular connections'.[20] From this Marxist perspective, individuals are not causally significant; men (or as Poulantzas refers to them, 'agents') are merely bearers (*träger*) of objective structures of social formations, which are determined by modes of production. Whereas sociology is an ideological practice because it fails to make an epistemological break with common-sense assumptions concerning the causal significance of human agency, Marxism (specifically, historical materialism) is a deterministic science whose theoretical object is not men but modes of production.

This adherence to structural determinism in *Political Power and Social Classes* clearly illustrates the general dependence of Poulantzas's theory on the work of Louis Althusser. The early work of Marx is rejected as a proper basis for a Marxist science of modes, since the writing of the 'young Marx' was itself locked within a problematic of the subject. This recognition of the crucial scientific significance of *Capital* entailed a rejection of the humanism of the *Theses of Feuerbach* and *The German Ideology*. It also involves an implicit criticism of the analysis of social classes and economic base in, for example, *The Communist Manifesto*. The view that social classes are the effects of the complex determination of the three structures is not easily reconciled with the economic definition of classes, the technological determinism by which the contradiction between forces and relations of production is characterised or with the claim that 'The history of all hitherto existing society is the history of class struggle' in the *Manifesto*. The idea that social revolution is most likely in the most developed capitalist societies where the bourgeosie digs its own grave through the unintentional creation of a disciplined and concentrated working class is jettisoned by Althusser and Poulantzas in favour of Lenin's views on 'conjunctures'. In *For Marx*, Althusser argues that revolution is never simply the outcome of 'the beautiful contradiction of Capital and Labour', but rather the determined consequence of a 'ruptural conjuncture' of contradictions.[21] The multiple contradictions of these conjunctures involve contradictions within the imperialist links between social formations, contradictions between modes of production within social formations and finally class contradictions. This view of revolutions not only implies that revolutions are characteristic of the margins or weakest links of capitalism; it also carries with it a clear rejection of the teleological and historicist implications of conventional Marxism. Socialism is not the inevitable outcome of the unfolding of some essence of capitalism; there is no historical ladder up which all societies must inevitably move. The anti-teleological views of Althusser and Poulantzas are directed against various forms of economic reductionism ('economism'), rather than against determinism. For example, Poulantzas, whose views on specific aspects of this problem have been directly influenced by the analyses of Charles Bettelheim, wants to draw attention to certain problems in transitional periods where the dominance of one mode in a social formation is replaced by some other mode.[22] A change in the dominance of modes does not bring about an automatic change in politics and ideology, since the economic is not the sole factor. Indeed, the capitalist mode of production may conserve elements from the feudal mode of production after capitalism has become the dominant mode of a given social formation. Poulantzas's elaborated determinism does not, by rejecting teleological theories, thereby open a back-door for human agency or voluntarism.

Uncompromising determinism does, however, traditionally create a range of crucial problems of a basically political nature. If men are determined by forces or structures which exist independently of their wills, outside their control and probably beyond their comprehension, then what is the point of organising men for political action? Does the conscious activity of Communists merely aid the progress of social transformation or does it merely underline existing contradictions? It may be that social-class analysis is less disconcerted by this apparent dilemma than the mode-theoretical approach, since the former might claim that, if class conflict changes society, then it is important to organise men in terms of class consciousness, revolutionary ideologies and political parties. If, according to mode of production analysis, classes are simply effects of the determination of three objective structures, then what happens to conventional Marxist interest in political struggle? Poulantzas attempts to cope with this issue in a variety of ways, but the overall effect of these conceptual adjustments is to weaken the claims of mode of production analysis, if not to abandon them altogether. Poulantzas, for example, makes a distinction between structures and practices. Although the mode determines the class structure, these structures set the limits within which class practices take place. Thus, political practice involves the leadership of the class struggle within and for the control of the state apparatus. Such an interpretation would make it difficult to distinguish Poulantzas's science from the so-called ideology of sociology or political philosophy. For example, Steven Lukes's three-dimensional theory of power, in which human agency is exercised within the interstices of given structures, bears a close formal relationship to

Poulantzas's distinction between structures and class practices.[23] A similar distinction is made by Poulantzas between class places which are determined by structures and class positions which are associated with unique historical exigencies. Thus, the class place of the labour aristocracy was determined by the structures of the capitalist mode of production, but its class position, namely an alliance with the bourgeoisie, was the consequence of the peculiar features of the British social formation at a given point in the development of the capitalist mode of production. It is conceivable that the determinism of mode of production analysis is compatible with the view that political practice has an effect on structural change by making a distinction between the abstract analysis of modes at the level of theory and the application of that analysis in the case of concrete social formations. One implication of Poulantzas's position would be that the abstract analysis of modes should not be (indeed could not be) a substitute for the comprehension of specific conjunctures of contradictions within a concrete social formation. For example, Poulantzas denies that there was such a thing as a 'pure' bourgeois revolution and points to the failures of the Third International to grasp the specific nature of fascism in Germany and Italy because of blind theoretical adherence to economism in *Fascism and Dictatorship*.[24] Poulantzas indemnifies this stance by an appeal to Lenin's claim that the heart of Marxism is the concrete analysis of a concrete situation. It appears, however, that these adjustments to the deterministic implications of modes of production analysis may not be wholly satisfactory. It cannot solve the problem of whether revolutions are the outcome of the logic of modes or of class struggles or both. Class practices are, in *Political Power and Social Classes*, residual phenomena which exist, as it were, in the gaps left over from structures. Furthermore, a political agent might reasonably ask whether political experience and acumen might be as valuable in the analysis of concrete political conjunctures as the abstract theory of modes. In short, how exactly does historical materialism bear on the analysis of the concrete?

A more radical solution for Poulantzas would be to deny that social classes are merely effects, that is, he could substitute class analysis for mode of production analysis. This solution is precisely the one adopted by Poulantzas, but the consequence is to drive a coach and horses through his determinism. While social classes in *Political Power and Social Classes* are effects of structural determination and while Poulantzas criticizes Lukács for treating classes as the subjects of history, in *Classes in Contemporary Capitalism* he appears to abandon this position implicitly by stating that a mode of production 'does not reproduce itself, or even exist, in the pure state, and still less can it be historically periodized as such. It is the class struggle in the social formations which is the motor of history; the process of history has those formations as its locus of existence.'[25] How can Poulantzas believe (a) that classes are effects which are caused in Plamenatz's words by 'something more "fundamental" than themselves' and (b) that classes are causes ('the motor of history')? In *Political Power and Social Classes* and *Classes in Contemporary Capitalism*, proposition (b) is simply tacked onto proposition (a) without any real attempt at a rigorous theoretical resolution of these difficulties. The class struggle disappears in these two works partly because they are concerned primarily with the relationship between the bourgeoisie and its fractions with the state. The working class and its struggle with the bourgeoisie hardly plays any part in the overall analysis of the state in capitalist society. In *Fascism and Dictatorship*, it is true that class struggle as the 'motor of history' is more prominent in the analysis, but, since Poulantzas believes that the defeat of the working class precedes the rise of fascism, the book is again mainly interested in the crisis in the power bloc and the role of the petty bourgeoisie as a governing class. The result is that, although Poulantzas occasionally appeals to the theoretical importance of 'class struggle', his actual analysis focuses on crises in the dominant class as effects of the contradictions between competitive and monopoly capitalism. In other words, the three major works of Poulantzas are conducted in terms of mode of production analysis with occasional appeals to the possibility or importance of social-class analysis.

Poulantzas, of course, is clearly aware of the contradictions between these forms of analysis and conscious of the political embarrassments of determinism from the point of view of working-class mobilisation. Poulantzas has been criticised for various forms of 'structural super-determinism' in the past by Miliband, and in a recent article in *New Left Review* Poulantzas has attempted to defend himself against the criticism that he has neglected the crucial role of class struggle in the production and transformation of social formations. Poulantzas defends himself by arguing that the dichotomy between choice and necessity is simply an aspect of bourgeois idealism and by claiming that in his various publications he has always comprehended 'the relations of power as class relations'.

Another feature of his defence is to contrast his conception of the transformation of structures with that presented by Etienne Balibar in the discussion of 'transitional modes of production' in *Reading Capital*.[26] Balibar is accused of neglecting the class struggle, which is a consequence of Balibar's formalism and economism. Poulantzas thus asserts that Balibar fails to make a rigorous distinction between modes of production at the level of theory and concrete social formations. If such a distinction had been made, then Balibar would have been able 'to grasp the precise role, in the reproduction/transformation of social relations, of the class struggle – that class struggle which, in point of fact, operates within concrete social formations'.[27] One possible implication of this claim is that the class struggle cannot be theorised at the level of abstract modes of production; the class struggle can only be grasped at the level of concrete social conjunctures in actual social formations. This implication would mean either that 'modes' and 'classes' exist at different theoretical levels or that no theory of classes exists. Does the notion of 'the concrete analysis of concrete problems' mean that no deterministic structural account of class is required for the understanding of transformations? Whatever the implications of Poulantzas's assertion, it does mean that the theory that social classes are the effects of the determination of structures has been abandoned. The problem is that Poulantzas provides no theory to plug that gap and thereby invites the accusation that his recent concern for class struggle is a form of empiricism.

Balibar's theory of the transitional mode has also been criticised by Barry Hindess and Paul Q. Hirst, who demonstrate the teleological features of Balibar's argument which fails to recognise that changes in the structure of social formations are the outcome of class struggles.[28] Elsewhere Hindess subjects Bettelheim's analysis of 'non-correspondence' between relations and forces of production in transitional periods to the same type of criticism. Hindess insists that:

> the transition from one mode of production to another necessarily involves the transformation of a complex structure of political, economic and ideological social relations. This transformation is effected by the means of the class struggle in the course of a series of displacements as the social formation moves from one transitional conjuncture to another.[29]

Although Hindess and Hirst do not attempt to expose the basis of Poulantzas's theory in the analyses of Balibar and Bettelheim, they do criticise Poulantzas for failing to provide a coherent theory of the effect of the political level on class interests. The result is that Poulantzas's theory, despite all appearances, is a 'complicated form of reductionism', specifically economic reductionism.[30] Although their criticisms of contemporary structural Marxism may well be valid, it is not exactly clear how Hindess and Hirst themselves escape the problem of attempting to reconcile the analysis of classes with the analysis of modes of production within a single, coherent theory of modes and social formations. They assert that the transformations of social formations are ultimately effects of the class struggle in 'transitional conjunctures'; this assertion refers to social relations in concrete social formations, but, since their main text on this subject (*Pre-Capitalist Modes of Production*) is a theoretical analysis of modes, they have not yet provided a detailed, rigorous account of the class struggle in concrete social formations. In short, they have not shown how in precise terms their theoretical analysis of modes relates to class struggles. Since in my view there is considerable difficulty involved in reconciling the analysis of modes at the theoretical level and the analysis of class struggles in concrete social formations, one solution for Hindess and Hirst would be to abandon their existing theoretical position on modes of production in favour of the analysis of class struggle.

These critical observations can be summarised by briefly considering the implications of mode of production analysis for conventional Marxist theories of revolution in order to bring out clearly the political consequences of a deterministic theory of modes of production. For example, in a conventional Marxist interpretation of revolutions, a revolution occurs when a previously dominated class replaces a dominant class by gaining effective control of the state, and by radically changing the nature of relations of production. Poulantzas has elaborated this primitive model of revolution by making a distinction between a governing class which runs the state apparatus on behalf of a dominant or ruling class and by arguing that various elements of pre-revolutionary society may be conserved by subsequent modes of production. However, it can be claimed that mode of production analysis has far more radical implications for the traditional view of revolutions. The theory of the capitalist mode of production identifies two sets of functions, namely capital accumulation and surplus-value production, but the theory does not have to specify which particular classes or class fractions are the bearers of these functions.[31] In actual capitalist societies, the capital-accumulation function may, for example, be differentiated between managers and owners. Furthermore, the replacement of one mode by some other mode in a social formation does not necessarily require a radical replacement of classes. The capitalist mode of production does not require a situation in which peasants in the feudal mode of production become capitalists, and it does not rule out the possibility that feudal landlords, who once existed by extracting surplus labour in the form of rent, can exercise the capital function in social formations dominated by the capitalist mode of production. Thus, transformations of modes appear to have no necessary consequences for the nature of class formations or for the class character of the power bloc. One might say that modes of production are theoretically indifferent to which classes exercise the various functions of accumulation, exploitation or political surveillance. One implication of this perspective is that there is a relative disjuncture between the transformation of modes and the struggle for the control of the state. Changes in the dominance of a mode of production within a social formation or transitions in terms of phases of a mode (such as the development of monopoly capitalism) may have a variety of effects at the political level in the constitution of the power bloc – no one class exercises hegemonic control over the state apparatus or a previously dominant class continues to exercise political control under new relations of production or a hegemonic class employs the services of a governing class or, by a political revolution, a new class gains control of the state apparatus. A variety of contingent class alliances within the power bloc is possible, following transformations of dominant modes within a given social formation. Thus, Marx's *Capital* offers a theory of the general crisis within the capitalist mode of production as a theoretical construct, but it does not require that particular classes should be the bearers of particular economic functions. The theory of the capitalist mode of production does not preclude the possibility that feudal landlords can act as a capitalist class. This theoretical possibility that dominant classes in one mode of production can be the dominant class in some other mode, rather than being replaced by a previously dominated class, is in fact relatively close to what actually takes place in concrete social formations in the transition to capitalism. In Britain the establishment of capitalism involved the destruction of the peasantry who became wage-labourers and the conversion of the countryside to capitalist agriculture. Some feudal lords turned to extraction industries and to commodity production for the market, thereby becoming a fraction of the capitalist class and exercising control over the state apparatus. The revolutions of the seventeenth century and the political struggles of the eighteenth and nineteenth centuries were merely contingent upon changes in the dominance of modes of production; they were not required by the capitalist mode as conditions of its existence. The political and ideological consequences of this type of analysis, which treats classes as effects of and revolutions as contingent upon the mode of production, are critical for the conventional Marxist view of the causal significance of class consciousness, political organisation and leadership of the class struggle. It is hardly surprising, therefore, that in recent years structural Marxists have begun to have second thoughts about a theory which regards classes as effects of structural determination.

In this discussion of structural Marxism, I have attempted to pinpoint some of the ambiguities that arise in connection with treating social classes as the primary motor of history or the contradiction between relations and forces of production within a mode of production as the cause of social change. A more elaborate analysis of Marx's theory of social change has been suggested by Robert Holton, who identifies four alternative explanations of social change in Marx's work.[32] These are (1) change results from the universalisation of the division of labour and the emergence of a global system of exchange relations, (2) change is the result of changes in the technological basis of society ('The handmill gives you a society with the feudal lord; the steammill society with the industrial capitalist'[33]), (3) change is brought about by the expansion of the productive forces in general (in terms of skills, knowledge, experience as well as technology), and (4) change is the product of class conflict over property relations within a society. These different approaches to the analysis of social change in the work of Marx are to some extent reflected in modern Marxist debates over the collapse of feudalism and the rise of capitalism. Of particular importance for the sociology of development has been the debate between so-called neo-Smithians like Frank, Sweezy and Wallerstein[34] and the class-relations approach of Hilton, Dobb and Brenner.[35] The former stress the importance of world trade in the development of capitalism, whereas the latter treat class conflicts as the crucial feature in the dissolution of feudalism.

Regardless of the merits or failures of individual contributions to recent debates in Marxism as to the nature of capitalist development, there are a number of general conclusions that emerge from the debate as a whole. The first is that there is no royal road to capitalism and therefore no general theory of capitalist development. The nature of class alliances that develop with the transition from feudalism to capitalism vary considerably between societies; it is not necessarily the case that the rising bourgeoisie decisively sweeps aside the traditional feudal landlords. There is no necessity for capitalism to develop as a parliamentary democracy expressing the individualistic ideology of the bourgeois class. Capitalism in southern Europe was often combined with fascist corporatism, based on an alliance between landlords, industrialists and financiers, who controlled the state through the medium of the army and a service class.[36] The variety of ideologies, political institutions and class relations that can be combined with capitalist economic relations is very considerable. Since there is no royal road to capitalism, it is difficult to make any clear-cut distinction between the stationary East and the dynamic West. Such global contrasts are the product of traditional Orientalist discourse and cannot be supported empirically or theoretically by sociological investigation.

The articles on Middle East societies and culture contained in this book were written over a period of ten years, but they share a number of general arguments which provide a linking theme. They are, first, a reflection on the notion that Oriental societies are stationary, a notion shared not only by sociologists and historians, but by Marxists and missionaries. The contrast between Occidental dynamism and Oriental stagnation is the product of a special discourse which has remained remarkably resilient in European thought over many centuries. Second, these papers attempt to criticise any form of evolutionary or teleological analysis of social change, stressing in contrast the contingent, diverse and complex nature of social development and underdevelopment. Third, these arguments are based on the assumption that the analysis of change has to be transnational and global. Throughout these studies, I have attempted to criticise internalist theories of change which treat the problem of change in terms of certain flaws or blockages within a given society, and to criticise externalist theories which approach the problem of development at the level of external constraints within the global market. An adequate theory of social change will have to combine these two perspectives to show how economic development is constrained by external restrictions and how these external constraints are conjoined with the internal class structure of a society. The analysis of Bangladesh and

Egypt in Chapter 10 attempts to vindicate this approach. Fourth, these chapters are further unified by the assumption that attempts to force a clear division between sociology and Marxist theory (in particular, between Weber and Marx) are largely fruitless and misguided. At one level, Marx and Weber shared many common prejudices about Oriental Despotisms, Islamic fatalism and Asiatic tradition. They also adopted rather similar explanations of Oriental stagnation. Although Weber was often misguided about the nature of Islam as a fetter on economic growth, his theory of prebendal political structure has much to commend it. Many of these papers are thus metatheoretical in the sense that they are concerned with procedural problems, what can or cannot be said, and with the nature of value judgements and ethnocentrism. However, the intention is that these articles also convey a substantial amount of empirical information (about Israel, Islamic history, Iranian politics, the class structure of Bangladesh, Egyptian agriculture and nomadic societies) which will be of interest to the general reader. This collection of papers as a whole is addressed to a traditional philosophical and humanistic problem, namely how can we understand others? First, we can never understand others *de nouveau*, but only in terms of cultural framework and discourses which filter and distribute our knowledge. Second, the Orient is essentially a subjective mirror of the Occident; we see ourselves in trying to see others.[37] Into the Orient, we have projected our fears and anxieties about absolutism, fatalism, stagnation, corrupting eroticism, sensuality and violence. Understanding others is a will-'o-the-wisp; understanding ourselves is at least a possibility.

This collection of essays is thus negative in intention; it sets out to show the failures of traditional Orientalist assumptions which characterised the Middle East as a region without history and which emphasised the progressive nature of western capitalist development. The early sections of this study (Chapters 2–6) outline the principal features of Orientalism and attempt to demonstrate the inadequacy of such a perspective. The second half of this study is more positive in intention by showing how the dialectic of external and internal constraints has structured the particular development of the Middle East. The essays on Israel, Iran, Bangladesh and Egypt examine historically the problems of modernisation in the context of global capitalist relations. The history of the Orient cannot be written independently of the Occident, but it is not enough to suggest that the development problems of the contemporary Middle East are simply a direct consequence of nineteenth-century colonialism and twentieth-century neo-colonialism. The social structure of the Middle East has also to be understood in terms of the transnational trade that provided the economic basis of the Islamic ruling class in the Middle Ages. In turn, these external relations of exchange have to be set in the context of internal class relations within Islamic societies. Chapters 4, 9 and 10 are specifically addressed to the question of historical change in the setting of global economic relationships. Finally, this collection of essays has an underlying moral objective: to promote a greater sociological appreciation of the Middle East without the prejudicial limitations of the Orientalist assumption of social stagnation as the essential feature of Oriental societies.

Notes

1 R. Fletcher (ed.), *The Science of Society and the Unity of Mankind*, London, 1974.
2 J.D.Y. Peel, *Herbert Spencer, the Evolution of a Sociologist*, London, 1971.
3 E. Durkheim, *The Division of Labour in Society*, Glencoe, Ill., 1964.
4 R. Nisbet, *The Sociological Tradition*, London, 1967.
5 V.G. Kiernan, *European Empires from Conquest to Collapse 1815–1960*, London, 1982.
6 Ernest Renan, 'Islamism and science', in *The Poetry of the Celtic Races and Other Studies*, London, 1896, p. 85.
7 K. Bock, 'Theories of progress, development, evolution', in T. Bottomore and R. Nisbet (eds), *A History of Sociological Analysis*, London, 1979, pp. 39–79.
8 T. Parsons, *Social Systems and the Evolution of Action Theory*, New York, 1977.
9 B. Hoselitz and W.E. Moore (eds), *Industrialization and Society*, The Hague, 1963.
10 D. Lerner, *The Passing of Traditional Society*, New York, 1964.
11 R. Dahrendorf, *Essays in the Theory of Society*, Stanford, 1968.
12 J.D. Crockcroft, A.G. Frank and D.L. Johnson (eds), *Dependence and Underdevelopment, Latin America's Political Economy*, New York, 1972.
13 S. Amin, *Accumulating on a World Scale*, London, 1974.
14 A.M. Bailey and J.R. Llobera (eds), *The Asiatic Mode of Production, Science and Politics*, London, 1981.
15 B.S. Turner, *Marx and the End of Orientalism*, London, 1978.
16 A. Giddens, *A Contemporary Critique of Historical Materialism*, London, 1981.
17 J. Plamenatz, *German Marxism and Russian Communism*, London, 1954, p. 29.
18 ibid., p. 33.
19 N. Poulantzas, *Political Power and Social Classes*, London, 1973.
20 N. Poulantzas, 'The problem of the capitalist state' and R. Miliband, 'The capitalist state: a reply to Nicos Poulantzas', reprinted in J. Urry and J. Wakeford (eds), *Power in Britain*, London, 1973.

21 L. Althusser, *For Marx*, Harmondsworth, 1969.
22 C. Bettelheim, *Economic Calculation and Forms of Property*, London, 1976.
23 S. Lukes, *Power, a Radical View*, London, 1974.
24 N. Poulantzas, *Fascism and Dictatorship*, London, 1974.
25 N. Poulantzas, *Classes in Contemporary Capitalism*, London, 1975, p. 23.
26 L. Althusser and E. Balibar, *Reading Capital*, 1970.
27 N. Poulantzas, 'The capitalist state: a reply to Miliband and Laclau', *New Left Review*, no. 95 (1976), p. 78.
28 B. Hindess and P.Q. Hirst, *Pre-Capitalist Modes of Production*, London, 1975, pp. 262 ff.
29 B. Hindess, 'Introduction', in Bettelheim, *Economic Calculation and Forms of Property*, p. 9.
30 Hindess and Hirst, *Pre-Capitalist Modes of Production*, p. 38.
31 For a discussion of classes as bearers of functions in modes of production, cf. J. Urry, 'Towards a structural theory of the middle class', *Acta Sociologica*, vol. 16 (1973), pp. 182 ff.
32 R.J. Holton, 'Marxist theories of social change and the transition from feudalism to capitalism', *Theory and Society*, vol. 10 (1981), pp. 833–67.
33 K. Marx, *The Poverty of Philosophy*, New York, 1966, p. 95.
34 R. Brenner, 'The origins of capitalist development: a critique of neo-Smithian Marxism', *New Left Review*, no. 104 (1977), pp. 25–92.
35 R. Hilton (ed), *The Transition from Feudalism to Capitalism*, London, 1976; R. Brenner, 'Agrarian class structure and economic development in pre-industrial Europe', *Past and Present*, vol. 70 (1976), pp. 30–74.
36 S. Giner, 'Political economy, legitimation and the state in southern Europe', *British Journal of Sociology*, vol. 32 (1982), pp. 172–99.
37 J.P. Charnay, *Les Contre-Orients ou comment penser l'Autre selon soi*, Paris, 1980.

2 Marx on Social Stationariness

The dual revolution, political and industrial, which ushered in the modern period fundamentally transformed the rural, structurally stable communities of eighteenth-century Europe. Since the basic ingredients of modern industrial society were forged in the period between 1789 and 1848, it is not surprising that much nineteenth-century social theory was an attempt to come to terms with these dramatic social transformations. One of the recurrent characteristics of early social theory was therefore an attempt to formulate dichotomous ideal types which would summarize the dominant features of the transition from rural to industrial society. For example, in German social thought, the breakdown of rural communities and the emergence of individualism, competition and egoism was analysed by Ferdinand Tönnies in terms of *Gemeinschaft* and *Gesellschaft* relationships.[1] Similarly, Max Weber was concerned with the transition in patterns of political domination from societies based on charisma and tradition to those based on legal-rational authority with the growth of bureaucratic political parties and trade unions in capitalism.[2] In France, social theorists were more exercised by the problem of discovering a moral basis for social order in a post-revolutionary secular society. Émile Durkheim, heavily influenced by Fustel de Coulanges's historical analysis of the sacred in *La Cité Antique* (1864), contrasted those societies based on a common morality and repressive law ('mechanical solidarity') with modern society based on the division of labour and restitutive law ('organic solidarity') in *De la division du travail social* (1893).[3] Finally, in Britain one can discern similar attempts to speculate upon the loss of pre-industrial social certainty, notably in Edmund Burke's *Reflections on the Revolution in France* (1790) and Henry Maine's *Ancient Law* (1861).

The similarities between the classic ideal types in sociological thought have prompted many writers to argue that the origins and nature of sociology as a whole can be seen as a common response to the problem of order generated by the dual revolution of the nineteenth century. In particular, Robert A. Nisbet has asserted that it 'would be hard indeed to account for the principle themes and emphases of the entire sociological tradition in the nineteenth century without citing the disruptive effect of the two revolutions on European society'.[4] Perhaps the main objection to Nisbet's thesis is that the process of industrialization and political change assumed very different forms in different parts of Europe. British society and social theory were in many respects very different from the social structures and their related sociologies which emerged on the continent. Unlike France and Germany, British industrialization was not accompanied in the nineteenth century by massive political turmoil. Both Barrington Moore and Perry Anderson have pointed out that Britain achieved a profound capitalist revolution in the seventeenth and eighteenth centuries without a revolution of its social structure.[5] Although Britain produced democratic institutions, politics continued to be 'the privilege of an antiquated aristocracy.'[6] The transition in Britain from *Gemeinschaft* to *Gesellschaft* was largely peaceful and gradual. Social thought was less concerned with systematic conceptualization of the problem of moral order; instead, utilitarianism and liberalism centred far more on the practical issue of incorporating the urban working class within the institutions of political democracy.

Because the British bourgeoisie did not achieve the status of a dominant hegemonic class, Anderson argued that the main social theory of the bourgeoisie (utilitarianism) was itself partial and parochial: 'its fanatically bleak materialism *ipso facto* precluded it from creating that cultural and value system which is the mark of a hegemonic ideology'.[7] While Anderson has provided a perceptive commentary on utilitarianism within the British class structure, there was at least one area in which utilitarianism did achieve something approaching hegemonic authority, namely, in its legitimation of British imperialism. Although British social theorists did not work in a social context of catastrophic transformations, they did reflect continuously on the great differences between industrial society and the traditional societies which had come within the orbit of Britain's world market. In the process of that reflection, utilitarianism produced a dichotomous ideal type which has been largely neglected by historians of sociological theory. This persistent dichotomy attempted to conceptualize the basic social differences separating East and West in terms of social 'stationariness', as J. S. Mill called it, and social dynamism. Of course, the concept of 'oriental despotism', which treated Asian society as a stagnant social entity, had been important in European political thought for centuries, but the debate about 'Asiatic society' came to have a special significance in British social theory in the nineteenth century.[8] An understanding of Asian societies was immediately important in the context of justifying British imperialism, but it also produced a yardstick for comprehending the problems of industrialism and democracy in Britain itself. While continental sociologists were busy developing a set of contrasts (sacred–secular, community–association, status–class) to analyse their own societies, British social theory was engaged much more in understanding the impact of capitalist economies on traditional Asiatic communities. Utilitarians perceived, however dimly, a parallel between the proper government of the new colonies and the proper regulation of the working class at home.

In this discussion, I shall attempt to outline the theory of Asiatic social stagnation as it appeared in British social theory between approximately 1818–67 with special reference to utilitarianism and Marxism. While both 'schools' shared common assumptions about the absence of indigenous forces of progress in Asia, their attitudes toward the causes and consequences of imperialism were very different. In the course of this study, it will be possible to indicate the continuities and breaks between utilitarian political economy and Marx's model of Asiatic production. One can treat Marx and Engels as part of the main stream of nineteenth-century British social theory not simply because they happened to live in Britain, but because they borrowed their factual information about Asia from utilitarian sources; there was also a remarkable conceptual overlap.

The connection between utilitarianism and the British empire, especially India, was highly formative, and one cannot understand the utilitarian view of society without examining its setting in imperial expansion. Both James Mill and J. S. Mill served as examiners at East India House and this position gave them first-hand experience of the practice of colonial-commercial administration, but it was also perfectly suited to the needs of 'amateur' bourgeois intellectuals.[9] It was partly because of this strategic position in the East India Company that utilitarianism came to have a direct impact on the government of India. The colonies provided a social laboratory in which the rational principles of utility could be applied and tested. Whereas in the early period of the Company's relationships with India under the guidance of Robert Clive and Warren Hastings, the main principle was indirect government and conservation of India's traditional culture and social structure, this policy was replaced in the nineteenth century by a movement for social reform and direct intervention. Much of the theoretical and practical content of the reformist movement was supplied by utilitarians.

James Mill's *The History of British India* (1818) provided a catalogue of the social ailments of despotical government, along with the practical remedies which would transform India into a progressive society. Native government was absolute and arbitrary, but at the same time ineffectual and inefficient:

> Among the Hindus, according to the Asiatic model, the government was monarchical, and, with the usual exception of religion and its ministers, absolute. No idea of any system of rule, different from the will of a single person, appears to have entered the minds of them, or their legislators.[10]

Political absolutism was combined with an all-embracing legal system which failed to make adequate distinctions between law, religion, morality and etiquette. Hindu culture failed to distinguish between public regulation and private conscience, which was so dear to the utilitarian programme. The formal legal tradition was administered inefficiently so that it left men 'no liberty even in their private and ordinary transactions'. The peculiar feature of Asiatic despotism was social stagnation conjoined with the insecurity of person and property. While dynastic personnel changed, the despotic structure went unaltered. Hence, the great Asian paradox: rapid turnover of personnel with complete rigidity of social roles and social structure. Part of the explanation for social stagnation was to be found in village organization, and Mill quoted with approval the fifth report of the House of Commons committee into East India affairs of 1810:

> The boundaries of the village have been seldom altered... The inhabitants give themselves no trouble about the breaking up and divisions of kingdoms; while the village remains entire, they care not to what power it is transferred, or to what sovereign it devolves; its internal economy remains unchanged... [11]

The enclosed, stagnant village life was wrapped within a system of religious beliefs which to Mill were 'all vagueness and darkness, incoherence, inconsistency and confusion', administered by the worst form of priestcraft. Since they lived under a combination of despotism and priestcraft, it is no wonder that Mill came to the conclusion that the Hindus were 'the most enslaved portion of the human race'. Mill's utilitarian programme for wrenching this stagnant society out of its enclosure within tradition was deceptively simple, namely, 'light taxes and good laws'. This combination would provide the security of property and liberty of the private individual which for Mill were the hallmark of progressive societies. In fact, this simple formula implied a total reconstruction of Indian society: the creation of a central, strong government; modernization of law and administration; registration and regulation of all land rights.

It has often been observed that, despite their emphasis on the individual and his personal happiness, there was a strong authoritarian, anti-liberal theme in the philosophical radicalism preached by Jeremy Bentham and James Mill.[12] Although utilitarians appeared to put happiness at the centre of their picture of human activity, their real concern was pain and the protection of men by efficient laws and government institutions. Men were to enjoy their pleasures only when the social world had been made safe from dangers. The world of liberalism is not one of confident men in pursuit of gain: '*homo economicus* of liberal theory was a creature not so much obsessed by the quest for gain as frightened by the ever-present prospect of loss'.[13] Tenuous social relations were to be made secure by considerable social control exercised through law and public opinion.

It is not surprising that this authoritarian theme in utilitarian thought should be present in Mill's scheme for Indian reform. Mill argued against those reformers who advocated extensive education for Indians and their employment in government positions. The people of India, in Mill's view, wanted good government, not representative government. In an article attributed to Mill, we find him arguing the case for effective, but arbitrary control: 'A simple form of arbitrary government, tempered by European honour and simple European intelligence, is the only form which is now fit for Hindustan.'[14] Although Mill, following Bentham, argued that the best way to curb the influence of 'sinister interests' (the aristocracy) in Britain was by an extension of popular control, in dealing with Indian society he advocated a form of benevolent despotism. The greatest happiness of the people of India was to be secured by reform of taxation and law brought about by an English autocracy. Since happiness was taken to be the self-evident end of human activity, the incorporation of despotism into the utilitarian scheme of Indian reform was easily justified by reference to the Benthamite view of human psychology. British despotism in India would limit the pains and insecurities of traditional Hindu despotism.

J. S. Mill departed from philosophical radicalism over the issue of pleasure and culture. For Mill, pushpin was not as good as poetry. One might suspect that J. S. Mill would have concluded that the happiness of Indians could not be dictated by the British. In fact, the younger Mill had little interest in the issue of British control in India. What bothered Mill was not the self-government of India, but the dangers of mass democracy in Britain. Mill used his father's analysis of despotic government in India as a model for the analysis of social 'stationariness' in western democracy. With the extension of the franchise and the reform of Parliament, Mill feared that the stagnation which typified Asian history would eventually overtake the hitherto dynamic societies of America and Britain. His anxieties over the 'omnipotence of the majority' were exacerbated by reading Alexis de Tocqueville's *Democracy in America* in the spring of 1835. The dangers of majority rule as outlined by de Tocqueville prompted Mill to define what he meant by 'democracy', namely, a social order in which people have 'security for good government'. Such a social order could be achieved only by the government of 'the wisest, and these must always be the few'.[15] There is in these remarks a continuity between James Mill and J. S. Mill in that both were more concerned with 'security for good government' than with political freedom. What J. S. Mill wanted to preserve, however, was the development and cultivation of individual opinion free from majority control.

Government by the people would, for Mill, produce a deadening conformity, just as custom had produced 'stationariness' in Asia: 'The despotism of custom is everywhere the standing hindrance to human advancement, being in unceasing antagonism to that disposition to aim at something better than customary . . .'[16] Asian society was static and had 'no history, because the despotism of Custom is complete'. Although Europe had been progressive, the new institutions of democracy threatened its capacity to encourage individuality and Mill found a suitable warning in the history of China. The Chinese, despite being a 'nation of much talent', had become stationary: 'and if they are ever to be farther improved, it must be by foreigners'.[17] Mill summarized his position by claiming that his fears were 'not of too great liberty, but of too ready submission; not of anarchy, but of servility; not of too rapid change, but of Chinese stationariness'.[18]

Mill's insistence that certain political devices were necessary to check the uniformities which went with popular democracy was a consistent aspect of his whole political outlook. His attitude towards Britain's role in Asia was, by contrast, shifting and contradictory. In his essay 'On Liberty' (1859), Mill took it for granted that backward nations can only be developed by 'foreigners'. In the same essay, in reference to the Mormon institution of polygamy (for which he had the greatest dislike), Mill argued that no one had the right to intervene. Although a contemporary writer had urged a 'civilisade' against Mormonism, Mill protested that no community has 'a right to force another to be civilised'. Yet Mill felt no compunction in arguing that the British colonies could be improved by benevolent despotism. In 'Representative Government' (1861), Mill asserted that in backward societies, 'a good despot is a rare and transitory accident: but when the dominion they are under is that of a more civilised people, that people ought to supply it constantly. . . . The only choice the case admits is a choice of despotisms'.[19] Mill could justify despotic interference in backward colonies on the grounds that 'barbarous' natives are incapable of judging for themselves. A wise ruler has a duty to protect his subjects from their own ignorance when the social causes of their historical stagnation 'are too far off to be within their ken'.

It has often been claimed that Mill broke with the basic principles of philosophical radicalism over the Benthamite doctrine of happiness, but this intellectual break was only apparent. Mill implicitly assumed that we can know what is good for others and that we have a duty to enforce happiness. In particular, it is Mill's commentary on Asiatic 'stationariness' that brings out the authoritarian underside of liberal policies in the nineteenth century. Just as Mill feared 'the mob' in British democracy, arguing for the maintenance of a 'leisured class' (an idea which united him with Coleridge's view of a 'clerisy'), so Mill feared that civilization would be contaminated by barbarous standards abroad. It is for this reason that there was no contradiction between utilitarian support for democratic liberty and despotic imperialism. The combination of opposites took place because of Mill's fear of 'stationariness' in Europe and Asia.

There are important connections between Marx's sociology and utilitarian theory. Marx himself pointed to one aspect of this relationship when, in a letter to J. Weydemeyer, he declared that 'long before me bourgeois historians had described the historical development of this class struggle'. One of the central tasks of Marx's intellectual development, after his arrival in Britain in 1849, involved a systematic critique of the foundations of utilitarian political economy as represented by Smith, Ricardo, Malthus and Mill. A major similarity between utilitarianism and Marxism centred on the analysis of social stagnation in Asiatic society and the progressive role of international capitalism. A minor reason for this similarity is that Marx and Engels had to rely upon information gathered by classical economists and upon the Blue Books and other official sources.

The theme of Asian societies as static and western society as dynamic runs through all Marx's writing. Like Mill, Marx was convinced that significant change (the transformation of the economic basis of Asian society and the emergence of classes) could come only from outside, as a consequence of the development of capitalism as a world economy. In 1848, Marx and Engels claimed that the bourgeoisie as part of its historical role 'draws all, even the most barbarian, nations into civilisation. The cheap commodities are the heavy artillery with which it batters down all Chinese walls, with which it forces the barbarians' intensely obstinate hatred of foreigners to capitulate.'[20] It was after Marx's move to London that he became increasingly sensitive to the significance of Asian social systems for his own theoretical interests. Between 1853 and 1859, Marx wrote a series of articles for the *New York Daily Tribune* in which he elaborated his view of Asian economies and the relationship between capitalism and the transformation of the Asiatic mode of production.[21]

Following a suggestion made by Engels to Marx that the absence of private property in land was 'the key to the whole of the East', Marx at first stressed the significance of environmental factors for property relations. The centralized state in Asia dominated the whole social order because of the peculiar requirements of large-scale public works:

> Climate and territorial conditions, especially the vast tracts of desert, extending from the Sahara, through Arabia, Persia, India and Tartary, to the most elevated Asiatic highlands, constituted artificial irrigation by canals and waterworks the basis of Oriental agriculture.[22]

The permanency of large-scale social and economic functions in the hands of a centralized state contributed to a static social structure. Here Marx underlined the common theme of social 'stationariness' which we have already seen developed by utilitarians. While the political superstructure was in a state of flux, India's 'social conditions remained unaltered since its remotest antiquity'. State regulation of public works was combined with the 'village system', uniting agriculture and manufacture, which produced a self-sufficient social unity. The English cotton industry undermined the 'hand-weaving, hand-spinning and hand-tilling agricultural system': 'blowing up their economical basis, and thus produced the greatest and . . . the only social revolution ever heard of in Asia'.[23] While Marx used the same sources as Mill on village life and public works, the main concern for Marx was the nature of property and ownership of the means of agricultural production. Mill's major focus in his approach to Asian society was on custom and opinion. Hence the real clue to Asian history in Marx's perspective lay in the fact that the state was the only 'real landlord'. Referring to Francöis Bernier's *Voyages contenant la description des états du Grand Mogol*, Marx wrote to Engels in 1853 claiming that the 'absence of private property in land' was the basis of Asian social structure and 'the real key, even to the Oriental heaven'. On the basis of these observations Marx came to the conclusion that the Asiatic mode of production could not be equated with European feudalism. The Indian 'zamindars' were 'native tax-gatherers', not feudal landlords. Similarly, the Asiatic mode of production was very different from the private slavery which characterized classical antiquity. Under conditions of centralized control, necessitated by extensive irrigation works, the mass of the population was subjected to 'general (state) slavery'.

Because of these distinctive features, Marx came to regard Asiatic society as a unique mode of production with a history totally different from that of the Occident. Whereas prior to 1853 Marx and Engels saw history unfolding in terms of slave, feudal and capitalist society, after Marx's 'discovery' of societies without private property in land, the Asiatic mode of production was added to the original model of social change and social types. What Marx came to emphasize was a crucial difference between Oriental and Occidental social development. The contradictions of capitalist economy produced conflict and progress, but Asia 'has no history at all, at least no known history. What we call its history, is but the history of successive intruders who founded their empires on the passive basis of that unresisting and unchanging society.'[24] Asian society has no economic class, since the state as the 'real landlord' faces a population in general, public slavery. Therefore, there could be no class conflict along Occidental lines producing a dynamic historical force. Since Marx and Engels were committed to the view that history is 'the history of class struggles', Asia had no history based on progressive social conflicts. Hence, change can only come, as the utilitarians had argued, from outside by fundamental changes in the economic foundations of Asian society. This was the 'historic mission' of international capitalism.[25]

When Marx came to draft some notes for his projected six-volume *Economics* in 1857–8 (the *Grundrisse*), the Hegelian theme of increasing freedom and human consciousness in history was fresh in his mind after he had 'leafed through Hegel's *Logic* again'. Once more, Marx was struck by the fact that the economic structures of Asian societies had not been conducive to general human development. In the *Grundrisse*, social 'stationariness' was traced back to tribal organization, in which the social unity was realized in a personal overlord. Marx attempted to show that despotism and absence of private property were connected with the combination of manufacture and agriculture at the village level so that surplus production could not escape from its narrow social confines. However,

> a part of this surplus labour belongs to the higher community. which exists ultimately as a person, and this surplus labour takes the form of tribute, etc., as well as of common labour for the exaltation of the unity, partly of the real despot, partly of the imagined clan-being, the god.[26]

This situation did not contribute to the emergence of autocephalous urban communes and thereby blocked the growth of an independent burgher culture which Marx suggested was an important ingredient of progress in Occidental history.[27] Finally, we may note that Marx returned to the same theme of political uncertainty joined with structural rigidity in writing *Capital*, where he discussed the 'simplicity of the productive organism in these self-sufficient communities'; 'this simplicity unlocks for us the mystery of the unchangeableness of Asiatic society, which contrasts so strongly with the perpetual dissolutions and reconstructions of Asiatic states, and with the unceasing changes of dynasties'.[28]

In describing Asiatic stagnation in terms of 'this undignified, stagnatory and vegetative life' and in asserting the absence of 'real' history in the Indian continent, Marx and Engels found themselves associated with an established tradition of political thought which had been puzzled by the extreme acquiescence of Asian peoples in despotic government.[29] The parallel between Marx's view of Asia and that of the utilitarians is, at least superficially, complete. Both agreed that Asian 'stationariness' could only become dynamic by exogenous forces. For Marx, colonialism was a necessary and largely progressive force. To some extent, Engels was more explicit than Marx on the revolutionary force of colonial and imperial expansion into backward markets. Writing about French colonialism in Algeria in the *Northern Star*, Engels had stated that 'the modern bourgeois, with civilisation, industry, order, and at least relative enlightenment following him, is preferable to the feudal lord or to the marauding robber, with the barbarian state of society to which they belong'.[30] The question to be explored, then, is whether there were discernible differences between the view of imperialism presented by the utilitarians and by Marx. They were in agreement that Asia was stagnant; did they also agree on the nature of imperial penetration?

George Lichtheim has claimed that in the 1850s Marx saw imperialism as a progressive force, but by 1867 Marx's standpoint had become 'one of unqualified hostility and contempt'.[31] Yet, even in his articles for the *Tribune* in the 1850s, Marx was unsparing in his condemnation of British methods, particularly of British brutality.[32] Marx held consistently to the position that while capitalism was ultimately a progressive force, it was also destructive. Marx asked his readers whether the bourgeoisie had ever brought about progress without 'dragging individuals and peoples through blood and dirt', and indicated that the people of India:

> will not reap the fruits of the new elements of society scattered among them by the British bourgeoisie, till in Great Britain itself the now ruling classes shall have been supplanted by the industrial proletariat, or till the Hindus themselves shall have grown strong enough to throw off the English yoke altogether.[33]

Marx differed from the utilitarians in that, in addition to his critique of Asian 'stationariness', he was a persistent critic of the destructive brutality of British colonial methods. Yet, in another sense, Marx was neutral about colonial expansion and felt no need to raise the question of justifying on moral grounds the whole development of colonialism. Capitalist expansion and the creation of new markets was an inevitable outcome of the contradictions of the capitalist economy. Imperialism was not a moral mission against arbitrary Asian governments, but an economic consequence of, among other things, overproduction in capitalist Europe. Indeed, Marx was contemptuous of any attempt to cloak economic exploitation in moral sentiments, referring on one occasion to 'the Christian-canting and civilization-mongering British Government'. By contrast, the utilitarians treated Christianity as false, but useful.

Marx remained optimistic about British involvement in India, however, because he believed it would intentionally create the conditions of India's self-development and independence. Whereas all previous conquerors had been eventually assimilated into existing Hindu culture, Marx saw that the British would not be accommodated because they had succeeded in destroying the traditional economic foundations of Asia. The emergence of modernized systems of communication, a British-trained army and a free press would create the conditions for India's final emancipation. (Hence, Marx and Engels's interest in the Mutiny.)[34] Above all, the introduction of the railway system would galvanize Indian society by creating 'those industrial processes necessary to meet the immediate and current wants of railway locomotion.... The railway system will therefore become, in India, truly the forerunner of modern industry.'[35] In his analysis of India's potential to transcend its 'stationariness' and colonial dependency, Marx was once more stressing an essentially Hegelian view of imperialism. Britain was paradoxically introducing into India the very conditions for its own removal and for the abolition and transcendence (the Hegelian notion of *Aufhebung*) of static despotism. Here Marx stood clearly aside from the main utilitarian commentators. Marx treated colonial dependence as merely a step towards a dynamic, independent society; the best Mill could offer was strong government within federal commonwealth.

In conclusion, we might note that Asia was not so much an object of analysis, but a mirror in which nineteenth-century theorists saw the dynamic nature of western capitalism. In that Asian mirror, J. S. Mill saw multiple dangers for the leisured intellectual class in a mass democracy. Marx noted two things. He saw a parallel between the stagnant societies of Asia and the reactionary role of the rural peasantry in revolutionary France. For Marx, the 'vegetative life' of Asian villages was yet another example of the backwardness of the European peasantry ('the barbarism within civilization'). Marx also saw a parallel between the emergence of a progressive Asia and the growth of a revolutionary urban proletariat in Europe. The basic difference between Marx and utilitarianism was that Marx, despite later Popperian critics, saw a necessary relationship between conflict and freedom, whereas the utilitarians, despite their *laissez-faire* ideology, worked for oppressive forms of institutional regulation. What brought them together was a common grounding in a prevalent typology in British social theory based on the notion of social 'stationariness'.

Notes

1 Ferdinand Tönnies, *Gemeinschaft und Gesellschaft: Abhandlung des Kommunismus und Socialismus als empirische Kulturformen* (Leipzig, 1887). For a recent commentary, cf. Arthur Mitzman, 'Tönnies and German Society, 1887–1914: from cultural pessimism to celebration of the Volksgemeinschaft', *Journal for the History of Ideas*, vol. 32 (1971), pp. 507–24.

2 Max Weber, *Wirtschaft und Gesellschaft* (Tübingen, 1925); *Gesammelte politische Schriften* (Munich, 1921).

3 Some aspects of the moral conflicts in nineteenth-century France are discussed in Theodore Zeldin (ed.), *Conflicts in French Society* (London, 1970) and Bruce Brown, 'The French Revolution and the rise of social theory', *Science and Society*, XXX (Fall, 1966), 385–432.

4 Robert A. Nisbet (ed.), *Émile Durkheim* (Englewood Cliffs, New Jersey, 1965), p. 19.

5 Barrington Moore, Jr, *Social Origins of Dictatorship and Democracy* (Harmondsworth, 1966), ch. 1; Perry Anderson, 'The origins of the present crisis', in *Towards Socialism* (London, 1966), pp. 11–52.

6 Jacques Droz, *Europe between Revolutions, 1815-1844* (London, 1967), p. 129.

7 Anderson, 'Origins of the present crisis', p. 33.

8 Cf. R. Koebner, 'Despot and despotism: vicissitudes of a political

term', *Journal of the Warburg and Courtauld Institutes*, vol. 14 (1951), pp. 275–302.

9 J. S. Mill said the occupation suited anyone 'not being in independent circumstances' who had 'private intellectual pursuits'. *Autobiography* (London, 1971), p. 51.

10 James Mill, *The History of British India* (London, 1848), 4th edn, Vol. 1, pp. 202–3.

11 Ibid., p. 314.

12 For discussions of the authoritarian side of philosophical radicalism and utilitarianism, cf. Alisdair MacIntyre, *A Short History of Ethics* (London, 1967), pp. 227 ff.; Eric Stokes, *The English Utilitarians and India* (Oxford, 1959), pp. xi. ff.; J. W. Burrow, *Evolution and Society* (Cambridge, 1966), ch. 5.

13 Sheldon S. Wolin, *Politics and Vision* (London, 1961), p. 328.

14 *Edinburgh Review*, vol. 16 (1819); attributed by A. Bain, *James Mill* (London, 1882), p. 109.

15 John Stuart Mill, *Dissertations and Discussions* (London, 1875), 3rd edn, Vol. 1, p. 471. For a discussion of Mill on democracy, J. H. Burns, 'J. S. Mill and democracy, 1829–1861', *Political Studies*, vol. 5 (1957), and reprinted in J. B. Schneewind (ed.), *Mill, a Collection of Critical Essays* (London, 1969), pp. 280–328.

16 J. S. Mill, 'On Liberty' (1859) in *Utilitarianism, Liberty and Representative Government* (London, 1962), p. 127.

17 Ibid., p. 129.

18 J. S. Mill, *Dissertations and Discussions*, Vol. 2, p. 56.

19 J. S. Mill, 'Representative Government' (1861), in *Utilitarianism, Liberty and Representative Government*, pp. 382–3.

20 K. Marx and F. Engels, *The Communist Manifesto* (1848) (Moscow, n.d.), p. 55.

21 On the Asiatic mode of production, Karl A. Wittfogel, *Oriental Despotism: a Comparative Study of Total Power* (New Haven, 1957); George Lichtheim, 'Marx and the Asiatic mode of production', *St. Antony's Papers*, vol. 14 (1963), pp. 86–112; Jean Chesneaux, 'Le Mode de production asiatique: quelques perspectives de recherche', *La Pensée*, vol. 114 (1964), pp. 33–55; Maurice Godelier, 'La Notion de mode de production asiatique', *Les Temps Modernes*, vol. 20 (1965), pp. 2002–27.

22 K. Marx, 'The British rule in India' (1853), in K. Marx and F. Engels, *On Colonialism* (New York, 1972), p. 37.

23 Ibid., p. 40.

24 K. Marx, 'The future results of the British rule in India' (1853), *On Colonialism*, p. 81.

25 For further discussion of Marx's view of the historical and progressive

role of capitalism, cf. Schlomo Avineri's introductory essay in *Karl Marx on Colonialism and Modernization* (New York, 1969).

26 K. Marx, *Grundrisse: Foundations of the Critique of Political Economy* (translated by Martin Nicolaus) (Harmondsworth, 1973), p. 473.

27 It would be interesting to develop this argument showing Marx's theoretical relations with Max Weber's views on capitalism and urban culture. Cf. Max Weber, *The City* (Glencoe, 1958). Some of the issues are raised in Vatro Murvar, 'Some tentative modifications of Weber's typology: Occidental versus Oriental city', *Social Forces*, vol. 44 (1966), pp. 381–9.

28 K. Marx, *Capital*, 4th edn (London, 1957), Vol. 1, pp. 378–9.

29 Although I have tried to show Marx's relationship with utilitarianism, it would also be necessary in a complete analysis to show Marx's indebtedness to Hegel's analysis of the master–serf relation in antiquity and in Oriental society: Georg Hegel, *The Philosophy of History* (translated by J. Sibree) (New York, 1956).

30 Lewis F. Feuer (ed.), *Marx and Engels: Basic Writings on Politics and Philosophy* (London, 1969), p. 489.

31 Lichtheim, 'Marx and the Asiatic mode of production', p. 98.

32 Cf. Marx's comments in 'The Annexation of Oudh' (1858), reprinted in *On Colonialism*.

33 Marx, 'The future results of the British rule in India', p. 85.

34 K. Marx and F. Engels, *The First Indian War of Independence, 1857–59* (Moscow, 1959).

35 Marx, 'The future results of the British rule in India', p. 85.

3 Islam, Capitalism and the Weber Theses

Over the last half century a substantial tradition of Weberian scholarship has developed in Europe which is focused on elaborate analyses of Weber's exploration of the relationship between religion and capitalism. Naturally, this scholarship has involved examinations of Weber's basic contrast between the European tradition of Puritan asceticism and the mystical ethics of Asian religions. One consequence of this dominant sociological tradition has been a relative neglect of Weber's treatment of Islam.[1] Although Weber died before completing his sociology of religion with a full study of Islam, his comments on early Islam and his more elaborate inquiry into Islamic law are sufficiently interesting to warrant a closer inspection than they have hitherto received. As a prophetic, egalitarian, salvation religion with close derivation from Judaism and Christianity, Islam is a significant test of Weber's thesis on asceticism and rational economic activity. Before turning to Weber's argument that Islam was not a salvation religion, it will be useful to clarify the kaleidoscopic interpretations which exist concerning Weber's analysis of religion and capitalism.

In this study of Weber on Islam, there are three related arguments which need to be distinguished at the outset. The first line of argument is that one can detect at least four different Weberian theses about the connection between religious beliefs and capitalism; these four theses cannot be successfully reconciled in one coherent Weberian theory about the secular significance of religious doctrines. Hence any attempt to consider Islam as a test case of Weber's sociology must be a complex process. My contention is that at least three of Weber's theses are either false or trivial. The fourth thesis, which examines the consequences of patrimonial domination, can be employed as a plausible explanation of some Islamic developments. My second argument is that, apart from factual mistakes about Islam, Weber stressed the wrong question about Islam. His main concern was to explain the absence of rational capitalism outside Europe, but the real sociological issue is to explain the transition of Islam from a monetary economy to an agricultural, military regime. Thirdly, Weber's analysis of Islam was not particularly successful; it is ironic that when Islamic reformers came to explain the decay of Islam, they employed implicitly Weberian arguments.

It would, however, be naive to accept this situation as proof of the validity of Weber's Protestant Ethic thesis.

Considerable differences of opinion among sociologists have arisen over the interpretation of Weber's Protestant Ethic thesis. These disagreements could emerge either through gross misunderstanding of Weber's sociology or because Weber's sociology itself contains different theses which are not necessarily consistent. Although there certainly has been misconception, it can also be shown that a number of distinct theories emerge from Weber's sociology.[2] The temptation is always to read consistency into a sociologist, particularly a great sociologist, when one is concerned with the history of ideas.[3] There are a number of ways by which one could bring out these different arguments which Weber entertained, often simultaneously. Here it will be fruitful to refer to Alisdair MacIntyre's argument in 'A mistake about causality in the social sciences', where he observed that, in attempting to demonstrate the relation between beliefs and actions, sociologists have often started with a strong thesis and ended with a compromise.[4] The strong thesis is that beliefs are secondary (Marx and Pareto) or that beliefs are independent (Weber). Most sociologists finish by eating their own words; thus, in MacIntyre's view, Weber slips into 'facile interactionism', in which beliefs cause actions and vice versa. This framework can be used to illustrate four different arguments in Weber's sociology of religion.

The first interpretation of the Protestant Ethic thesis (PE) is that it entails an idealistic theory of values. The second thesis (PE^{i}) is that it is an argument about the necessary and sufficient conditions for the emergence of capitalism. The Weber thesis (W) takes a wider view of Weber's sociology of civilizations, stressing the importance of the concept of 'understanding' in Weber's philosophy of science. Finally, the second Weber thesis (W^{i}) underlines the continuity between Marx and Weber by showing that Weber continuously draws attention to the ways in which beliefs are shaped by their socio-economic contexts. Weber showed that Islamic institutions were incompatible with capitalism because they had been dominated by a long history of patrimonialism. Islamic beliefs were certainly influential, but still secondary to patrimonial conditioning. Unfortunately, this thesis was also held alongside other interpretations of Islamic history which make Weber's theoretical position unstable.

Economic and social historians were probably the first to treat the Protestant Ethic as a strong theory in which Calvinist beliefs caused modern capitalism. H. M. Robertson, for example, attempted to refute what he regarded as Weber's psychologism by showing that capitalism arose from 'material conditions', not from 'some religious impulse'.[5] More recently, H. R. Trevor-Roper asserted that Weber and Werner Sombart had reversed Marx's materialism.[6] In attempting to win support for this particular thesis

(PE), Syed Alatas claimed that Talcott Parsons, Pitrim Sorokin and Reinhard Bendix have all treated the Protestant Ethic thesis as an idealistic theory.[7] Although one can show that Weber thought that ideas were often causally significant, the main problem with this interpretation (PE) is that Weber himself denied that he held such a theory about Calvinism. In *The Protestant Ethic and the Spirit of Capitalism*, he insisted that the theory that capitalism was the creation of the Reformation would be 'a foolish and doctrinaire thesis'.[8] Evidence also comes from Weber's associates at Heidelberg that he was annoyed by 'idealistic' interpretations of the Protestant Ethic thesis.[9]

Sociologists who wish to reject the PE interpretation have normally claimed that the first essay on the Protestant Ethic was merely an early, trial monograph. In this perspective (PE^i), asceticism is a necessary and sufficient condition of rational capitalism, but asceticism needs to be placed with a number of other key variables.[10] Hence sociologists have turned, for example, to Weber's *General Economic History*, in which we find that the prerequisites of modern capitalism include capitalist modes of ownership, free labour, rational law and free market movements. It is sometimes argued in addition that Weber had a general scheme to set up an experimental test of PE^i by cross-cultural comparison. Thus Parsons has noted that Weber, turning from the method of agreement to the method of difference, embarked upon 'an ambitious series of comparative studies all directed to the question, why did modern rational bourgeois capitalism appear as a dominant phenomenon only in the modern West?'[11] Although this interpretation (PE^i) of Weber does more justice to Weber's sociology considered as a whole than with a simple 'idealist' perspective (PE), it contains at least two difficulties. First, it tends to assume that Weber accepted J. S. Mill's methodology and consequently understates Weber's *verstehende* sociology. Secondly, it assumes that the Protestant Ethic thesis is continuous and central in Weber's later sociology. The issues raised, however, in *Ancient Judaism*, *The Religion of China* and *The Religion of India* concerning bureaucracy, patrimonialism and village organization are far wider than the restricted theme of the Protestant Ethic thesis. In some respects, the problem of asceticism as an aspect of radical social change is tangential to Weber's analysis of Asian society.[12]

Sociologists who hold that Weber's main concern was to explore historical connections of values and meaning have rejected the view that Weber attempted, by cross-cultural comparison, to demonstrate the causal primacy of values. Rather than seeking any over-simplified causal chain, Weber was concerned, according to this view (W), to elaborate complex 'affinities' or 'congruencies' between social meanings. For example, Peter Berger argued that Weber's first concern was with 'elective affinity' (*Wahlverwandtschaft*), namely, with the ways in which 'certain ideas and certain social processes "seek each other out" in history'.[13] Similarly, Ferdinand Kolegar has criticized those commentators who treat Weber's theory of capitalism and Protestantism as a simple causal account of economic development. For Kolegar, Weber attempted to demonstrate the 'mutual reinforcement' between economic and religious ethics.[14] Weber is said to hold not a positivist or Humean view of causality; rather, Weber sought to explain actions by grasping their subjective meaning.

Clearly, this view (W) does give legitimate weight to Weber's own methodological position, but this emphasis on 'elective affinity' rather than 'empirical cause' does run into three problems. It assumes a very debatable issue, namely, that Weber followed consistently his own methodological guidelines. Weber's 'interpretative explanation' (*verstehende Erklärung*) involves the philological interpretation of the actor's concepts and terms. Yet Weber never faced the problem of whether a complex meaning system such as 'Islam' can be unambiguously treated as a 'religion'. Uncovering the multiplicity of meanings encased in the term 'Islam' is part of the sociologist's fundamental task.[15] A further difficulty with explanations in terms of subjective meaning is that they rarely get beyond plausible descriptions of subjective states without relating these meanings to their social structural settings.[16] Finally, by giving priority to meaningful causality over empirical causality, this interpretation (W) finds it difficult to rescue Weber from the charge of 'facile interactionism'. It could be argued that Weber regarded these problems by showing, in specific examples, how social groups acted as carriers of values and beliefs and how 'elective affinities' developed between the socio-economic basis of carrier groups and particular constellations of beliefs. However, such an interpretation of 'elective affinity' comes very close to a Marxist view that beliefs are socially constructed in terms of dominant economic interests.

The fourth view of Weber's (W^{i}) often starts by refuting the facile notion that Weber was arguing with 'the ghost of Marx'. For example, Hans Gerth and C. Wright Mills claimed that Weber's task was partly to complement Marx's economic materialism 'by a political and military materialism'.[17] They also suggested that as Weber became more embittered by German politics, he gave increasing prominence to 'material' factors. A consideration of Weber's public lecture at Freiburg in 1896 on ancient civilization shows, however, a consistent Marxist undercurrent in Weber's sociology.[18] Similarly, Norman Birnbaum has argued that Weber contributed a sophisticated sociology of motives to Marx's analysis of interests and ideologies.[19] While contemporary reappraisals of Marx's Paris manuscripts and *Grundrisse* have enormously complicated our conception of the relationship between Marx and Weber, Weber's view of motive remains an important issue.[20] Recently, Paul Walton has suggested that Weber's sociology enables us to study 'the possession by particular actors or groups of vocabularies, phrases or outlooks, which, far from being rationalizations or mystifications of interests, act as motive forces for action itself'.[21] Walton's statement follows C. Wright Mills's theory that groups exercise social control, linguistically, by imputing good or bad motives to actions.[22] Mills pointed out that his approach was compatible with Weber's definition of a motive as 'a complex of subjective meaning'.[23]

The theory of motive implicit in Weber and elaborated by Mills is not incompatible with a Marxist treatment of ideas and ideology. There is no contradiction in saying that vocabularies of motive determine social actions, but these vocabularies are locked within specific socio-economic contexts. Indeed, Mills was at pains to point out that certain social settings exclude certain types of motive. In secular settings, a religious vocabulary of motives is either inappropriate or unavailable. It would not be difficult to imagine a situation in which traditional religious languages for describing and influencing social activities became obsolete with the decline in social power of religious élites. Like Weber, Marx thought that the religious culture of feudalism was wholly irrelevant under capitalist conditions: new motives appropriate to capitalist social relations would evolve without an atheistic campaign.[24] It is not difficult to interpret Weber's analysis of ascetic motives in precisely these terms. Weber himself claimed that it was necessary to investigate how ascetic motives were shaped by 'the totality of social conditions, especially economic'.[25] The fourth Weber thesis (W^i) thus asserts that to explain actions we need to understand the subjective meaning of social actions, but the languages which are available for describing and explaining actions are determined by socio-economic settings.

Weber started by recognizing that Meccan Islam was a monotheistic religion based on ethical prophecy which rejected magic. Given that Allah was all powerful and omniscient, and man predestined, asceticism could have emerged as a solution to a potential 'salvation anxiety'. Weber argued that asceticism was blocked by two important social groups: the warrior group, which was the main social carrier of Islam, and the Sufi brotherhoods, which developed a mystical religiosity. In adapting Muhammad's monotheistic Koran to the socio-economic interests of a warrior life-style, the quest for salvation was reinterpreted through the notion of *jihad* (holy war) to the quest for land. Islam was turned into a 'national Arabic warrior religion'. The concept of inner salvation never fully developed and adherence to the outward rituals of the community became more significant than inward conversion: 'Ancient Islam contented itself with confessions of loyalty to god and to the prophet, together with a few practical and ritual primary commandments, as the basis of membership.'[26] Weber concluded that despite Islam's origins in Jewish-Christian monotheism, 'Islam was never really a religion of salvation'.[27]

The warrior group turned the religious quest into a territorial adventure and Islamic asceticism was basically the rigour and simplicity of a military caste. Islam did, however, develop a genuine salvation path with ultimately religious goals, but this quest was mystical and other-worldly. Weber regarded Sufism as a mass religiosity which enabled Islam to reach its conquered subjects through their indigenous symbolism and ritual. Sufi mysticism thus introduced magical, orgiastic elements into Islam and watered down its monotheism. The combination of a warrior religiosity with mystical acceptance of the world produced all the:

> characteristics of a distinctively feudal spirit; the obviously unquestioned acceptance of slavery, serfdom and polygamy . . . the great simplicity of religious requirements and the even greater simplicity of the modest ethical requirements.[28]

Given this religious ethic, Islam could not provide the social leverage whereby the Muslim Middle East could be lifted out of feudal stagnation. At this level of argument it would be all too easy to interpret Weber as postulating that Islam did not produce capitalism because it had a culture incompatible with the spirit of capitalism (PE thesis). Alternatively, one could conclude that Weber is claiming (W thesis) that there was an elective affinity between the needs of a warrior group and the militaristic values which developed from pristine Islam. Weber's argument was, in fact, far more complex; when Weber turned to an analysis of Islamic law, it appears that his argument was constructed in terms of a string of prerequisites which are necessary for capitalist development (PE^i thesis).

At the centre of Weber's sociology of law is a distinction between arbitrary, *ad hoc* law-making and legal judgements which are derived logically from general laws. In the case of substantive, irrational law, law-makers do not follow general principles, but judge each case according to purely arbitrary factors. The paradigmatic case of such law, in Weber's view, was that of the qadi (or cadi) who judges each case on personal, particularistic grounds. The law resulting from qadi decisions lacks generality and stability. However, Islam did possess a universal legal code, despite different legal schools, in the form of the Sharia (Holy Law), which Weber categorized as substantive, rational law. Law of this kind follows principles which are derived from sacred revelation, ideology or a belief system imposed by conquest. The norm of the Sharia were 'extra legal' in the sense of being derived ultimately from prophecy and divine revelation. Whereas qadi justice was unstable, sacred justice was inherently inflexible and could not be readily extended systematically to meet new cases and situations. After the first three centuries of Islam, the Sharia was treated as complete and hence there emerged a hiatus between theory and practice which was bridged by *hiyal* (legal devices): 'innovations had to be supported either by a *fetwa*, which could almost always be obtained in a particular case, sometimes in good faith and sometimes through trickery, or by the disputatious casuistry of the several competing orthodox schools'.[29] Therefore, Islam lacked a necessary condition for capitalist development, namely a systematic formal law tradition (PE^{i} thesis).

The standard sociological interpretation of Weber on law is that he held a strong thesis (PE^{i}) that rational formal law is a necessary prerequisite of rational capitalism and, as a result, crude economic explanations of capitalism are inadequate. Despite the explicit strong thesis (PE^{i}), Weber admitted that, in the case of English judge-made law, the absence of a gapless system of law had not held back the progress of English capitalism. In England, the courts of justice of the peace resembled 'qadi-justice to an extent unknown on the Continent'. Weber went on to observe that 'adjudication by honoratores' on continental lines 'may thus well stand in the way of the interests of the bourgeois classes and it may indeed be said that England achieved capitalistic supremacy among the nations not because but rather in spite of its judicial system'.[30]

English capitalism did not suffer in this way for two reasons, in Weber's view. Lawyers and entrepreneurs were drawn from the same social class and shared common interests; as a professional body, lawyers enjoyed considerable political autonomy. Weber appears, therefore, to have argued that it was not the content of law, but the social context and institutionalization of law which was crucial for capitalist contractual relations. Similarly, the instability of qadi justice and the inflexibility of the Sharia are products of patrimonial rulership, rather than irreducible facts about Islamic culture. A close reading of Weber suggests this final interpretation (W^{i} thesis). Whereas Occidental bourgeois strata preferred formal rational law, Oriental patrimonial rulers 'are better served' by substantive qadi justice, which represents 'the likelihood of absolute arbitrariness and subjective instability'.[31]

Viewing Weber's treatment of law in this light takes us to a final interpretation of Weber's analysis of Islam. This final thesis (W^{i}) seems to be that Islam did not generate capitalist industrialization because for centuries the Muslim homelands had been dominated by a system of patrimonial bureaucracy controlled by foreign troops. It is the patrimonial economic and political structure which explains the absence of a capitalist spirit, of rational law and of independent cities. Furthermore, although Weber's dominant theoretical problem seems to be that of explaining the absence of capitalism outside Europe, Weber does appreciate that one major issue in Islamic history is to explain the relative stagnation of the economy between the twelfth and nineteenth centuries. Weber attempted to suggest an explanation in terms of the problems of financing patrimonial troops:

> the feudalization of the economy was facilitated when the Seljuk troops and Mamelukes were assigned the tax yield of land and subjects; eventually land was transferred to them as service holdings... The extraordinary legal insecurity of the taxpaying population *vis-à-vis* the arbitrariness of the troops to whom their tax capacity was mortgaged could paralyze commerce and hence the money economy; indeed, since the period of the Seljuks (ca. 1050–1150) the Oriental market economy declined or stagnated.[32]

The decline of the money economy was accompanied by increasing arbitrariness in law, land rights, property and civic relations. Weber summarized these political conditions under the term 'sultanism', which described purely arbitrary decisions of a patrimonial ruler. Since property holding became uncertain, the urban merchants invested in *waqfs* (family trusts consecrated to pious works), which were comparatively safe from interference. These investments encouraged an extensive immobilization of capital which 'corresponded fully to the spirit of the ancient economy which used accumulated wealth as a source of rent, not as acquisitive capital'.[33] Since towns were merely army camps for patrimonial troops and since patrimonial interference discouraged investments in trade and craft industry, a bourgeois lifestyle and ethic did not develop in Islam. Thus, Weber concluded that the prebendal feudalism of imperial Islam 'is inherently contemptuous of bourgeois-commercial utilitarianism and considers it as sordid greediness and as the life force specifically hostile to it'.[34]

According to this thesis (W^i), Islamic values and motives certainly influenced the way in which Muslims behaved in their economic, political and social activities, but we can only understand why these values and motives were present by studying the socio-economic conditions (patrimonial dominance and prebendal feudalism) which determined Islamic history.

Weber's theory that the 'feudal ethic' of Islam was the result of Islam being dependent on a warrior stratum as its social carrier (PE or W) is factually wrong. Islam was primarily urban, commercial and literate. Mecca was strategically placed on the trade routes between the Mediterranean and the Indian Ocean; Muhammad's own tribe, the Quraysh, had achieved a dominant political position based on their commercial strength in the region. The Prophet himself had been employed on the caravans which brought Byzantine commodities to the Meccan market. The Koran itself is steeped in a commercial terminology.[35] There has been a continuous conflict in Islam between the dominant urban piety and the values of the desert, but this conflict was also economic. Desert tribes threatened the trade routes and extracted taxation from merchants. Islam provided a culture which was capable of uniting Bedouins and urban merchants within a single community. Islam was thus as much a triumph of town over desert as Arab over Persian and Christian.

Weber's description of Islamic law was far more valid and accurate. Most scholars have recognized that the Sharia was an ideal law which allowed a gap to grow between ideal and practice.[36] The gap could only be filled by the most complex institutions and legal devices. The problem, then, lies not so much with Weber's description of Islamic law, but with how that account will fit into his explanation of Islamic social backwardness. It is not easy to insert this view of Islamic law into a theory that rational law is a necessary condition for capitalist development (PE^{i} thesis). Weber has already shown that English capitalism developed despite its judge-made legal system, so that formal rational law may help capitalist development, but it cannot be a necessary condition. Furthermore, a number of scholars have concluded that the rigidity of Islamic law and its prohibition of usury never really interfered with commerce.[37] The main problem in commercial life was the threat that patrimonial rulers would seize property and goods to pay off their troops.

There does, therefore, seem to be empirical support for Weber's final thesis (W^{i}) that the decline of Islam's money economy is to be explained in terms of its patrimonial structure. While there have been many different explanations of Islamic decline in terms of international trade, demographic crises and even climate, there is a widely held theory that the failure of the ruling institutions of Islam was closely connected with problems of military finance.[38] There is an old Oriental maxim which says that 'a ruler can have no power without soldiers, no soldiers without money, no money without the well-being of his subjects, and no popular well-being without justice'.[39] By 'justice' the Ottoman jurists meant that the sultanate should maintain a balance between the two halves of society, between *askeri* (military, civil service and *ulama*) and *reaya* (Muslim and non-Muslim tax-payers). It was the inability of the sultanate to ensure that each social stratum fulfilled its special functions, the inability to satisfy justice, which weakened the fabric of Islamic society, particularly under Ottoman rule.

Ultimately, justice was dependent on successful warfare and a powerful sultanate. Warfare provided booty and land by which the sultanate could reward and pay off retainers. Without new land, tax-farming and bribery became major means of political influence and reward. Without a powerful sultanate, the complex bureaucratic machinery of the Ottoman state lacked direction and purpose. Failure to extend Islam, the withdrawal of the sultan from public life and the increasing inefficiency of the military were interrelated aspects of social decline. When the Ottoman empire reached its territorial limits in 1570, the state in search of revenue to pay off the standing army was forced to let imperial fiefs to tax-farmers. The *sipahi* (land-owning cavalry) went into decline because of the growing use of firearms, but also because when a *sipahi* died without heir, his lands were appropriated by the Treasury and let out for tax-farming. With the decline of the *sipahi*, the peasantry were at the mercy of the growing class of *multezims* (tax-farmers). As the *sipahi*, peasantry and merchants declined with the failure of the ruling institutions, local magnates (Ayan) and small dynasts (Dere-beyis) arose to terrorize the provinces. As a political entity, Islam was unable to prevent nationalist movements in the Balkans, unable to exclude European colonists and unable to develop its own industry and trade.[40] These developments in Islam were explained by Weber in terms of the contradictions and imbalances of 'sultanism' as a political system (W^{i} thesis).

There are a number of theses in Weber's sociology which give different explanations of social, especially capitalist, development. I have suggested that only the final thesis, which explains the decline of Islamic society in terms of certain military-economic contradictions (W^{i}), has the support of modern research. The other three theses (PE, PE^{i} and W) suffer from damaging theoretical ambiguity and circularity or they are factually false. It is ironic, therefore, that when Muslim reformers came to explain for themselves the apparent failures of Islamic civilization, they used implicitly Weberian arguments, especially theories of individual ascetic motivation (theses PE and PE^{i}), rather than structural explanations (W^{i}).

The colonial expansion of Europe created an acute problem of theodicy: if Islam is the true religion, how are infidels so successful in this world? The Muslim answer to this issue has been shared by the most diverse reformist movements, namely, 'Christians are strong because they are not really Christian; Muslims are weak because they are not really Muslim'.[41] In order to become 'really Muslim', it is necessary to rid Islam of foreign accretions and to discover original, pure Islam, which is seen to be completely compatible with the modern, scientific world. Pure Islam is based on an ascetic, activist, this-worldly ethic. The enemy of both pure Islam and modern society is a set of attitudes – fatalism, passivity, mysticism – which was introduced into Islam by the Sufis, Berber marabouts and related groups. Criticism of Sufism has been, of course, a persistent aspect of orthodox Islam over the centuries, but there is a new emphasis in the contemporary rejection of Sufi mysticism, namely, that it is a drain on economic resources and is incompatible with asceticism and activism. Expenditure on tombs and festivals has been widely criticized, particularly in North Africa. Active involvement in this world thus became a major theme of Islamic reform directed against Sufi quietism. A favourite koranic text of the reformer Jamal al-Din al-Afghani (1839–97) was 'Verily, God does not change the state of a people until they have changed themselves inwardly.[42] Similarly, Rashid Rida asserted that the first principle of Islam was 'positive effort'.

There are, therefore, certain interesting parallels between Weber's account of Protestantism (PE and PE^{i}) and the basic themes of Islamic reform. Pure Islam and Puritanism sought in the basic scriptures of their religion an ethic which would be free from mystical, ritualistic accretions. The result was a set of norms prescribing asceticism, activism and responsibility. Yet the connection between Puritan asceticism in Europe and Islamic modernism in the Middle East is superficial and derivative. Probably the most significant difference is the social context in which Islamic 'puritanism' is located. Islamic reform was a response, often apologetic, to an external military and cultural threat; it was an attempt to answer a feeling of inferiority and frustration resulting from western colonialism. Despite the existence of pre-colonial Islamic 'puritanism (Wahhabism, Hanbalitism), Islamic reform in the modern period was not so much an autonomous development as an attempt to legitimate the social consequences of an exogenous capitalism. Basic Islamic terms were conveniently translated into European ones without much respect for etymology:

> Ibn Khaldun's umran gradually turned into Guizot's 'civilization', the maslaha of the Maliki jurists and Ibn Taymiyya into the 'utility' of John Stuart Mill, the ijma of Islamic jurisprudence into the 'public opinion' of democratic theory . . .[43]

The 'Protestant Ethic' of Islam was second-hand and it was such because the leaders of Islamic modernism were either educated by Europeans or accepted European traditions. Weber's Protestant Ethic theory (theses PE and PE^{i}) came to fit Islamic modernization simply because Muslims came to accept a European view of how to achieve capitalist development. Reformers like al-Afghani, Muhammad Abduh and Rashid Rida accepted the view, especially as expressed by M. Guizot (*General History of Civilization in Europe*), that social progress in Europe had followed the Protestant Reformation. It is no surprise that al-Afghani saw himself as the Luther of Islam.

In this inquiry into Weber's view of Islam, I have attempted to show that we can plausibly perceive four different theses in Weber's sociology of civilizations. On the basis of contemporary research and theoretical discussion, three theses can be dismissed as either false or theoretically weak. The fourth thesis is that Islam declined and was eventually forced into economic dependence on Europe because it could not solve an inherent weakness in what Weber called 'sultanism'. In this final perspective, Islamic beliefs are still treated as influential, but the presence of these beliefs, rather than some other beliefs, is explained by the social and economic structure of patrimonialism. When Muslim reformers came to understand their own economic decline, they often employed theories of ascetic motivation, but this fact cannot be taken as evidence that asceticism is a necessary aspect of capitalist development. The ideology of hard work in modern Islam was largely a colonial importation.

Notes

1 The exceptions include Maxime Rodinson, *Islam et capitalisme*, Paris, 1966; Ernest Gellner, 'Sanctity, puritanism, secularization, and nationalism in North Africa', *Archives de Sociologie des Religions*, vol. 8 (1963), pp. 71–86; Sami Zubaida, 'Economic and political activism in Islam', *Economy and Society*, vol. 1 (1972), pp. 308–38; Robert J. Bocock, 'The Ismailis in Tanzania: a Weberian Analysis', *British Journal of Sociology*, vol. 22 (1971), pp. 365–80.

2 A range of these misconceptions has been exposed and criticized in Michael Hill, *A Sociology of Religion*, London, 1973.

3 Some of these issues are discussed in Quentin Skinner, 'The history of ideas', *History and Theory*, vol. 8 (1969), pp. 3–53.

4 A.MacIntyre, 'A mistake about causality in social science' in P. Laslett and W. G. Runciman (eds) *Philosophy, Politics and Society*, (Second Series), Oxford, 1962, pp. 48–70.

5 H. M. Robertson, *Aspects of the Rise of Economic Individualism*, Cambridge, 1935, p. xiii.

6 H. R. Trevor-Roper, *Religion, Reformation and Social Change*, London, 1967, p. 4.

7 Syed Hussein Alatas, 'The Weber thesis and South East Asia', *Archives de Sociologie des Religions*, vol. 8 (1963), pp. 21–35.

8 Max Weber, *The Protestant Ethic and the Spirit of Capitalism* (translated by Talcott Parsons), London, 1965, p. 91.

9 Cf. Weber's comments on Hans Delbruck, in Paul Honigsheim, *On Max Weber*, New York, 1968, p. 43.

10 For an example of this viewpoint, cf. Niles M. Hansen, 'The Protestant Ethic as a general precondition for economic development', *Canadian Journal of Economics and Political Science*, vol. 24 (1963), pp. 462–74.

11 Talcot Parsons, *The Structure of Social Action*, Glencoe, Ill., 1949, p. 512.

12 For a commentary, cf. Hisao Otsuka, 'Max Weber's view of Asian society', *The Developing Economies*, vol. 4 (1966), pp. 275–98.

13 Peter Berger 'Charisma and religious innovation: the social location of Israelite prophecy', *American Sociological Review*, vol. 28 (1963), p. 950.

14 Ferdinand Kolegar, 'The concept of "rationalization" and cultural pessimism in Max Weber's sociology', *The Sociological Quarterly*, vol. 5 (1964), p. 362.

15 For an analysis of the meaning of Islam, cf. Wilfred Cantwell Smith, *The Meaning and End of Religion*, New York, 1964.

16 On this problem, cf. John Rex, 'Typology and objectivity: a comment on Weber's four sociological methods', in Arun Sahay (ed.), *Max Weber and Modern Sociology*, London, 1971, pp. 17–36.

17 H. H. Gerth and C. Wright Mills (eds.), *From Max Weber: Essays in Sociology*, London, 1961, p. 47.
18 Max Weber, 'The social causes of the decay of ancient civilization' (translated by Christian Mackauer), *Journal of General Education*, vol. 5 (1950), pp. 75–88.
19 Norman Birnbaum, 'Conflicting interpretations of the rise of capitalism: Marx and Weber', *British Journal of Sociology*, vol. 4 (1953), pp. 125–41.
20 Much of the complexity is discussed in Anthony Giddens, 'Marx, Weber and the development of capitalism', *Sociology*, vol. 4 (1970), pp. 289–310.
21 Paul Walton, 'Ideology and the middle class in Marx and Weber', *Sociology*, vol. 5 (1971), p. 391.
22 C. Wright Mills, 'Situated actions and vocabularies of motive', *American Sociological Review*, vol. 5 (1940), pp. 904–13.
23 Max Weber, *Theory of Social and Economic Organization* (translated by A. M. Henderson and Talcott Parsons), New York, 1966, p. 98.
24 Cf. Nicholas Lobkowicz, 'Marx's attitude towards religion', *The Review of Politics*, vol. 26 (1964), pp. 319–52.
25 Max Weber, *The Protestant Ethic and the Spirit of Capitalism*, 1965, p. 183.
26 Max Weber, *The Sociology of Religion* (translated by Ephraim Fischoff), London, 1965, p. 72.
27 ibid., p. 263.
28 ibid., p. 264.
29 Max Rheinstein (ed.), *Max Weber on Law in Economy and Society* (translated by Edward Shils and Max Rheinstein), Cambridge, Mass., 1964, p. 241.
30 ibid., pp. 230–1.
31 ibid., p. 229.
32 Max Weber, *Economy and Society* (Guenther Roth and Claus Wittich, eds) Vol. 3, New York, 1968, p. 1016.
33 ibid., p. 1097.
34 ibid., p. 1106.
35 This terminology is analysed in Charles C. Torrey, *The Commercial-Theological Terms in the Koran*, Leiden, 1892.
36 Various statements of this situation in Islamic law can be found in J. Schacht, *An Introduction to Islamic Law*, Oxford, 1964; N. J. Coulson, *A History of Islamic Law*, Edinburgh, 1964; N. J. Coulson, 'Doctrine and practice in Islamic law: one aspect of the problem', *Bulletin of the School of Oriental and African Studies*, vol. 18 (1956), pp. 211–26.
37 This point is emphasized by Rodinson, *Islam et capitalisme*. Some aspects of the legal perspective on usury can be found in J. Schacht's

comments on 'riba' in *Encyclopaedia of Islam* (1st edn).

38 Different perspectives on Islamic decline can be found in Hamilton Gibb and Harold Bowen, *Islamic Society and the West*, Oxford, Vol. 1, pt 1, 1960; Halil Inalcik, *The Ottoman Empire: the classical age 1300–1600*, London, 1973; Claude Cahen, 'Quelques mots sur le déclin commercial du monde musulman à la fin du moyen age' in M. A. Cook (ed.), *Studies in the Economic History of the Middle East*, London, 1970, pp. 31–6; J. J. Saunders, 'The problem of Islamic decadence', *Journal of World History*, vol. 7 (1963), pp. 701–20.

39 Halil Inalcik, 'Turkey', in Robert Ward and Dankwart A. Rustow (eds), *Political Modernization in Japan and Turkey*, New Jersey, 1964, p. 43.

40 The control of trade fell into the hands of Jews, Greeks, Armenians and non-Ottoman merchants. Cf. Traian Stoianovich, 'The conquering Balkan orthodox merchant', *Journal of Economic History*, vol. 20 (1960), pp. 234–313.

41 Albert Hourani, *Arabic Thought in the Liberal Age*, London, 1962, p. 129.

42 Cf. Nikki R. Keddie, *An Islamic Response to Imperialism*, Berkeley and Los Angeles, 1968.

43 Hourani, *Arabic Thought in the Liberal Age*, p. 344. On Islamic reform in Asia, cf. W. F. Wertheim, 'Religious reform movements in South and Southeast Asia', *Archives de Sociologie des Religions*, vol. 12 (1961), pp. 52–62.

4 Middle Classes and Entrepreneurship in Capitalism

It has often been suggested that the generally slow and limited industrialization of the Middle East can be explained by sociological rather than economic causes. That Islamic values did not produce a social climate in which innovative entrepreneurship could flourish, but, on the contrary, inhibited commercial development. That the political insecurity of the Islamic empires made investment in productive industrial capital too hazardous. That Muslim merchants instead sought quick profits from trading in luxury goods, short-term speculative investment or investment in *waqf* property. This sociological account attempts to establish a clear dichotomy between European and Arab societies. In the capitalist West, one crucial cause of the industrial revolution of the nineteenth century was the existence of an autonomous, vigorous middle class willing to invest in new technology. By contrast, one of the peculiarities of the class structure of Arab societies has been the absence or weakness of an independent, urban middle class. There is a shortage of managerial and entrepreneurial talent because the real middle class is a thin stratum wedged between the salariat of the bureaucratic state and the mass of the population. Proponents of this view are sceptical as to the capacity of the so-called 'new middle class' of state functionaries to act as a vehicle for innovative entrepreneurship. According to this theory, the ultimate roots of economic backwardness in the Middle East are located within certain features of the systems of social stratification. For the purpose of my argument, I shall call this perspective 'the problematic of the missing middle class'.

The aim of this essay is to provide a hostile critique of the general argument that entrepreneurship is causally important for the emergence of capitalist production and to reject *in toto* the specific thesis that the missing middle class may explain the relatively tardy industrialization of the Middle East. In rejecting these conventional sociological standpoints, it will also be necessary to attack a range of assumptions about the nature of competitive capitalism. I will raise some fundamental issues in the theory of modes of production and their transformations. Because of the scope of these criticisms and the necessarily convoluted nature of some of these arguments, it will prove convenient to take the peculiar step of presenting my conclusions at the beginning rather than at the end.

As a general principle, it is a mistake to exaggerate the causal significance of entrepreneurship in the emergence of capitalism. In general, societies do not lack creative individuals, but whether that innovative effort will be directed toward military achievement, artistic expression, trade or productive investment will depend on structurally determined, objective conditions. The existence of the 'entrepreneurial role' is sociologically determined, not generated by the creative activities of individuals. Entrepreneurship is an effect of capitalist structures and not vice versa. This argument was clearly expressed by Baran (1973, pp. 385 ff), who asserted that the idea that the entrepreneur was the central figure in economics was a tautology, which could be boiled down to 'in the absence of industrial capitalism there are no industrial capitalists'. In most underdeveloped societies there is no shortage of supply of entrepreneurial skills, but, given the objective circumstances of a backward economy, these talents are exercised in the field of circulation rather than in industrial production (Elkan, 1973).

The preconditions of capitalist development in Britain in the eighteenth and nineteenth centuries cannot be repeated by underdeveloped countries in the twentieth century, precisely because the conditions for development are transformed by the existence of capitalism in Europe and North America. This notion is, of course, central to the sociology of underdevelopment (Frank, 1969) and to dependency theory (Dos Santos, 1970). The success of competitive capitalism in Britain meant that very different development paths had to be followed in France, Germany and Italy. Thus, the thesis that entrepreneurship is a 'missing link' in the Middle East has to assume that there is only one viable route to industrialization, namely *laissez-faire* British capitalism. The economic history of Europe in fact demonstrates that industrial growth can be achieved by a great variety of development pathways (Cipolla, 1973). There is, as it were, no 'royal road' to bourgeois capitalism along which the innovative middle class is a necessary step (Poulantzas, 1973).

The functions of entrepreneurship (innovation, risk-taking, management) have been performed by a great variety of agencies. In Britain, in the early stages of capitalist development, the functions of ownership and management were concentrated within the capitalist family and investment funds were acquired through company profits. This paradigmatic instance of free-enterprise capitalism was rarely replicated elsewhere. Where competition from imported commodities threatened to kill infant, indigenous industry or where the local bourgeoisie was particularly weak, or where the costs of technological advance were prohibitive, some public institution took on the role of entrepreneur. In Germany, this role was fulfilled by the banks, whereas in Russia it was occupied by the state (Gerschenkron, 1962). In short, even within the sphere of European capitalist development, the middle-class entrepreneur was far from being the unique carrier of the industrial process. Moreover, the middle-class entrepreneur was not necessarily the solvent of pre-capitalist culture and social structure, as depicted in the more lyrical passages of the *Communist Manifesto*. Although the European bourgeoisie may have played a radical role in economic affairs, it was often politically and culturally conservative.

Recent scholarship demonstrates that Islam was not hostile to commercial activity and that Islamic culture (especially legal relations) did not block the development of commercial institutions (Rodinson, 1974). Evidence can be found to suggest the existence of an Islamic 'bourgeoisie' from early times (Goitein, 1957). There is also the very obvious example of Lebanon as the great entrepôt of East–West trade (Issawi, 1968). Although these objections to the missing middle-class thesis are valid at a descriptive level, they are ultimately unsatisfactory as a theoretical critique. They adequately illustrate the existence of merchants and commercial institutions in medieval Islam, but they illegitimately confuse 'merchant' with 'capitalist'. The existence of merchants is never a guide to the presence of capitalist relations of production. Merchants exist under conditions of many modes of production (slave, feudal, ancient). To prove that Islamic values were not hostile to the commercial practice of merchants is to prove nothing about Islam as a catalyst or depressant of capitalist activity.

The problematic of the missing middle class rests inevitably on a general theory of the relationship between social classes and modes of production, namely, that the struggle between classes or the activity of social classes brings about transformations in the modes of production. Thus, the absence of radical transformations in the modes of production of Middle East societies is a consequence of the absence of a radical, innovative middle class. My thesis is based on the opposite assumption: social classes are the effects of the structures of modes of production. In order to make a comparison between 'the middle class' in Europe and 'the middle class' in the Middle East, we must establish a comparison of modes of production. The problematic of the missing middle class seeks to compare the bourgeois class of competitive capitalism in nineteenth-century Britain with the new middle class of the post-colonial Middle East. It is not surprising that family capitalism is not flourishing under conditions of state socialism or under various forms of capitalism, where state intervention is a necessary feature of the cycle of capital. The social pre-eminence of the state bureaucracy and the new middle class in the Middle East is hardly peculiar since most developing societies are forced by historical conditions and by reason of the character of global capitalism to protect their markets and their indigenous industries from foreign control. As a general rule, few backward societies can afford the luxury of competitive capitalism as a stage in their industrial development. Most societies (including such European illustrations as Spain and Italy) are forced by the objective conditions of international development to proceed from pre-capitalist to monopoly capitalist modes. Centrality of the state to capitalist investment, separation of control and ownership, concentration and centralization of production in large units, complex division of social and technical labour – these are features of monopoly capitalism. They are by no means incompatible with military dictatorship; the advance of monopoly capitalism does not necessarily require the presence of an active middle class within a democratic framework. It can be argued that the dominance of fascism in Europe actually enhanced the spread of capitalist relations of production, particularly in agriculture (Poulantzas, 1974). Middle East experts who have been struck by the role of the army as an agent of modernization have not discovered anything peculiar to the Middle East.

At one level my argument may look like the conventional 'environmentalist' position which asserts that the peculiar amalgam of resources, human attitudes and historical background in the Middle East necessitates centralized planning efforts which will utilize the profit-seeking entrepreneur much less than did the capitalist West (Meyer, 1959, p. 33). While this observation may be perfectly correct, it seems to carry the incorrect implication that the profit-seeking entrepreneur is the normal channel for industrial capitalist development. Historically, the independent capitalist entrepreneur may have played a role in British industrialization, but was less important in continental Europe as a whole. Recent studies suggest that in the Netherlands the main burden of entrepreneurial activity was borne by efficient administrators of the republic, not by autonomous Calvinistic merchants (Wertheim, 1964). From this perspective, the apparently peculiar absence of the middle-class entrepreneur from Middle East economies and the associated dependence on state guidance in economic affairs begins to look historically normal. The steady decline of profitability of capitalist investment, the increasing costs of development research and the pressure for welfare expenditure have contributed to the growth of state expenditure as a percentage of gross national product in the advanced societies. These illustrations point to the fact that those who insist on the irreducible importance of the independent businessman and the virtues of the small family business belong to a particular school of economic philosophy according to which any state interference is a check to sound economic growth.

Disagreements in sociology over the nature of capitalist development and, specifically, over the issue of retarded industrialization in Islamic societies can be traced back to Weber and Marx. Weber's two essays on the Protestant Ethic and the spirit of capitalism provided a profound statement of the centrality of private entrepreneurship, rational calculation and achievement motivation in the process of capital accumulation (Weber, 1930). The

Calvinistic capitalist provided Weber with his principal criterion for analysing the relationship between Islamic values and economic change. Weber's explanation can be divided into two components.

First, although Muhammad's koranic monotheism contained a this-worldly ascetic ethos (*innerweltliche Askese*), the pristine revelation was transformed by the material interests of the warriors who became the primary carriers of Islam. The result was that the initial religious drive for salvation was converted into a military quest for land and Islam became what Weber referred to as 'a national Arabic warrior religion'. The religious tensions which in Calvinism drove men to a calling in the world were consequently absent in Islam. While Puritanism was hostile to the values and institutions of pre-capitalist Europe, Islam had the 'characteristics of a distinctively feudal spirit' (Weber, 1968, p. 626). The societies in which Islam came to be the hegemonic culture did not, therefore, possess an internal mechanism for demolishing this pre-capitalist heritage.

Second, in European feudalism the feu was an inherited right to land, in Islamic societies the prebend could not be inherited. In Weber's view this arrangement implied a greater concentration of power at the centre around the patrimonial household of the ruler, whereas in feudalism under conditions of 'parcellized sovereignty' (Anderson, 1974) the periphery possessed a relative political autonomy. Perhaps the most crucial difference between the Arab Middle East and Christendom was that in Europe there developed autocephalus townships which were not internally divided by ethnic, religious or cultural differences (Weber, 1958). The legal and political autonomy of European cities encouraged the development of a rich associational life of guilds and professional groups. This provided the ideal social milieu for the development of urban piety, bourgeois rationalism, commercial stability and an independent legal system. By contrast, these prerequisites of capitalist development were absent in Islam because the city was primarily a military outpost of the state within which guilds and merchants were closely supervised by the state bureaucracy. Furthermore, cities in Islam were internally divided into subcommunities and did not develop integrated institutions. These general characteristics – a centralized state apparatus, prebendal land rights, bureaucratically controlled guilds – Weber summarized as 'sultanism', a system of authority which encouraged the promotion of officials by arbitrary decision-making, rather than rational, universal norms, and resulted in instability in legal and financial conditions. Rather than invest their wealth in productive capital, merchants were more likely to seek security in *waqf* property. This immobilization of capital 'corresponded fully to the spirit of the ancient economy which used accumulated wealth as a source of rent, not as acquisitive capital' (Weber, 1968a, p. 1097).

This second argument was certainly not original. Weber's ideas about sultanism were simply one version of the well-established theory that the backwardness of Islam was the outcome of Oriental Despotism (Koebner, 1951; Venturi, 1963). From Montesquieu onwards it had been generally believed that the backwardness of Oriental societies resulted from three conditions: (1) the absence of private property in land; (2) the stultifying uniformity of belief and tradition, which resulted from the absence of class distinctions; and (3) the arbitrary power of the despotic ruler. This traditional theory was developed by social scientists like J. S. Mill and Weber around the notion that the crucial ingredient for a society which aimed to be simultaneously capitalist and democratic was a strong, politically active middle class. Mill saw the educated British middle class as the main bastion against the growing tide of cultural uniformity and illiberality. In a similar mood, Weber had chronicled the massive contribution of the Protestant middle classes to European economic development, but in Germany Weber recognized that political unification and economic strength owed more to Bismarck, the military and the Junker class than to the leadership of the bourgeoisie. The problem facing Germany was the decline of the traditional Junkers and the failure of the middle class to develop any political consciousness and leadership (Giddens, 1972). When Mill and Weber, therefore, reflected on the implications of the absence of a middle class in Asia, they were also deeply concerned by the ambiguities of the location of the middle class in their own societies.

It is generally agreed that, for an alternative to Weber, we have to turn to Marx and Engels. There is the conventional notion that, whereas Weber founded his sociology on the subjective orientation of social actors, Marx by contrast established his materialistic analysis on the objective structures of modes of production. In crude terms, Marx treated Protestantism as an effect of the economic interests of the rising bourgeois class in their struggle with the dominant class of the feudal mode of production (Birnbaum, 1953). For our purpose, a more significant difference between Marx and Weber lies in Marx's rejection of the idea that the origins of capitalist accumulation are to be found in innovative entrepreneurial activity. Marx scornfully demolished the myth that 'the so-called primitive accumulation' of capital was made possible by a virtuous minority who were 'industrious, intelligent, and, above all, thrifty' and who were consequently distinguished from the mass of 'lazy rascals [that] wasted their substance in riotous living' (Marx, 1930, p. 790). In opposition to this myth, Marx attempted to show that the capitalist system emerged with the brutal separation of independent peasants from the means of production (the land) in order to transform them into landless wage-earners. At the same time, the industrial capitalist had to destroy the privileges of the feudal lords and the restrictive guild organization of the traditional master craftsmen. The real origins of capitalism were not in the thrifty, calculating activity of entrepreneurs, but in 'the historical process whereby the producer is divorced from the means of production' and 'this exploitation is written in the annals of mankind in letters of blood and fire' (Marx, 1930, p. 792).

Without raking over the venerable arguments about Marx's relationship to Weber, it is important to note two aspects of Marx's treatment of the rise of global capitalism. First, in his early work, Marx did ascribe a historically creative, dynamic role to the bourgeoisie as the great solvent of traditional relationships. In the *Communist Manifesto*, Marx and Engels were quite explicit in their claim that the 'bourgeoisie, historically, has played a most revolutionary part.... It has accomplished wonders far surpassing Egyptian pyramids, Roman aqueducts and Gothic cathedrals' (Marx and Engels, 1973, p. 70). Second, in their commentaries on the Middle East and Asia, Marx and Engels developed the concept of an Asiatic mode of production in which the state was the real landlord and there was no private property in the means of production. Asia lacked the critical mechanism for radical change, namely, the struggle between classes for the control of property. In a society dominated by the state and the official bureaucracy, the imperial cities were merely 'royal camps' (Marx, 1973, p. 479) in which a burgher class could not flourish. Just as Mill and Weber had thought that it was political instability which accounted for the lack of productive investment in Oriental society, so Engels in his commentary on Turkey came to the same conclusion: that the economic surplus was not 'safe from the hands of greedy satraps and pashas. The first basic condition of bourgeois acquisition is lacking, the security of the person and the property of the trader' (Marx and Engels, 1953, p. 40).

Because of their internally static condition, the societies of the Orient could only be changed by exogenous forces, namely, capitalist imperialism and colonialism. In China, the English bourgeoisie had brought down the 'most imperturbable empire on earth' by the simple expedient bales of calico (Marx and Engels, 1972, p. 18). Cheap commodities were the heavy artillery by which the English capitalists had forced all nations to accept 'the bourgeois mode of production' (Marx and Engels, 1973, p. 71). It was in India in particular that the British had brought about the only social revolution in Asia, by transforming land into a commodity, organizing a modern army, building a railway system and modernizing communication. Similar results followed in the Middle East with French colonialism. Thus, in his article for the *Northern Star* on the revolt of Abd el Kader against the French invasion from 1832 to 1847, Engels referred to the revolt as 'hopeless'. He welcomed the French conquest as 'an important and fortunate fact for the progress of civilization' directed against 'the barbarian state of society' (Feuer, 1971, p. 489). Marx and Engels consistently maintained that the stationary societies of the Middle East and Asia could only be transformed by the destructive effects of capitalist expansion. This belief was combined with the notion that the struggle of small nations or minorities against this historical growth of the capitalist mode of production was, by definition, a reactionary struggle.

During the eighteenth and nineteenth centuries the major figures of sociology and political economy – Engels, Hegel, Marx, Mill, Montesquieu and Weber – came to the conclusion that the economic backwardness of the Middle East resulted from a combination of social and political causes, of which the absence of a strong middle class of capitalist entrepreneurs was especially important. Their view of the social stratification of Middle East societies was confirmed by the fact that the traditional penetration of Islamic commercial life by minorities (Greeks, Jews, Armenians, South Slavs) steadily increased in the period following the Capitulations. The presence of foreign entrepreneurs in the commercial life of the Middle East has been explained in terms of a variety of factors. Weber claimed that a 'martial religion' was hostile to the rational economic ethos and 'inherently contemptuous of bourgeois-commercial utilitarianism' (Weber, 1968, p. 1106). Muslim intellectuals and professionals preferred government service as the only honourable employment for their social class. The foreign trade of the Ottoman empire tended to come under the control of Jewish, Christian and non-Ottoman merchants, while the political and administrative tasks of the empire remained far more under the control of indigenous Muslim strata. A simpler explanation might be that through a series of Capitulation agreements foreign groups were able to establish a wide range of privileges which gave them substantial control over Ottoman commerce. The early Capitulations of 1535, granting security to French traders, were gradually extended to English merchants in 1580 and to Dutch traders in 1612. In the eighteenth century, these agreements were steadily abused by the practice of awarding privileges of consular (*berâts*) to numerous protégés (Gibb and Bowen, 1950; Hodgson, 1974).

The contemporary scholarly debate provides three areas for discussion: (1) studies on psychological motivation and value commitment as preconditions for economic 'take-off', (2) studies of the continuing absence of an autonomous middle class; and (3) investigations of the emerging new middle class, with special reference to the potential role of the army as a modernizing agency.

The Weberian tradition has been clearly upheld by the research of American sociologists, in particular Daniel Lerner (1958) and David C. McClelland (1961, 1963). In Lerner's theory of the breakdown of traditional society, urbanization and social mobility encourage the development of empathy, namely, the ability to imagine and occupy new and varied social roles. This social-psychological transition from a rigid to empathetic character-type is important for the construction of an open, democratic society in which people have to acquire and express preferences for different commodities, political leaders and social structures. The general problem in the Middle East is that expectations have grown too rapidly in a situation where the objective structures of modern society have been inadequately developed. This gap between expectation and provision was a typical experience of the young middle class, which had abandoned traditional life-styles. In Syria, after the removal of the mandate in 1941, a new middle class emerged but 'the number of educated young aspirants for social mobility is increasing at a much faster rate than the capacity of Syrian institutions to absorb them satisfactorily' (Lerner, 1958, p. 276). Their access to top social positions was blocked by the political control of the established oligarchy. Furthermore, until 1950 over one-half of the university students graduated in law, while posts in agriculture and engineering could not be filled. The majority of students wanted secure posts in government service, since 'outside the bureaucracy, there is little opportunity to utilize the skills acquired by legal or humanistic training' (Lerner, 1958, pp. 276–7). The frustration of the middle class resulted in disaffection with the existing government and a drift toward radical and extremist parties. The dilemma of the Syrian middle class is in fact the problem of modern, educated men whose rising expectations are circumscribed by the presence of a largely rural and traditional environment. In Lerner's model, the transition to modernity requires a thorough secularization of the traditional Islamic environment.

A similar theory is presented in McClelland's studies of achievement motivation and increased economic output. In this theory, the principal motivation of entrepreneurship is the need for achievement, which is created during early socialization, when the child is exposed to demands for high standards of performance and self-reliance. Although McClelland's view of entrepreneurship has been influential in sociology as a whole (Kilby, 1971; Smelser, 1976), specific applications in the Middle East have not been attempted. Furthermore, McClelland's own view of entrepreneurship in backward societies is highly contradictory. In 1950, he found that n-Achievement in poor countries was generally higher than in the more developed countries. McClelland's explanation was that, realizing their backwardness in international terms, these societies 'are now motivated to close the gap between themselves and the more industrially developed countries' (McClelland, 1961, p. 102). Yet, when McClelland discovered that n-Achievement levels were lower in Italy and Turkey than in the United States, he provided the convenient explanation that this finding was not unusual since it 'agrees with the level of development of those countries' (McClelland, 1961, p. 287).

While Lerner and McClelland came to the conclusion that the cultural and familial environment of the Middle East (apart from Lebanon) was not conducive to middle-class entrepreneurship, other sociologists have confirmed this argument by showing that Middle East entrepreneurship is less organized and rational than European capitalist behaviour. Business is not organized around rational, universalistic principles, but around traditional and particularistic norms. Research into Lebanese business structure suggested that there was a marked reluctance to accept the corporate form of business, factory organization and labour discipline, and that there was a clear preference for business partnership based on kinship ties (Sayigh, 1962 and 1963). Sayigh also claimed that in Arab society generally there was a careless attitude to the timetable requirements of industrial production and commercial life. The shift from rule-of-thumb techniques to proper rational business calculation was slow. The tardy development of commercial rationality was attributed to 'suspicion of the unfamiliar processes of calculation, belief that elaborate data collection and calculation are not really needed, traditionalism, and hesitation to surrender still one more area of action to the expert in the business establishment' (Sayigh, 1965, p. 65).

A similar picture has been offered by A. J. Meyer, who commented that, by Weber's standards of rational bureaucratic organization, most Middle East companies would be regarded as traditional (Meyer, 1958 and 1959). In Middle East capitalism, there is little differentiation between retail and wholesale, low specialization in one brand of product and scant delegation of authority. The absence of any rational organization of the firm was largely accounted for by the preference for the family firm, on the one hand, and for farming and land investment rather than industry, on the other. Meyer suggested that it was much easier for rich Arabs to preserve the extended family in a rural, farming context than in an urban, industrial environment. Although Meyer's view that the family firm is incompatible with capitalist rationality can be challenged with specific reference, for example, to Lebanon (Khalaf and Shwayri, 1966), his position falls into line with the general consensus that in backward societies entrepreneurial skill is directed toward trade or land rather than industry – 'into trade, where the turnover of capital is rapid, into land which is both secure and more liquid than factories' (Habakkuk, 1971, p. 48).

Another group of historians and social scientists has suggested that the historically missing bourgeoisie has not emerged within the contemporary system of social stratification. The historical claim is linked to the notion that in Middle East societies, although the state apparatus was overdeveloped, there was virtually no development of a 'civil society'. In the classical accounts of Oriental Despotism, the problem of Oriental stagnation was a consequence of the absence of intervening, intermediate institutions (in Weber's terms, the absence of *Rechtsgemeinschaften*). Islamic societies were, so to speak, all state and no society. Thus, 'the Ottoman empire lacked those "intermediate" structures which both Machiavelli and Montesquieu regarded as constituting the difference between Eastern despotism and Western feudalism' (Mardin, 1969, p. 264). This contrast between East and West in terms of intermediate (particularly bourgeois) institutions has been repeated in much of the contemporary literature. Alfred Bonné provided a list of causes which inhibited the emergence of capitalism in the Middle East: the low density of population, restrictions on the scope of the market, the control of commerce by foreigners and the impact of cheap European commodities on local markets which had no adequate protection. But at the top of his list came the missing middle-class entrepreneur (Bonné, 1960, p. 217).

In the two decades after the Second World War, in most Middle East societies over one-half the employed population were located in agriculture; the industrial working class remained relatively insignificant. For example, the Egyptian census of 1947 showed that the urban working class in industrial occupations represented 6 per cent of the employed population (Gordon and Fridman, 1964). The Egyptian case is instructive because, even in a Middle East society where industrialization has gone further than in other societies within the region, the middle class of self-employed, small capitalists and professional people was approximately 6–10 per cent of the population (Berger, 1957, 1958 and 1964). The middle class was both small and internally fragmented by its differentiation into an urban and rural sector (Hussein, 1973; van Nieuwenhuijze, 1965). The most significant change has been the emergence of a new middle class of state employees, rather than the development of the small capitalist class. These developments are indicated by the growth of professional associations in law, medicine and the technical professions (Reid, 1974; Ziadeh, 1968). Although the increase in the middle-class salariat was a consequence of a rapid expansion in the role of the state in the economy, the new middle class was also brought into existence by the growth of the petroleum industry. A particularly clear illustration of this process has been documented in the case of Saudi Arabia (Rugh, 1973).

Although the process of industrialization has produced a new middle class, most research suggests that it does not possess any social integration. There is no single group within the class which is capable of exercising any decisive political leadership. The new professional groups tend to divide into traditional and modern wings. Thus, 'it would be misleading to suggest that the professionals were a cohesive group with a shared social outlook. Many had sprung from the landed upper class and continued to identify with it despite their education and professional experience' (Reid, 1974, p. 56). In the absence of an integrated élite within the civilian middle class, it has become common for social scientists to consider the Middle East army as an alternative force for innovation and modernization.

The argument about the army as the spearhead of the political interests of the new middle class has been closely associated with the research of Halpern, whose primary thesis is that 'the army has become the principal actor and instrument of a new middle class' (Halpern, 1962, p. 278). The army can play this modernizing role because it has been exposed to advanced technology, a modern education and principles of rational organization and efficiency. The failure of the traditional élite and the small capitalist class to develop Arab societies attracted the new middle class to the army as an alternative institution for stimulating rapid social change. The army has adhered to the ideology that it alone represents the nation and remains outside the context of party politics, but in practice the army is not immune from the 'factionalism within the ruling junta' (Halpern, 1962, p. 304). Although there is a wide consensus that the military does indeed play a significant social role, there has been a marked divergence of opinion regarding the social conditions which produce military intervention. Halpern has analysed the Middle Eastern army as the coherent instrument of an integrated new middle class.

In contrast to Halpern, Perlmutter (1967, 1970) demonstrated that it was the very weakness of the new middle class, the existence of class conflict and the absence of any political authority which propelled the army into politics. Once in power, the army has not been a cohesive social factor and has not enjoyed any lasting success as an agent of rapid modernization. It is the 'absence of a strong, cohesive, and articulate middle class which is a condition for praetorian government' (Perlmutter, 1977, p. 97). The army cannot directly represent the new middle class because the interests of that class are divided and the class is politically underdeveloped. The recent history of military intervention in Syria, Iraq and Egypt indicates the loss of political power by the middle class. Rather than represent it, the army subordinates the weak middle class (Hottinger, 1968, p. 124).

From this perspective, a variety of social scientists have been struck not by the social changes which are implied by the relationship between the new middle class and the army, but by the massive historical continuity of the army's social hegemony. This particular interpretation can be connected with Weber's view that Middle East societies were founded by conquest in the name of a religion for which *jihad* was an institution of major salvational significance. From the earliest times, military virtues were more important than bourgeois virtues. This emphasis on social continuity also connects contemporary analysis with the writing of Hegel and Marx on Oriental stagnation.

The absence of a property-owning middle class has also been regarded as an element in the absence of a genuine revolutionary tradition in Middle Eastern societies. Avineri's observation about the failure of the nationalist movement to bring off a real social revolution (1970, p. 34) has received widespread support from political scientists (Zartman, 1976). Whereas the

West has undergone a series of revolutionary struggles based on class conflict, involving the mass of society equipped with a revolutionary ideology, Middle East society has only experienced political struggles between social élites. The military *coup d'état* has resulted in changes of ruling personnel and political alliance, but it has not produced radical changes in social structure. A recent symposium on revolutions concluded that 'struggles for independence and radical movements in the Middle East, *coups d'état*, insurrections and rebellions so far do not constitute revolutions' (Vatikiotis, 1972, pp. 12—13). The struggles of the nineteenth and twentieth centuries were feuds between political notables (Hourani, 1968), rather than revolutionary conflicts of a class nature. This absence has also been regarded as a function of the missing middle class. Because of the failure of an urban autonomous middle class to develop as a dynamic force in society, there has been no corresponding radical bourgeois tradition in ideology and law. In the West the bougeois class developed a radical critique of feudalism: the theory of the right to resist bad government, the doctrine of the separation of powers, the theory of individual rights and the corpus of beliefs which arose with bourgeois society (social contract, individualism, equality, freedom of exchange). In the Middle East, the concepts of radical social change were imported from revolutionary Europe, but although the intelligentsia acquired a new set of slogans, the institutions of bourgeois radicalism (parliament, independent judiciary, free press and secular university) remained underdeveloped (Lewis, 1953).

In summary, the modern version of the theory of Oriental Despotism states that Oriental societies have been dominated by highly centralized, but despotic and arbitrary states, founded on public control of land through prebendal land rights. This centralized state apparatus ruled out the development of independent cities, autonomous guilds and an urban middle class of property-owning capitalists. Characteristic bourgeois institutions and virtues did not develop. The Middle East stagnated because of this missing link. The transformations of the Middle East in the modern period are merely appearances. The underlying continuity of the centralized state, the state bureaucracy and the military is the all-pervasive feature of the Middle East. The arrival of a new middle class has done little to alter the fundamental structure and ethos of Arabic society. The new salariat has been too weak and divided to shoulder the task of social reconstruction.

In opposition to the theory of Oriental Despotism, it is conventional to argue that there was nothing in traditional Islamic culture and social arrangements that inhibited the development of an industrial, capitalist society. It is possible to point to the development of a mercantile culture from early Islamic times, the commercialization of Middle East society, the rapid development of banking and the centrality of trade to Islamic societies.

Weber's view that the social carriers of Islamic values were warriors and that Islam failed to elaborate an ascetic calling in business cannot be supported (Turner, 1974a).

The most systematic criticism of the Weberian tradition as a whole has been developed by Rodinson. From the Koran and *hadith*, Rodinson demonstrates that, far from discouraging economic involvement, Islam provides an explicit legitimation of trade and commerce: 'Economic activity, the search for profit, trade, and consequently, production for the market, are looked upon with no less favour by Muslim tradition than by the Koran itself. We even find eulogistic formulations about merchants' (Rodinson, 1974, p. 16). The regulations controlling *riba* did not hinder investment and entrepreneurship. From the time of the Prophet, merchants conformed exactly to the requirements of the Weberian typology; commercial capital was extensively developed and petty commodity production was dominant, although craftsmen did hire wage-workers (Rodinson, 1974, p. 51). A capitalist sector developed alongside existing pre-capitalist agrarian modes of production and these early industrial enterprises (especially in textiles) were well provided for in terms of commercial, banking institutions.

The first check to this commercial development was the result of external forces such as the Crusades and Mongol invasions. The early period of cultural and economic expansion gave way to patrimonial empires with a greater emphasis on discipline, conformity and imitation. In the seventeenth century European societies began to gain an economic and military advantage over the Islamic Middle East. By the nineteenth century the economic growth of industrial enterprises was 'only in accordance with the European model, imitating it, and generally speaking, under its domination. The preponderance of Europe made this development very difficult, especially owing to the lead that European technique had acquired, the lack of protection, free trade imposed by force, and the subjection of those states that had remained independent, through the mechanism of the public debt and owing to their economic and military weakness' (Rodinson, 1974, pp. 130–1). Rodinson's central thesis is that Islam did not stand in the way of capitalist development, but that capitalism did not emerge as the dominant mode of production until it was implanted by the West under highly unfavourable conditions. The Middle East was forced into a path of dependent capitalist development in the first half of the twentieth century.

These criticisms of the Weberian tradition are valid in their own terms, but they do not go far enough as a critique of the total Orientalist perspective (Turner, 1979) because many of its primary assumptions have remained unchallenged. In order to refute the argument that Islam blocked the development of the capitalist mode of production, these authors characteristically proceed by attempting to establish the presence of Muslim merchants and traders. The assumption here is that merchants will develop into capitalists. In volume three of *Capital*, Marx showed that the existence of merchants cannot contribute to the overthrow of pre-capitalist modes of production, but may in fact conserve archaic economic conditions. Capitalists must constantly revolutionize the means of production in order to ensure the production of capital to produce more capital ('Accumulate! Accumulate! That is Moses and all the prophets!'). By contrast, the merchant who buys and sells operates within circulation rather than production. The development of trade under merchant control in pre-capitalist empires was not a forewarning of the birth of capitalism: 'the mere presence of monetary wealth and even the achievement of a kind of supremacy on its part, is in no way sufficient for this dissolution into capital to happen. Or else ancient Rome, Byzantium, etc.... would have ended their history with free labor and capital' (Marx, 1973, p. 506). The wealth of merchants 'remained always within the sphere of circulation, was never applied either to agricultural or industrial production in any innovative fashion. The so-called commercial revolution in no way altered the feudal mode of production' (Hilton, 1976, p. 23). The attempts by Oriental historians to refute Weber by demonstrating the existence of Muslim merchants are, therefore, simply irrelevant.

The issue has been further confused by the tendency of Oriental historians to utilize the terms 'merchant' and 'bourgeoisie' interchangeably. Merchants operate in the sphere of circulation, not production. More importantly, it is impossible to identify social classes without a prior identification of modes of production – classes are determined by their functions within modes of production. In order to provide a critique of existing approaches to the problem of Middle Eastern capitalism, it will be necessary to go beyond the state of identifying the presence of merchants or attitudes favourable to interests or institutions which stimulated trade. It is necessary to undermine much of the mythological history of European capitalism as a supposed model for Middle Eastern development.

All the European capitalist societies industrialized either before or without a bourgeois revolution. In Britain, the foundations of capitalism were established in the countryside in the sixteenth century by landlords, who enclosed the land for sheep in response to the demand for wool. The system of enclosures had destroyed the peasantry as a class by 1600, thereby laying the basis for landless wage-labour. Agrarian capitalism was brought about by an alliance between the rural gentry and the upper ranks of the townsmen (Moore, 1967). Capitalist relations had already penetrated the countryside long before the revolutions of 1640 and 1688; these were not bourgeois revolutions against a reactionary feudal nobility. The seventeenth-century struggles established certain juridical and political conditions for the spread of capitalism, but they did not result in the political dominance of the bourgeoisie. The control of the state remained in the hands of the traditional nobility, a large section of which had gone over to agrarian capitalism. This alliance between agrarian and industrial capitalists gave British capitalism its stability. The industrial revolution of 1780–1840 took place before the bourgeoisie had achieved political hegemony between 1832 and 1850. It has often been observed that many of the archaic features of British society – the survival of privileges, the lack of professionalism in business, the monarchy, the Established Church and the House of Lords – can be attributed to the fact that Britain achieved capitalist industrialization without a bourgeois revolution (Anderson, 1964).

The French Revolution has been traditionally regarded as the example of a successful bourgeois revolution, because it brought the bourgeoisie to power, transformed the state and created in Jacobinism a typical ideology of the bourgeoisie (Poulantzas, 1973). However, the triumph of the bourgeoisie over the nobility was achieved by consolidating the economic and political position of the peasantry and the petty bourgeoisie. Although the French Revolution may have created the conditions for capitalist development, large-scale industrial production was slow to emerge in an economy dominated by the small family enterprise. A banking system linked to the needs of industry was also lacking. In the countryside, the continuity of the peasant farm contributed to the immobility of labour and the limitations of the home market for capitalist commodities. From this point of view, the French Revolution represented the premature political victory of the bourgeoisie; it did not correspond to a clear industrial revolution. Even its political aspect was limited by the necessity for alliances with the peasantry and the petty bourgeoisie. This special combination of features led Marx to believe that the French Revolution was politically precocious, a tragedy followed by the farce of 1848.

The absence of an unambiguous bourgeois revolution coupled with rapid capitalist expansion was also repeated in the cases of Germany, Italy and Russia. The industrialization of Germany is a particularly eloquent example of capitalist expansion conducted under the auspices of the state. The bourgeois class never replaced the political control of the Junker class. There was obviously 'no close correspondence between economic growth and democratisation. It may even be justifiable to attribute economic advance at least partly to political retardation' (Borchardt, 1973, p. 115). A similar disjuncture between economic, political and social developments exists in the instances of Italy and Russia (Gerschenkron, 1962). Throughout western Europe 'one very striking point common to every case should perhaps be noted: namely the bourgeoisie's lack of political capacity (because of its class constitution) successfully to lead its own revolution in open action' (Poulantzas, 1973, p. 183). In short, there are no historical grounds by which it can be claimed that the Middle East does not possess a characteristic which was decisive in European capitalist development. On the contrary, what both share is a process of industrialization in which the bourgeoisie is typically 'missing'.

These different paths to capitalist development in Europe also established different conditions under which entrepreneurship could operate. Again, England provided the exceptional case. Capitalist development in coal-mining, engineering, textiles, agricultural improvement and shipbuilding were all undertaken without a significant state intervention in the economy. British capitalism, furthermore, did not possess a banking system which was geared to long-term industrial investment requirements. It is also significant that Britain's industrial revolution was over long before the first attempt was made in 1870 to create a system of universal education at an elementary level. It does not follow that Britain was blessed with an abundance of achievement-motivated, innovative entrepreneurs ready to risk their capital in uncertain industrial inventions. More important was the fact that Britain enjoyed enormous advantages as the first industrial nation – a stable political environment, an expanding home market, cheap transport, cheap sources of energy and, above all, a virtual monopoly of overseas markets. Thus, the British cotton industry did not rely on its 'competitive superiority but on a monopoly of the colonial and underdeveloped markets which the British Empire, the British navy and British commercial supremacy gave it' (Hobsbawm, 1969, p. 58).

The existence of Britain as a capitalist society changed the conditions for similar developments in Europe. The relatively backward societies of France, Germany and Italy were forced to adopt different development strategies. They concentrated on the introduction of the most advanced and expensive technology, introducing large-scale plants and fostering investment-goods industries (Gerschenkron, 1962). These strategies were financed not by the private family capitalist of the British experience, but by the state and the banks and, in Italy, foreign investment.

The main conclusion of this sketch of European economic development is that the economic revolution (to establish the dominance of the capitalist mode of production) and the political revolution (to establish the political dominance of the bourgeoisie over liberal, parliamentary democracy) very rarely coincide. The argument presented by Vatikiotis, Lewis, Avineri and others that in the Middle East industrial development has not been accompanied by a middle-class dominated democracy also applies in the case of European development. Indeed, the very uneven and backward nature of development in the competitive phase of capitalism and the peculiarly unstable alliances between fractions of the dominant class has led theorists like Poulantzas (1974) to the conclusion that the economic concentrations of monopoly capital and the capitalist development of the countryside requires fascism.

It is characteristic of the advanced industrial societies that the system of family capitalism (competitive capitalism) is subordinated to a system of monopoly capitalism, based on large international corporations where investment for capital restructuring is financed through the multinational companies and public agencies such as investment banks, pension funds and the state. Advanced capitalism requires the services of the state to supply unprofitable aspects of the infrastructure, to assist in the crises of capitalism, to redress the uneven distribution of regional resources and to discipline labour (Holloway and Picciotto, 1978).

The growth of the state in the operations of modern economies has also been associated with the growth of a new middle class. In part, this new middle class has emerged with the growing technical sophistication of industrial production, but its presence is also explained by the division between industrial management and ownership. The growth of a professional class of managers, supervisors, accountants, planners and service workers corresponds to the new requirements of capital accumulation in advanced capitalism. While state expenditure as a percentage of gross national product in many advanced capitalist societies has reached very high levels (52 per cent in Britain in the 1960s), there has been a profound change in the class structure so that the new middle class in America and Britain represents between 48 per cent and 54 per cent of all employees. Correspondingly, the percentage of productive manual workers in America, Europe and Japan continues to decline relative to other social classes.

Against this background of capitalist development in the West, we can develop a more realistic appraisal of the nature of industrialization in the Middle East. The industrial development of Britain radically changed the conditions for 'spontaneous capitalism' in all other societies. In particular, this meant that the possibilities of industrialization under competitive capitalist conditions for relatively backward societies were severely limited. Most developing societies have been forced to opt for a strategy of 'development from above' under the guidance of the state or the party or the army. In this respect, the central role of the state, the absence of a powerful middle class and the rise of a new middle class in the Middle East does not appear to be as historically peculiar as commonplace. The really unique case remains Britain, in which competitive capitalism had a very long history and in which the funds for new investments were provided out of the profits of the family firm. The existence of monopoly capitalism on a global scale in the twentieth century has made the likelihood of industrial success under *laissez-faire* conditions with private entrepreneurship rather limited. The recent history of President Sadat's 'open-door policy' which, rather than stimulating industrial investment in Egypt, created a boom in imported luxury goods, is a particularly good illustration of the effects of free entrepreneurship in a developing society (Aulas, 1976). Most Middle East societies, because of their colonial heritage, their relative backwardness, the role of multinationals in the control of world trade and the strength of international competition, have opted for some form of state management, usually state capitalism with an Arab socialist ideology. In this regard, the post-independence development of Algeria is an instructive example. Centralized industrial development in Algeria was based on the realization that full independence could only be achieved on the basis of economic self-sufficiency and that, if Algeria's oil resources are exhausted in 1984, alternative means of production must be developed very rapidly (Clegg, 1971; Farsoun, 1975). Apart from Lebanon, the majority of Middle East societies (especially Turkey, Iraq, Syria, Egypt, Algeria and Tunisia) have begun the process of industrialization under state intervention without a phase of competitive capitalism. This is a typical, not peculiar, development strategy.

All the conditions which are conventionally said to have prevented the emergence of capitalism in Islamic lands – unfavourable religious attitudes to wealth, the preference for honorific professions over business occupations, the scarcity of entrepreneurial talent, arbitrary law-making procedures – were also present in European societies. The indigenous middle class was politically weak or economically backward; entrepreneurial roles, as in the Middle East, were often filled by foreign migrants (Trevor-Roper, 1967). If bourgeois revolutions did not take place in Arab societies, they were similarly missing in Europe in the sense that the bourgeois political revolution did not coincide with the industrial revolutions. In both regions, the state, the army or the banks have been the main vehicle for entrepreneurial functions in societies faced by the task of rapid political unification, social development and capital accumulation. The important differences between the north European societies and the Middle East are to be found in the very different conditions for development which are inevitably posed for 'late developers'. In facing the problem of rapid, intensive industrialization, 'late developers' will be typically forced to solve the problem of accumulation not through external colonies, but through their own agricultural and pre-capitalist sectors. The solution does not lie in the behaviour of risk-taking entrepreneurs.

References and Further Reading

Al-Azmeh, Aziz. 'What is the Islamic city?' *Review of Middle East Studies*, 2(1976): 1–12.

Alexander, A.D. 'Industrial entrepreneurship in Turkey: origins and growth', *Economic Development and Cultural Change*, 8(1960): 349–65.

Anderson, Perry. 'Origins of the present crisis', *New Left Review*, 23(1964): 26–54.

__*Lineages of the Absolutist State*, London, 1974.

Aulas, Marie-Christine, 'Sadat's Egypt', *New Left Review*, 98(1976): 84–97.

Avineri, Shlomo. 'The Palestinians and Israel'. *Commentary*, 49(1970): 31–44.

__'Modernization and Arab society: some reflections', in Irving Howe and Carl Gershman, (eds), *Israel, the Arabs and the Middle East*, New York, 1972.

Baran, Paul A. *The Political Economy of Growth*, Harmondsworth, 1973.

Bellah, Robert N. (ed.) *Religion and Progress in Modern Asia*, New York, 1965.

Berger, M. *Bureaucracy and Society in Modern Egypt*, Princeton, N.J., 1957.

__'The middle class in the Arab world', in W. Z. Laqueur (ed.), *The Middle East in Transition*, London, 1958.

__*The Arab World Today*, New York, 1964.

Binder, L. (ed.), *The Study of the Middle East*, New York, 1976.

Birnbaum, Norman. 'Conflicting interpretations of the rise of capitalism: Marx and Weber', *British Journal of Sociology*, 4(1953): 125–40.

Bonné, Alfred. *State and Economics in the Middle East*, London, 1960.

Borchardt, Kurt. 'The industrial Revolution in Germany 1700–1914', in Carlo M. Cipolla (ed.), *The Emergence of Industrial Societies*, London, 1973.

Burns, J. H. 'J. S. Mill and democracy 1829–61', in J. B. Schneewind (ed.), *Mill*, London, 1968.

Cipolla, Carlo M. (ed), *The Emergence of Industrial Societies*, London, 1973.

Clegg, Ian. *Workers' Self-Management in Algeria*, New York, 1971.

Clough, S. B. *The Economic History of Modern Italy*, London, 1964.

Elkan, Walter, *An Introduction to Development Economics*, Harmondsworth, 1973.

Farsoun, Karen, 'State capitalism in Algeria' *MERIP Reports* 35(1975): 3–30.

Feuer, Lewis S. (ed.), *Marx and Engels: Basic Writings in Politics and Philosophy*, London, 1971.

Fisher, S. N. (ed.), *Social Forces in the Middle East*, New York, 1968.

Frank, A. G. *Capitalism and Underdevelopment in Latin America*, New York, 1969.

Gerschenkron, A. *Economic Backwardness in Historical Perspective*, Cambridge, Mass., 1962.

Gibb, H. A. R. and Bowen, H. *Islamic Society and the West*, Vol. 1, London, 1950.

Giddens, A. *Politics and Sociology in the Thought of Max Weber*, London, 1972.

Goitein, S. D. 'The rise of the Near-Eastern bourgeoisie in early Islamic times', '*Journal of World History* 3(1957): 583–604.

Gordon, L. A. and Fridman, L. A. 'Peculiarities in the composition and structure of the working class in the economically underdeveloped countries of Asia and Africa (the example of India and the UAR)', in T. P. Thornton (ed.), *The Third World in Soviet Perspective*, Princeton, N. J., 1964.

Gramsci, Antonio. *Quaderni del Carcere. (Il Risorgimento)*, Vol. 3, Turin, 1949.

Habakkuk, J. 'Lectures on economic development', in I. Livingstone (ed.), *Economic Policy for Development*, Harmondsworth, 1971.

Halpern, Manfred. 'Middle Eastern armies and the new middle class', in J. J. Johnson, (ed.), *The Role of the Military in Underdeveloped Countries*, Princeton, N. J., 1962.

Hilton, R., (ed.), *The Transition from Feudalism to Capitalism*, London, 1976.

Hobsbawm, E. J. *Industry and Empire*, Harmondsworth, 1969.

Hodgson, Marshall G. S. *The Venture of Islam*, Chicago and London, 1974, 3 vols.

Holloway, John and Picciotto, Sol (eds.), *State and Capital: a Marxist Debate*, London, 1978.

Hoselitz, Bert F. 'Entrepreneurship and economic growth', *American Journal of Economics and Sociology*, 12(1952): 97–110.

Hottinger, Arnold. 'How the Arab bourgeoisie lost power', *Journal of Contemporary History*, 3(1968): 111–28.

Hourani, A. 'Ottoman reform and the politics of notables' in W. R. Polk and R. C. Chambers (eds.), *The Beginnings of Modernization in the Middle East*, Chicago, 1968.

Howe, Irving and Gershman, Carl (eds.), *Israel, the Arabs and the Middle East*, New York, 1972.

Hussein, Mahmoud. *Class Conflict in Egypt: 1945–1970*, New York, 1973.

Issawi, Charles. 'The entrepreneur class', in S. N. Fisher (ed.), *Social Forces in the Middle East*, New York, 1968.

Johnson, J. J. (ed.), *The Role of the Military in Underdeveloped Countries*, Princeton, N. J., 1962.

Khalaf, Samir and Shwayri, Emilie. 'Family firms and industrial development: the Lebanese case', *Economic Development and Cultural Change*, 15(1966): 59–69.

Kilby, Peter (ed.), *Entrepreneurship and Economic Development*, New York, 1971.

Koebner, R. 'Despot and Despotism: vicissitudes of a political term', *Journal of the Warburg and Courtauld Institute*, 14(1951): 275–302.

Laqueur, W. Z. (ed.), *The Middle East in Transition*, London, 1958.

Lerner, Daniel. *The Passing of Traditional Society*, New York, 1958.

Lewis, Bernard. 'The impact of the French Revolution on Turkey', *Journal of World History*, 1(1953): 105–25.

Livingstone, I. (ed.), *Economic Policy for Development*, Harmondsworth, 1971.

Mardin, S. 'Power, civil society and culture in the Ottoman Empire', *Comparative Studies in Society and History*, 11(1969): 258–81.

Marx, K. *Capital*, London, 1930, 2 vols.

__*Grundrisse*, Harmondsworth, 1973.

Marx. K. and Engels, F. *The Russian Menace to Europe*, London, 1953.

__*On Colonialism*, New York, 1972.

__*The Revolution of 1848*, Harmondsworth, 1973.

McClelland, David C. *The Achieving Society*, Princeton, N.J., 1961.

__'National character and economic growth in Turkey and Iran', in Lucian W. Pye (ed.), *Communications and Political Development*, Princeton, N.J., 1963.

Meyer, A.J. *Middle Eastern Capitalism*, Cambridge, Mass., 1959.

__'Entrepreneurship and economic development in the Middle East', *Public Opinion Quarterly*, 22(1958): 391–6.

Moore, Barrington, Jr. *Social Origins of Dictatorship and Democracy*, Harmondsworth, 1967.

Owen, Roger, 'Islam and capitalism: a critique of Rodinson', *Review of Middle East Studies*, 2(1976): 85–93.

Perlmutter, Amos. 'Egypt and the Myth of the new middle class: a comparative analysis', *Comparative Studies in Society and History*, 10(1967): 46–65.

__'The myth of the myth of the new middle class: some lessons in social and political history', *Comparative Studies in Society and History*, 12(1970): 14–26.

__*The Military and Politics in Modern Times*, New Haven and London, 1977.

Polk, W.R. and Chambers, R.C. (eds.), *The Beginnings of Modernization in the Middle East*, Chicago, 1968.

Poulantzas, Nicos. *Political Power and Social Classes*, London, 1973.

__*Fascism and Dictatorship*, London, 1974.

Pye, Lucian W. (ed.), *Communications and Political Development*, Princeton, N.J., 1963.

Reid, D.M. 'The rise of professions and professional organization in modern Egypt', *Comparative Studies in Society and History*, 16(1974): 24–57.

Rodinson, Maxime. *Islam and Capitalism*, Harmondsworth, 1974.

Rugh, William. 'Emergence of a new middle class in Saudi Arabia', *Middle East Journal*, 27(1973): 7–20.

Santos, R. Dos. 'The structure of dependence', *American Economic Review*, 60(1970): 231–6.

Sayigh, Yusif A. *Entrepreneurs of Lebanon: the Role of the Business Leader in*

a Developing Economy, Harvard, 1962.
__'The modern merchant in the Middle East', in C.A.O. van Nieuwenhuijze (ed.), *Markets and Marketing as Factors of Development in the Mediterranean Basin*, The Hague, 1963.
__'Cultural problems and the economic development of the Arab World' in Robert N. Bellah (ed.), *Religion and Progress in Modern Asia*, New York, 1965.
Schatz, Sayne P. 'n-Achievement and economic growth: a critical appraisal', *Quarterly Journal of Economics*, 1965, 234–41.
Schneewind, J.B. (ed.), *Mill*, London, 1968.
Shinder, Joel. 'Career line formation in the Ottoman bureaucracy 1648–1750: a new perspective', *Journal of Economic and Social History of the Orient*, 16(1973): 217–37.
Smelser, Neil J. *The Sociology of Economic Life*, New Jersey, 1976.
Smith, Anthony D. *Theories of Nationalism*, London, 1971.
Stoianovich, Traian. 'The conquering Balkan orthodox merchants', *Journal of Economic History* 20(1960): 234–313.
Thornton, T.P. (ed.), *The Third World in Soviet Perspective*, Princeton, N.J. 1964.
Trevor-Roper, H.R. *Religion, the Reformation and Social Change*, London, 1967.
Turner, Bryan S. *Weber and Islam: a Critical Study*, London, 1974a.
__'The concept of 'social stationariness': utilitarianism and Marxism', *Science and Society*, 38(1974): 3–18.
__*Marx and the End of Orientalism*, London, 1979.
van Nieuwenhuijze, C.A.O. (ed.), *Markets and Marketing as Factors of Development in the Mediterranean Basin*, The Hague, 1963.
__*Social Stratification and the Middle East*, Leiden, 1965.
Vatikiotis, P.J. (ed.), *Revolutions in the Middle East and Other Case Studies*, London, 1972.
Venturi, Franco. 'Oriental despotism', *Journal for the History of Ideas*, 24(1963): 133–42.
Weber, Max. *The Protestant Ethic and the Spirit of Capitalism*, London, 1930.
__*Economy and Society*, New York, 1968a, 3 vols.
__*The City*, New York, 1968b.
Wertheim, W.F. 'Religion, bureaucracy and economic growth', *Transactions of the Fifth World Congress of Sociology*, 1964, 73–86.
Zartman, I. William. 'Political science' in L. Binder (ed.), *The Study of the Middle East*, New York, 1976.
Ziadeh, F. *Lawyers, the Rule of Law and Liberalism in Modern Egypt*, Stanford, 1968.

5 Orientalism, Islam and Capitalism

Any sociological attempt to determine whether Islam impeded the development of industrial capitalism cannot be separated from the larger, more complex analysis of the general social, political and economic characteristics of Islamic civilizations. In turn, this wider problem of comparative sociology cannot be separated from the traditional debate about the similarities and differences between the historical development of Christendom and Islamdom.[1] Thus, studies which appear to have the relatively narrow focus of establishing relationships between Islamic institutions and economic behaviour, such as entrepreneurial activities,[2] can only be properly understood as particular aspects of the complex, historical confrontation between Islamic and Christian cultures. Political and academic perceptions of the Islamic social reality have been profoundly moulded by centuries of military and economic struggle for dominance over global trade routes.[3] In addition, the typologies which have been used to conceptualize Islamic social structures have been elaborated in the context of political struggles in Europe with the rise of absolutism in the seventeenth century and parliamentary democracy in the nineteenth century. These observations merely illustrate the fact that any evaluation of the debate over Islam and capitalism must be simultaneously an exercise in the sociology of knowledge.

The analysis of Islam as a faith and Islamdom as a socio-cultural system has been dominated for centuries by a particular perspective which has determined the research topics, focus and conclusions of western scholarship. It is thus possible to consider the various disciplines which contribute to the study of Islam – theology, history, philology, sociology and so on – as different approaches within the same conceptual framework. This perspective or conceptual framework can be conveniently referred to as 'Orientalism'. Although there are a number of varieties of the Orientalist perspective, in this discussion of Islam and capitalism it will be adequate merely to distinguish between 'early' or 'classical' and 'contemporary Orientalism'. By this perspective, I mean a set of assumptions which dictates the sorts of theoretical questions that are posed of Islam and consequently the range of answers following from the boundaries established by the perspective. To employ a more sophisticated vocabulary, Orientalism is a 'problematic' which determines theoretical issues, approaches and conclusions within a given set of disciplines. Any theoretical advances beyond a problematic presuppose recognition and ultimate transcending of the limitations imposed by the traditional framework. My contention is that Orientalism dominates not only conventional Islamic studies, but also infects perspectives which are conventionally regarded as distinct and separate, namely, Weberian and Marxist sociology. In the field of Islamic studies, specifically with reference to the debate about Islam and capitalism, Marxist scholarship has not adequately transformed the limitations of Weber's sociology of development, because Marxism itself has followed the Orientalist tradition.

In the analysis of the social structure of Islamdom, Orientalism has adhered to a number of elementary propositions. The first is to make a dichotomous contrast between the static history and structure of Islamicate societies and the dynamic evolutionary character of Occidental Christian culture. The crucial feature of this dichotomy is that Christendom is homogeneously and uniformly progressive and dynamic: Islamdom is consistently static, after the initial outburst of the Islamic conquest from the Arabian peninsular. The problem posed by the initial dichotomy is to explain the decline of early Islam and its subsequent stagnation. The rise of Islam is thus the genesis of its demise.[4]

The second crucial feature of Orientalism is to provide a list of causes which explain the stationariness of Islamdom. The list typically includes the absence of private property, the presence of general slavery and the prominence of despotic government. The effect of these three features of Oriental society is to reduce the mass of the population to an abject dependence on the will of the ruler. The population lives in a condition of general uniformity in relation to the absolute will of the central, despotic power because there are no significant intervening institutions between the despot and the mass. All social institutions belong to the despot and are, therefore, 'ruling institutions'. Since the ruler appropriates all societal power, Oriental society possesses no autonomous organizations and institutions. In particular, autocephalous cities never fully developed under despotic conditions because the ancient cities of these societies were, in fact, merely military camps. These conditions combined to render social and economic life utterly precarious. No urban middle class could prosper in a situation where property could be confiscated by arbitrary political interventions. These features of Orientalist sociology could be summarized by the observation that the Oriental social formation possessed an overdeveloped state without an equivalent 'civil society'.

The third major dimension of the Orientalist problematic relates to the issue of the Muslim psychology. The account of despotism in Orientalist literature raises the difficulty of explaining how the society held together without constant turmoil, fractional conflicts and perennial social disturbance. The conventional solution was to treat Islam as an all-embracing, undifferentiated and timeless set of beliefs and practices which tied the people fissile?

to the ruler, who appeared under the guise of God's benevolent viceregent. Islam, in this perspective, was an essential social cement counter-balancing the fissiparous forces of the militarized cities.[5] The psychological effects of Islam were to foster attitudes of resignation, acceptance and fatalism. According to Orientalism, the Islamic faith generated no motivation for changing social arrangements or for opposing the political despotism of the ruler. Furthermore, it has been argued that, unlike Christianity, Islam did not develop an adequate legal doctrine of the right to resist unjust governments. No effective apparatus was ever developed to enforce the notion that the faithful need not submit to an impious ruler.[6] The absence of western motives – achievement motivation, innovation, anti-authoritarianism – has been connected sociologically with the failure of an entrepreneurial middle class to develop in despotic societies.

Finally, it is important to note that the Orientalist sociology of Islamdom was founded on a particular epistemology which was predominantly idealistic and essentialist. The failure of Islamdom to develop along Occidental historical lines towards a rational, democratic, industrial society was explained by reference to the inner essence of Islam itself. Islamicate history was flawed by the presence of an ethos – despotic, fatalistic, quiescent – which had the consequence of inhibiting innovation. This religious essence was manifest at the level of social structures and gave Islamdom its changeless characteristics. The Islamicate social system was conceptualized by Orientalism as an 'expressive totality', in the sense that the inner essence of Islam found its expression in all aspects of Islamdom and gave the social system its harmonious unity.[7] Islam was thus conceived as the essence which found its expression in the multitude of manifest phenomena. Similarly, Occidental society and history represented a teleological unfolding of an inner essence. From its foundation, Christendom contained the seeds of a rational, progressive society which unfolded and matured into democratic industrialism.[8] The unity of Occidental history was determined by this rational, essential core. It was this epistemology which lay behind the principal assumption of Orientalism, namely, that Islamdom was characterized by inertia, whereas Christendom was essentially dynamic.

The development of a political theory of Oriental Despotism cannot be separated from the emergence of absolutist states throughout Europe. In France, in particular, there was a lively debate throughout the seventeenth century over the characteristics of strong legitimate government and arbitrary despotic rule of 'L'Empire du Turc'.[9] Bossuet, the instructor of the young Louis XIV, attempted to distinguish between the legitimate absolutism of the royal household which was 'l'image de la grandeur de Dieu', and merely arbitrary power. According to Bossuet, there were four causes of arbitrary government: general slavery, absence of private property, absolute power of the ruler over his subjects and arbitrary law-making.[10] Bossuet's summary of the causes of arbitrary power and his general commentary on the imperial structures of Turkey and Russia provide a perfect illustration of the dominant motif of classical Orientalism which put the Aristotelian typology of governments to novel usage.[11] By far the most significant contributor to this tradition was Montesquieu in *The Spirit of the Laws* of 1748. Montesquieu distinguished three types of government: namely, republic, monarchy and despotism. Again, we find that the crucial difference between monarchy and despotism was that under a monarchy a single individual rules according to established laws, whereas in a despotic polity a single individual ruled in terms of personal caprice. The political sentiment behind monarchy was honour, but in despotism it was fear. Monarchy was based on inequality of social ranks; despotism involved extreme equality of an impotent human mass in relation to an arbitrary ruler. Under despotism, there were no social structures connecting the people to the ruler and, in the absence of a structure, precariousness and political passion dominated the social life.

The principal examples of despotism were drawn by Montesquieu from the empires of Asia, especially Turkey. Whether or not Montesquieu was referring to actual Asiatic societies or to a set of fictions is a matter of debate. For example, Althusser argues that, in Montesquieu's political sociology, despotism was 'only a geographical illusion', since the real object of Montesquieu's thought was absolute monarchy.[12] *The Spirit of the Laws* was thus a political tract against royal absolutism from the spokesman of the declining feudal nobility. This interpretation of the *parti pris* of Montesquieu's political theory has been challenged by Anderson who claimed that Montesquieu's analyses of despotism were more than allegorical devices.[13] The main point is that, regardless of Montesquieu's propagandist intentions, his account of Asiatic despotism was taken to be a real political system, rather than a mere fiction. Montesquieu's conception of the despotisms of the Orient eventually came to be attacked by writers with first-hand experience of actual Asiatic societies. In particular, Anquetil-Duperron from his own research and observation demonstrated the existence of legal contracts, private property and stable commercial relationships in Iran and India.[14] Writers like Boulanger and Bernier, who supported the view that private property did not exist in Asia, provided a thinly disguised pretext for the European exploitation of Asia.

The German contribution to classical Orientalism was amply illustrated by Hegel's *Philosophy of History*. The central aim of Hegel's social philosophy was to understand the conditions under which human beings could achieve self-consciousness in history. Hegel, therefore, applauded Montesquieu for not deducing political structures from asocial human nature.[15] Although Hegel made important distinctions between various regions within Asia, his general view was that the attainment of self-consciousness in the Orient was precluded by its structural features. In the Orient no conception of personal freedom and human individuality developed, so that despotism was the natural form of government. It was also typical for the despotic ruler to appear in the guise of a divine overlord. This situation stood in sharp contrast to the emergence of a subjective consciousness and political democracy in Greek culture. With reference to regional variations within Asiatic culture, Hegel claimed that India and China were stationary civilizations and, although at its inception Islam stood for a robust, creative spirit, it soon declined. In Hegel's view, Islam 'has long vanished from the stage of history at large, and has retreated into Oriental ease and repose'.[16]

Hegel's influence on Marx is a matter of acrimonious dispute.[17] In the field of the sociology of development, Marx can be interpreted in Hegelian terms to the effect that Occidental capitalism represented a dynamic, universal force in history and that capitalism resulted in the destruction of the stagnant, particularistic cultures of the Orient.[18] In the *Communist Manifesto*, Marx and Engels presented a view of Occidental capitalism as an inevitable and progressive force in history which brought about the liquidation of the stagnant economic systems of China and India. This view of the progressive nature of capitalism was further exemplified in the journalism of Marx and Engels, especially in their view of British colonial policy in respect of China and India.[19] On particular issues, such as the French invasion of Algeria, Engels was quite specific about the historical importance of the conquest of the barbaric societies of Arabia by the progressive forces of bourgeois capitalism.[20] Finally, it is important to note that Marx and Engels based their view of Asia on sources which were located at the centre of the Orientalist problematic, namely Bernier and the English utilitarians. Marx, writing to Engels in 1853, commented that Bernier was correct in thinking that the absence of private property was the basis of Oriental societies.[21] Marx and Engels reiterated in their treatment of the Asiatic mode of production the long heritage of Oriental Despotism which they acquired directly or indirectly from Montesquieu, Ferguson, James Mill and J. S. Mill.[22] Their view of Oriental society was in fact similar to that of Bossuet; Marx and Engels claimed that societies in which the Asiatic mode of production was dominant were characterized by an absence of private property (the state is 'the real landlord'), by 'general slavery' and by precarious political conditions. Their view of the relationship between Islamdom and economic stagnation was probably best summarized by Engels, who observed that Turkey, as with 'any other Oriental domination, is incompatible with a capitalistic economy' because there was no 'security of the person and the property of the trader'.[23]

The notion that Oriental societies were economically and historically stagnant was common intellectual currency amongst political economists in

Victorian Britain. In *The History of British India* (1818), Mill saw the problem of Indian inertia in terms of political despotism; in the absence of a system of political and legal rules, the ruler controlled society according to his own personal whims, so that no liberty of conscience could develop. J. S. Mill attributed 'Chinese stationariness' to the oppression of custom and tradition over individuality.[24] The servile equality of the mass under despotic conditions smothered any sign of creative genius in the individual. The implication of British political economy was that, given a combination of sloth, servility and various social arrangements preventing capital accumulation, Oriental societies could only be changed by foreign conquest. As with the French political writers of the eighteenth century, Victorian commentators thought that Turkey most fully exemplified the corruption of Oriental societies by indolence and lasciviousness. In popular literature, Thackeray in his *Journey from Cornhill to Cairo* referred to the 'cool sweet dreamy languor' which took possession of the unwary European in the Middle East. Like other writers of the period, Thackeray thought that European technology – the paddle-wheel, Fulton's boiler, the brougham – would inevitably destroy Turkish dominion in the Middle East or, to use his own expression, extinguish Mahomet's crescent.[25] The whole tenor of this popular, semi-educational travel literature (Browne's *A Year among the Persians*, Kinglake's *Eothen* or, at a more serious level, Lane's *Manners and Customs of the Modern Egyptians*) suggested that Muslims were simultaneously servile and vicious; they were down-trodden in a society which, without stable ranks or dignities, was a haphazard whirligig of ups and downs, entertaining in fiction but unbearable in fact.[26] The main difference between this quasi-fictional literature and the serious political-theory tradition from Hobbes to Jones is that the latter attempted to discover the social and structural conditions which prevented political and economic change in Asia, without dwelling too long on the supposed psychology of Muslims.[27]

Having outlined the principal assumptions of the classical contribution to the study of Islamdon, it is striking to realize how heavily dependent the major studies in contemporary sociology, economics and history are on this heritage. For example, one of the most influential studies in English of Islamicate civilization is Gibb and Bowen's *Islamic Society and the West*.[28] This book, which has achieved the status of a virtual textbook on the Arab provinces of the Ottoman empire and Anatolia, purports to be a sociology of the Ottoman social system, but it turns out to be merely a new version of Orientalism. The authors define Ottoman society by reference to its religious essence – hence the title of their study. As with traditional Orientalism, Gibb and Bowen concern themselves with tracing the historic rise and fall of this Islamic essence. They define Islamdom as a stationary and retrograde civilization whose governmental apparatus resulted in a 'stifling of initiative'.[29] There was a fundamental distinction between the rulers and their subjects with no intermediary institutions (with the possible except of the *ulama*). At the same time, at the village and city level there existed a ceaseless factional hostility which, in the famous quotation from Volney, constituted 'une guerre civile perpétuelle'. We have already observed this formulation in Montesquieu and Hegel to the effect that in Turkey the state was overdeveloped in relation to intervening institutions ('civil society'). Gibb and Bowen's version of this traditional view has been clearly influential in the analysis of the Ottoman system in the work of Mardin and Inalcik who treat society as a dichotomy between *askeri* (the military and *reaya* (subjects).[30] Gibb and Bowen's text also provides the major source for Anderson's study of the 'House of Islam' in *Lineages of the Absolutist State*. Anderson derives his distinction between 'civil society' and the 'state' from Gramsci, but his information on the general characteristics of Islamdom is heavily dependent on Gibb and Bowen's account. The oddity of this dependence is striking, since Anderson is explicitly aware of the dangers of the Orientalist tradition but continues to flirt with that perspective.

The difficulties which are inherent within the Gibb and Bowen perspective have not gone unnoticed in recent controversy. As Owen has, for instance, pointed out, the changes in the nature of Ottoman society cannot be understood without reference to the international context and external constraints – in particular, the development of a global economy centred on western Europe in the sixteenth century.[31] Furthermore, there was no simple social gulf between state bureaucrats and local populations; instead, there was a sociologically significant network of intermediaries and local interest groups which operated a brokerage function between the state and the immediate community. The arguments about the stationary nature of the society also ignore the readiness of local peasant communities to respond to new market forces. The rapid spread of maize cultivation in the seventeenth century is a case in point. Similarly, the thesis about the ineluctable decline of an Islamic essence has to ignore the significant economic progress that did take place in the Ottoman Middle East in the medieval period. The Orientalist problematic, however, is not amenable to empirical objections because, once the analysis of Islam has been formulated in terms of essentialism, decline follows automatically from a contaminated essence.

However influential Gibb and Bowen may have been among historians, the most profound Orientalist influence in the sociology of development and comparative sociology has been injected via the sociological writings of Weber. His fragmented commentary on Islam and more systematic analysis of patrimonial domination were aspects of his study of the conditions for the emergence and continuity of rational capitalist development. Weber's knowledge of Islam was much less substantial than his understanding of Judaism and Christianity. His information and perspective on Islamdom were derived from such writers as Snouck Hurgronje, C. H. Becker and Julius Wellhausen.[32] Despite the scattered quality of Weber's observations on Islam, it is still the case that Islam played a strategic part in his general argument about the relationship between religious values and capitalist institutions.[33] Although early Islam appeared to possess certain traits which could have favoured capitalist behaviour – asceticism, monotheism, predestination as a central belief, a prophetic vision – Islamicate societies did not generate or contribute to a rational 'spirit of capitalism'. In order to explain this paradox, Weber presented two separate arguments. In the first, which was concentrated in his account of the routinization of charisma in *The Sociology of Religion*, Weber attempted to show that the monotheistic asceticism of Muhammad's original koranic preaching was ultimately corrupted during its adoption by a warrior society. Weber's first argument was thus a version of the Orientalist decline thesis. The second argument which emerged in Weber's broader analysis of domination in *Economy and Society* was focused on the patrimonial aspects of the Islamicate social structure. It was this latter argument, rather than Weber's view of ascetic values and motives, which was central to his analysis of the contrast between feudal Europe and the patrimonial societies of the Middle East and Asia.

In feudalism, the title to land was held as an inheritable right on the part of a stratum of nobles in exchange for military service; in patrimonialism, the right to land was retained by the state and the right to the use of land in exchange for a service was not inherited. Thus, the system of prebends offered a much less secure property right than was the case for the feu, which was a perpetual lease. In Weber's treatment of this contrast, it followed that in feudalism the notables enjoyed relative autonomy from the demands of the central authority. In patrimonial empires, by contrast, the centre attempted to monopolize economic and political power at the imperial centre by controlling land, the imperial army and transit trade in opposition to the horse-born nobility. Under these conditions independent cities could not develop, and retained the status of imperial army camps.[34] Insecurity in the urban environment limited the possibility for the emergence of an autonomous, enterprising middle class. In addition, the Islamic guilds were under the control of state officials.[35] Although there was a class of merchants in medieval Islam connected with international trade, Weber argued that, because the *Sharia* did not protect the individual against *ad hoc* legal decisions, merchants invested in *waqf* property dedicated to some pious end. Such property was a source of rent rather than a component of 'acquisitive capital'. Such a society was subject to continual crises because the requirements of the central state always exceeded revenue from taxation and foreign booty. These fiscal crises of the patrimonial state were mitigated by resort to tax-farming and quasi-feudalization of land rights, on the one hand, and by increasing the rate of exploitation of the peasantry, on the other. These methods, however, often served to increase the level of uncertainty over property and trade. In the last analysis, therefore, this interpretation of Weber's sociology of Islam leads to the unfashionable conclusion that Weber's theory cannot be distinguished from Engel's view that in Turkey the basic prerequisite of capital accumulation - security of person and property - was absent.

At this stage, it will be sufficient to consider some of the principal criticisms of Weber's sociology of Islam. The first thesis about the diminution of the ascetic content of early Islamic monotheism by a carrier group of Muslim warriors is inadequate because it exaggerates the importance of warriors and militaristic values in early and medieval Islam. By contrast, merchants and mercantile values were far more decisive in shaping the culture of Islamicate societies.[37] In reply to Weber, Rodinson goes to great lengths to demonstrate that there was nothing in the prescriptions and proscriptions of Islam as a religion to inhibit the rise of a rational capitalist ethos.[38] Rodinson shows that the prohibitions on profits from certain types of usury never seriously affected investment and trade; in addition, he claims that Weber's view of the limitations on the rationality of koranic theology cannot be sustained. Although Weber's discussion of the weak development of an ascetic content to Islam as a causal factor in the absence of capitalism cannot be sustained, there are serious problems in the alternative theory presented by Rodinson which need to be considered.

Rodinson wants to argue that financial and commercial capitalism as well as petty commodity production developed in medieval Islam in a way which was broadly equivalent to similar capitalist sectors in feudal Europe prior to the dominance of the capitalist mode of production. This sector within pre-capitalist Islamdom failed to develop fully because it was undermined by the onslaught of European commodities in the period of western imperialism. In order to establish the existence of this capitalist sector, Rodinson quotes a diversity of examples from a wide range of Islamicate contexts - from Arabia in the time of the Prophet to the Gulf states of the modern period. Thus, in attempting to challenge the Orientalism of Weberian sociology, Rodinson employs the epistemology and theoretical assumptions of Orientalist history. Instead of providing an analysis of the specific structures and economic processes of particular societies for different periods in history, Rodinson contrasts one timeless, undifferentiated category ('Islam') with other vague categories ('European capitalism' or 'Christianity'). Rodinson provides no justification for regarding 'Islam' as a unitary concept denoting a homogeneous civilization regardless of social and economic differentiation.[39]

In addition, Rodinson concentrates mainly on Weber's first argument, which is concerned with the nature of values and motives favouring or impeding capitalist behaviour; Weber's analysis of the patrimonial structure of Islamicate empires is largely ignored. To criticize Weber's commentary on Islam and asceticism, Rodinson demonstrates the importance of the merchant class in the history of Islamic civilizations. Unfortunately, the importance of a merchant class for the subsequent dominance of the capitalist mode of production within a society is a matter of unresolved dispute. The fact is that merchants as a class appear in different societies under very different economic conditions and they are not, as it were, heralds proclaiming the dawn of a new mode of production. Referring to the relationship between feudalism and merchant capital, Marx observed that merchant capital 'cannot by itself contribute to the overthrow of the old mode of production but tends rather to preserve and retain it as its pre-condition'.[40] Merchants were not historically a dissolvent of pre-capitalist modes of production so that evidence about the compatibility of Islamic values and capitalist activities is often irrelevant for studying the conditions of the capitalist mode of production. In attempting to solve problems in Weberian sociology, Rodinson has uncovered a more fundamental and intractable issue, namely, the question of the transformation of a mode of production. The precise conditions and processes which result in the dissolution of pre-capitalist modes of production are still obscure.

The sociology of development has emerged under the auspices of two opposed theoretical frameworks. Within the internalist perspective, sociologists concentrate on the values and institutions of the *internal* structure of a society which is, for the purpose of analysis, treated as an isolated societal unit. The explanations for the growth or stagnation of an economy are consequently couched in terms of personal beliefs, family structures, patterns of inheritance and so on, rather than in terms of the global context of the society within the international division of labour. Weber's explanation of economic stagnation in terms of religious values in Islam is a typical example of an internalist theory, since it pays no attention to the peculiarities of the global situation of Islamicate societies. A contemporary illustration of internalist causal models of Middle East development is provided by Lerner's celebrated study of psychological empathy.[41] The transition from traditional to modern society is successful where there is a correct balance between the processes of urbanization, literacy, provision of mass media and political participation. Under optimum conditions, a growth in geographical mobility with the creation of new urban centres will coincide with the emergence of a new personality structure. Citizens with empathy can participate in the new social arrangements and contribute to the processes of democratization, secularization and commercialization of the traditional society. In Lerner's diagnosis, the Middle East is not developing adequately because it is out of step in terms of the modernization model. There is too much urbanization in relation to the growth of literacy; too little political participation in relation to the state's control of the media.[42]

In the sociology of development in general, any theory which concentrates on the characteristics of the human population of an underdeveloped society is an internalist perspective.[43] For example, Hershlag claims that the principal shortage facing the Middle East is not one of capital, but a shortage in terms of human resources.[44] There are too few risk-taking innovators. Muslim entrepreneurs have a low horizon of economic expectations, and are content with immediate profits rather than future returns. According to Hershlag, there is also a marked preference for the small, family enterprise, rather than large organizations with a rational investment programme.[45] These observations on the present situation must be located within the wider historical context. Given the patrimonial stucture of Islamdom, it has been traditionally argued that a strong middle class never developed in Islam. Internal and transit trade was typically controlled by religious minorities, especially the Jews and Christians.[46] In the modern period, political scientists have debated whether certain sections within the officer élite of Middle Eastern armies can perform the social and economic functions which were undertaken historically by the bourgeoisie in Europe.[47]

This treatment of the 'missing middle class' in Islam can be challenged on a number of grounds. These interpretations of Islamicate history tend to exaggerate the significance of bourgeois entrepreneurship in the emergence of European capitalism. An examination of the classic case of bourgeois development – nineteenth-century Britain – suggests that risk-taking innovators were not a crucial feature of industrialization. Hobsbawm, for example, shows how capitalist investment was protected from damaging competition and uncertain investment because of Britain's control over foreign markets.[48] Capitalists aimed at security of investment in guaranteed markets, rather than at the uncertainties of long-term investments which also required rational planning. Futhermore, those views of capitalism that emphasize the autonomy of the innovative capitalist underestimate the central importance of the state in the capitalist development, not only of Britain, but of Germany and Italy. In continental Europe, there was a critical need for economic protection from British finished goods and an equally important requirement for the state to contribute to the development of a sound economic infrastructure.[49] There is comparative evidence to support the view that, once capitalism was the dominant mode of production in Britain, all subsequent capitalist development outside Britain required massive support from the state.[50] Thus the importance of the state, bureaucracy and the new middle class in Middle East development in the modern period does not appear historically or structurally peculiar in the context of global capital development.

The principal objection to the internalist emphasis on the necessity for independent bourgeois entrepreneurship is of a more theoretical nature. The precise form taken by commercial activities in a society cannot be understood independently of the general economic circumstances pertaining in that society, and these general conditions are in turn dependent upon that society's temporal and spatial location within global capital accumulation. In this perspective, the presence or absence of opportunities for capitalist initiative, rational planning and long-term investment depends, not on human resources, but on the world economic context. The dominance of commercial against industrial capital in Lebanon, for example, is to be explained by historical and sociological causes relating to its proximity to Israel, its function in world trade and its internal class structure, rather than by reference to subjective preferences for small-scale family capitalism.[51] The argument about entrepreneurial skills and the poor quality of capitalist drive in underdeveloped societies is either false or tautological. It is fallacious because there are ample reservoirs of entrepreneurial skill in underdeveloped socieites, but they cannot find an outlet in capitalist roles.[52] It is tautological because the thesis about entrepreneurial skills is based ultimately on the claim that 'in the absence of industrial capitalism there are no industrial capitalists and vice versa'.[53] Although explanations for low economic performance in terms of the backward-bending supply curve of effort or high leisure preferences or the absence of a willingness to defer immediate gratification have been abandoned in the sociology of development for other regions, they still appear to enjoy credibility in Middle East studies.[54]

This specific issue in the analysis of Islamic entrepreneurs will serve to pinpoint general difficulties in the internalist explanations of capitalism in terms of cultural and institutional factors. By contrast, what can be referred to as the externalist approach of Frank, Magdoff, Dos Santos and Furtado concentrates on the international context of a society, rather than its internal characteristics.[55] More precisely, the internal features of a society are treated as effects of causes which are situated in the processes of capital accumulation on a world scale. In this perspective, societies on the periphery of capitalism are systematically underdeveloped by the advanced capitalist societies and by multinational corporations. For example, the failure of industrialization in Egypt, following the collapse of Muhammad Ali Pasha's reform programme, was simply a feature of Egypt's international dependency as a mono-crop exporting agricultural society. However, the economic surplus that was generated by cotton production was characteristically repatriated to foreign interests or reinvested in cotton production or diverted into banking and insurance.[56] The peculiarities of colonial agrarian capitalism have been adequately documented in the historical development of Algeria, Lebanon and the Gulf States.[57] From this externalist perspective, the question of the relevance of Islamic beliefs, institutions and general culture to capitalism is no longer regarded as a significant sociological issue. The question is, in part, treated as insignificant for epistemological reasons, namely, that the *structure* of the capitalist mode of production is taken as the real object of inquiry, rather than the beliefs of *individuals*. Furthermore, this perspective rejects attempts to analyse the causes of the spontaneous growth of capitalism as irrelevant to the question of the effects of capitalist colonialism on the periphery of world capitalism. The study of the origins of capitalism in Britain does not provide any insight into capitalist underdevelopment today because the conditions for capitalist development were fundamentally changed by the fact of British capitalist growth. The conditions for capitalist development in the eighteenth century cannot be reproduced as conditions for contemporary development.

Although the externalist critique of the work of sociologists like Lerner, McClelland, Inkeles and Smith is convincing, there are certain difficulties in the externalist approach.[58] Before addressing these analytical problems, it is important to realize that internalist explanations are typically regarded as Weberian, whereas externalist accounts of colonialism generally claim a Marxist parentage. In fact, as became clear in the previous discussion of Orientalism, Marx's Asiatic mode of production had pronounced internalist characteristics as an explanation of the backwardness of Asian societies. The stationariness of Asia was explained by reference to the absence of private property, the dominance of the state, and the constitution of the village economy. In the recent controversy over the Asiatic mode, it has been suggested that this theoretical mode should be expunged from the list of accepted Marxist categories because the Asiatic mode is analytically incoherent. If there are no classes in the Asiatic mode, then it is impossible to explain the presence of the state without resort to technological reductionist arguments about the hydraulic functions of the state.[59] It can also be claimed that the Asiatic mode of production that was discussed primarily in Marx's journalism belonged to Marx's pre-scientific period, before the rigorous concepts of *Capital* had been fully developed. While Marx's formulation of this mode remains highly contested, the applications of the Asiatic mode of production to the analysis of the Middle East have produced very uneven and problematic results.[60]

Regardless of the exact relationship of Marxism to contemporary externalist explanations of capital development, the externalist perspective has to be challenged in terms of its theoretical and explanatory validity. In criticizing the Weberian tradition in the sociology of development, the neo-Marxist externalist school has failed to realize that, to some extent, these two perspectives have two different objects of research. Weberian sociology has been directed towards questions about the *genesis* of capitalism in Europe and then to comparative research about the internal conditions for capital accumulation in other cultural contexts. The externalist school, by contrast, has tended to examine the conditions for the *persistence* of capitalism and its effects on the underdeveloped world in the aftermath of British capital development. Although Weber's account of the rise of capitalism may not provide very useful approaches for understanding the effects of neo-colonialism in modern Africa, it is not thereby ruled out as an orientation to the sociology of the genesis of capitalism. However, the conscious disregard for the analysis of the internal structure and culture of underdeveloped societies by externalist explanations raises serious difficulties. Frank's version of externalism, for example, cannot give a satisfactory account of why certain societies rather than others are forced on to the capitalist periphery. Furthermore, it cannot explain why certain societies which are deeply penetrated by multinational corporations (such as Canada or Scotland) manage to enjoy a high level of capitalist development (of an admittedly uneven variety). As Melotti observes in relation to Frank's model of capitalist underdevelopment, Frank completely overlooks 'the internal structures of the individual currently underdeveloped countries and tends to reduce the process of underdevelopment to a mere mechanistic concomitant of the development of capitalism'.[61] In short, an adequate explanation of the differences between socieites in terms of capital development would have to examine the location of the societies in terms of the international division of labour *and* to provide an analysis of the internal structure and cultural features of the societies. The internal structure would not be a mere effect of external economic conditions, and the analysis of the internal structure may include evidence on the class structure, mode of production and the ideological structure (including religion, morals and values).

A number of recent studies of Islamicate societies have provided illustrations of research based on the necessity of understanding the complex causal relationship between the total global structure and the minute details of the internal arrangements of given societies. Wallerstein, for example, sets his debate about the origins of the European world-economy in the context of the decline of ancient empires.[62] The disintegration of empires resulted in Europe in feudalization, whereas in the Turco-Muslim and Chinese cases there was a process of prebendalization. In feudalism, as Weber argued, the landlords have relatively high income, autonomy and power relative to the central state, whereas in prebendalism the land-owning class is weak and the state bureaucracy has considerable economic and military strength. Thus, feudalization in western Europe resulted in the dismantling of the imperial structure of Rome, but Chinese and Islamicate prebendalization resulted in the maintenance of an imperial structure. In Wallerstein's argument, the prebendal empires precluded or, more exactly, reduced the possibility of feudalization *and* of capitalism. In China, it was precisely the strength of the bureaucratic state that limited the spread and employment of technological change (in firearms, for example) which could have resulted in unfavourable political reorganization. Various contingent circumstances contributed to the different structural implications of these political systems. The European agricultural economy was based on wheat and cattle; this system encouraged outward geographical expansion, which favoured propertied classes in a situation where there was no strong imperial structure. By contrast, the rice economy of China required more men but less space. Social groups in China that might have benefited from cattle were restrained by the centralization of decision-making. The Islamicate and Chinese systems developed as world-empires within which nation-states, city-states and politically powerful bourgeois classes were relatively weak. Western Europe developed as a world-economy without a unified political structure, that is, without a world-empire. Capitalism flourished in a system where there was a multiplicity of political units, rather than a unifying political empire. Because an empire has to raise taxes in order to administer a large land mass, the economic surplus is directed away from capital accumulation. Thus, it was precisely the rationality of the advanced bureaucracy and political structure of the Chinese and Islamicate empires that inhibited economic changes in the direction of capital accumulation.

These two social systems - feudalism and prebendalism - are not, however, counterpoised as two static entities. Wallerstein presents a theoretical model of historical change in which uneven, contradictory transformations, rather than an evolutionary unfolding of an ethos, are central. In the emergence of capitalist relations in agriculture in the sixteenth and seventeenth centuries, England and the United Provinces successfully established themselves as national entities within a world-economy, but the efforts of France and Spain to create a world-empire were failures. Thus, the contrast between world-economy and world-empire is not simply a contrast between the dynamic Occident and a stagnant Orient. More significantly, the process of capitalist development is uneven in that, within the world-economy, there are strong core states which create subordinate peripheral and semi-peripheral regions. The core states enjoy the benefits which arise from the division of labour within the world-economy and they create a strong state apparatus to preserve these inequalities. Because there is no political mechanism within the world-economy as a whole, these global inequalities cannot be ameliorated and economic inequalities are continuously reinforced by the market. This perspective on the emergence of a world-economy provides a valuable method of analysing changes in the

Ottoman empire, which can be interpreted as one instance of a pre-capitalist formation being integrated into the world-economy.

In the Ottoman empire, the internal crisis of prebendalism, resulting in a feudalization of social relationships, was reinforced by external economic pressures of world trade which also undermined the authority of the central state apparatus in relation to local landlords. Before the expansion of European trade in the nineteenth century, the central government controlled the transit and export trade, supervised manufacture through the urban guilds and secured an adequate extraction of the mercantile surplus.[63] Thus the state raised revenue from the non-feudal, pre-capitalist agrarian sector, while the merchant class collected the surplus from commercialized agriculture which produced crops for the external market. These commercial crops were exchanged for imports of luxury goods which were then used by the merchants in exchanges with the bureaucrats and landlords. These reciprocal economic relationships between fractions of the dominant class were profoundly changed by important developments in the external context of the Ottoman empire. New sea routes, such as the Portuguese discovery of the Cape and the British entry into the Indian Ocean in the late seventeenth century, started a process which cut the international transit trade running traditionally through Ottoman territories. The precious goods trade came under the control of British and Dutch merchants, producing a profound reduction in Ottoman state revenue. Bursa and Aleppo declined as centres of trade and industry.[64] The growth of the European economies resulted in an increase of external trade in raw materials (grain and raw cotton) to satisfy the European demand. This new trade, however, went mainly through illegal channels, thereby avoiding official taxes, and the state control over external trade was continuously undermined. To meet this new demand for raw materials, more land came under the control of merchants in the commercial sector, thereby reducing the proportion of land in the state sector. This period of commercialization was accompanied by the rise of 'life-farms' (*malikane*) and commercial estates (*ciftlik*) to produce cash-crops on an extended scale with enserfed peasantry and share-croppers. The traditional land-holding class of cavalry (*sipahi*) went into decline as the *timariots* (land with fixed revenue in exchange for military service) were replaced by commercial estates. These changes are associated with the endemic revenue crisis of the Ottoman state, which was no longer able to control peripheral regions. The paralysis of state power provided conditions for the rise of independent lords (*derebeys*) in Anatolia and local notables (*ayans*) in Rumelia.

This process of proliferalization of Ottoman regions within the world-economy was completed in the nineteenth century. With new concessionary arrangements and improvements in communications (steam freighters, railways and telegraph), European manufactured imports destroyed the system of guild production and rural crafts. In order to increase revenue to deal with the fiscal crisis, the state was forced to increase taxation and this produced further discontent and political disaffection. Even 1875, with the rising in Herzegovina, to the Balkan War of 1912, the state was faced by continuous disruption of the European and Balkan provinces, which became satellite societies of the core states of the world-economy. The Ottoman prebendal system was thus dismantled by an internal process of class struggle between bureaucrats, landlords and merchants, but this process was reinforced by the effect of economic changes in the external environment resulting from the consolidation of capitalism as a world-economy.

In these studies of Islamdom which have been inspired by the work of Wallerstein and his students, there emerges a perspective on economic and social change that begins to break with the classical assumptions of Orientalism. These studies preserve much of the central theme of Weber's conceptualization of patrimonialism and its imperial crises, but the internal processes of change within the Ottoman structure are clearly set within the context of massive restructuring of the external context of the Ottoman economy. The commercialization of the Ottoman agrarian system was, furthermore, not a peculiar feature of a decadent Islamicate empire, but a process which was common to a variety of social systems under the impact of nineteenth-century capitalism. The subordination of the Islamicate economy to capitalist relationships of production and its peripheralization in the world economy does not require any Orientalist assumptions about essential differences between Oriental and Occidental culture in order for sociologists and historians to understand these processes of capital accumulation. The peripheralization and exploitation of regions by strong core states were social processes operating both within and between given societies. Furthermore, the Asiatic mode of production is not a mode of economic production that is in fact peculiar to Asian societies.[65] The rise and persistence of capitalist relations of production cannot be approached as a problem which presents itself merely at the level of religious culture, because the analysis of capitalist development cannot be conducted in terms of static comparisons between religious essences. Recent studies in the history of capital formation in dependent Islamicate societies therefore begin to point towards new ways of formulating the question of the relationship between Islam and economic change.

The conventional Orientalist approach to Islam and capitalism was centred on the problem of the causes of 'spontaneous' capitalist development.[66] Within Weberian sociology this inquiry took the form of discovering the crucial ingredients of western capitalist development – an independent bourgeoisie, rational law, freedom of the market and labour – in order to isolate those factors which appeared to be absent in Asian societies. From this perspective, one of the principal differences appeared to lie in the field of personal religious values. The systematic elaboration of neo-Marxist theories of development has provided a powerful critique of this approach. First, after the capitalist mode of production had been established in Europe, the conditions for subsequent economic development were radically changed. The result is that the conditions for 'spontaneous' capitalist development could no longer be repeated. Much of the debate in Orientalism about the 'missing middle class' has, as a result, been of little sociological value. Second, the analysis of capitalist development in India, Pakistan and Africa has shown that, when capitalist relations of production were inserted into underdeveloped societies, they typically had the paradoxical effect of conserving and reinforcing archaic, pre-capitalist forms of labour organization and general social relations.[67] In underdeveloped societies, social backwardness is often the effect, not of indigenous social relations and culture, but of colonial agrarian capitalist development. In this respect, the development of capitalism in Asia, especially in societies like India, has been contrary to the expectations of Weber *and* Marx.[68] Thus, the dominance of the capitalist mode of production does not automatically result in the destruction of pre-capitalist modes of production and, in general terms, it is important to conceptualize all social formations as combinations of overlapping modes of production.[69] The uneven development of capitalism in Islamicate societies has numerous parallels in European capitalism, where massive regional inequalities within societies – between the south and north in Italy, or between the south-east and north-west in Great Britain – and inter-social differences have been the common theme of capital accumulation. These approaches in the sociology of development underline the absurdity of naive contrasts between one homogeneous entity (the Christian West) and another uniform entity or essence (Islamic Asia). Furthermore, these contemporary reorientations in sociological thought indicate the fundamental difficulties of teleological perspectives on social change. The end of the Orientalist form of historicism will also involve a critique of those forms of Marxism which treat history as the inevitable march of progressive relations of production and advanced forms of material production. The effect of capitalist relations of production on Islamicate societies may well be various forms of underdevelopment.[70]

In reformulating the traditional problematic of contrasts between East and West in Orientalism, it will be necessary to pay regard to the specificity of given societies and their unique position within the world-economy. References to 'Islamic societies' ignore the obviously banal point that the development problems of northern Nigeria are very different from those of Bangladesh or Jordan or Tunisia. In attempting to criticize the Orientalist picture of Islam, I have by necessity been forced into adopting their terminology, but the distinctions between Islam, Islamdom and Islamicate are not wholly satisfactory. This terminology of the late Marshall Hodgson presupposes that, behind all the multifarious sociological phenomena of numerous Islamicate societies, there exists an inner common core which is personal piety or faith. Unfortunately, Hodgson's treatment of the phenomenon of faith takes us back to the realm of essences which are universal, immutable and uncaused.[71] Much of the traditional debate about Islam and capitalism has assumed that 'Islam' is a unitary object of study without providing a justification for this assumption. Furthermore, the debate assumes that the relationship between Islamic beliefs and capitalist behaviour or, more generally, between 'spiritual factors' and 'material factors' is one of externality, separation and contingency. Ironically, this particular formulation of the relationship between religious beliefs and economic actions parallels the distinction between the economic base and the superstructure in mechanistic versions of Marxism. In terms of simple distinctions between material factors and ideas, it is never possible to allocate unambiguously such phenomena as scientific knowledge or legal definitions of property or political institutions to the superstructure. For example, concepts of legal ownership are crucial to relations of production, which determine the nature of the mode of production. Thus, in attempting to speculate about the causal relationships between Islamic beliefs and capitalist actions, the Orientalist overlooks the fact that, given the nature of *social* actions, beliefs are necessarily constitutive of social interaction.[72]

These observations about the status of causal explanations within the Orientalist tradition also raise questions about the conventional approach of the sociology of religion when applied to the world of Islam. The implication of this critique of the conventional debate about capitalism and Islam is that it is not possible to isolate and extract an inner religious essence from Islam, which we then call 'Islamic piety' or 'faith' or the 'religious kernel', in order to compare this essence with an external phenomenon of capitalism. Not only does this methodology assume that western conceptions of private and public spheres have universal relevance, it assumes that the 'religious values' of Islam are themselves without social causes or historical determination. It is this problem which undermines the central theme of that modern classic of Islamic studies, Marshall G. S. Hodgson's *The Venture of Islam*. In the case of Islam, such distinctions between the inner religious life and the outer secular world have little sociological relevance because of certain crucial differences between the origins of the Christian religion and the foundations of Islamdom. It was this interpenetration of social and religious dimensions in Islamic history that led Marx and Engels to the observation that the history of Asia always appeared as the history of religions.[73] Furthermore, in view of the valid criticisms which have been raised against attempting to produce internalist explanations of economic stagnation by reference to culture or religious beliefs, many conventional contributions of the sociology of religion to the sociological analysis of underdevelopment must be treated as partial. In particular, the pursuit of analogies between the Protestant Ethic and the values of some brotherhood or sect in Islam must be regarded as a discredited research activity.[74]

By referring to Orientalism as a 'problematic', it is not implied that all the research of traditional Orientalism is false, misguided or ideological. The Orientalist tradition merely created a framework of concepts within which certain key issues were specified (such as the 'decline of Islam') and which indicated a range of possible solutions. One central feature of this framework was an attempt to explain a principal cultural variation between economic advances in European societies and stagnation in 'Islamic society'. This problematic has not been peculiar to one discipline (although it has been prominent in historical research) or to one perspective (occurring in both Marxist and Weberian sociologies). There was, for example, a significant conceptual overlap between Weber's patrimonial type of authority and Marx's Asiatic mode of production. The procedure for criticizing this Orientalist problematic involves both empirical and theoretical objections. It is possible to show that, following Rodinson, Islamic beliefs and legal codes did not hinder enterprise and that Islam possessed a rational core of values and attitudes. The main focus of criticism must, however, be couched at a more theoretical level by demonstrating the incoherence of the paradigm which generates a series of false problems about bourgeois entrepreneurship, Islamic cities, spontaneous capitalist development and stationary societies. The most cogent reply to the Orientalist inquiry into the relationship between Islam and capitalism is to demonstrate the incoherence and irrelevance of the original set of questions.

Notes

1 In this discussion I shall initially follow the distinctions between 'Islam' and 'Islamic,' 'Islamdom' and 'Islamicate' which are presented in Marshall G. S. Hodgson, *The Venture of Islam*, Chicago, 1974, 3 vols.

2 On entrepreneurial activity, C. Issawi, 'The entrepreneur class', in S. N. Fisher (ed.), *Social Forces in the Middle East*, Ithaca, 1955; A. J. Meyer, 'Entrepreneurship and economic development in the Middle East', *Public Opinion Quarterly*, vol. 22 (1958), pp. 391–6; A. J. Meyer, *Middle Eastern Capitalism*, Cambridge, 1959; Y. A. Sayigh, *Entrepreneurs of Lebanon*, Cambridge, 1962.

3 Norman Daniel, *Islam, Europe and Empire*, Edinburgh, 1966.

4 David Waines, 'Cultural anthropology and Islam: the contribution of G. E. von Grunebaum,' *Review of Middle East Studies*, no. 2 (1976), pp. 113–23.

5 For the Orientalist emphasis on factions in the Islamic city, see. I.M.

Lapidus, *Muslim Cities in the Later Middle Ages*, Cambridge, 1967; I.M. Lapidus (ed.), *Middle East Cities*, Berkeley and Los Angeles, 1969; A. Raymond, *Artisans et commercants au Caire au XVIIIe siècle*, Damascus, 1973–4, 2 vols.

6 This argument is central to B. Lewis, 'Islamic concepts of revolution', in P.J. Vatikiotis (ed.), *Revolution in the Middle East and other case studies*, London, 1972, pp. 30–40.

7 On the concepts of 'problematic', 'expressive totality' and 'idealism', cf. Louis Althusser and Etienne Balibar, *Reading Capital*, London, 1970.

8 For example, Talcott Parsons, 'Christianity and modern industrial society', in L. Schneider (ed.), *Religion, Culture and Society*, New York, 1965, pp. 273–98.

9 For a discussion, Sven Stelling-Michaud, 'Le mythe du despotisme oriental', *Schweizer Beiträge zur Allgemeinen Geschichte*, vols. XVIII–XIX, (1960–61), pp. 328–46.

10 J. Benigne-Bossuet, *Politique tirée des propres paroles de l'Écriture Sainte a Monsigneur le Dauphin*, 1709, quoted in R. Koebner, 'Despot and despotism: vicissitudes of a political term', *Journal of the Warburg and Courtauld Institutes*, vol. XIV (1951), pp. 275–302.

11 For a general discussion, Paul Hazard, *La Crise de la conscience européenne*, Paris, 1935. For commentary on the relationship between Greek and Islamic philosophy, W. Montgomery Watt, *Islamic Political Thought*, Edinburgh, 1968.

12 Louis Althusser, *Politics and History. Montesquieu, Rousseau, Hegel and Marx*, London, 1972.

13 Perry Anderson, *Lineages of the Absolutist State*, London, 1974; a similar approach is adopted by Raymond Aron, *Main Currents in Sociological Thought*, New York, 1965, vol. 1.

14 For a discussion, Franco Venturi, 'Oriental despotism', *Journal for the History of Ideas*, vol. 24 (1963), pp. 133–42; for a critical note on Venturi's interpretation of the politics of Anquetil-Duperron, cf. Anderson, *Lineages of the Absolutist State*, p. 466.

15 H. Nohl (ed.), *Hegels Theologische Jugendschriften*, Tübingen, 1907, p. 411; this aspect of Hegel's philosophy is considered by Raymond Plant, *Hegel*, London, 1973.

16 G.W.F. Hegel, *The Philosophy of History*, New York, 1956, p. 360.

17 Compare, for example, Louis Althusser, *For Marx*, Harmondsworth, 1969 and Jean Hyppolite, *Studies on Marx and Hegel*, London, 1969.

18 The Hegelian perspective is particularly apparent in Shlomo Avineri (ed.), *Karl Marx on Colonialism and Modernization*, New York, 1968; for a critical commentary, Bryan S. Turner, 'Avineri's view of Marx's theory of colonialism: Israel', *Science and Society*, vol. 40 (1976), pp. 385–409.

19 Henry M. Christman, *The American Journalism of Marx and Engels*, New York, 1966.
20 F. Engels's article from *The Northern Star*, in Lewis S. Feuer (ed.), *Marx and Engels: Basic writings on politics and philosophy*, London, 1971.
21 K. Marx and F. Engels, *On Colonialism*, New York, 1972, p. 313.
22 This dependence is discussed in Bryan S. Turner, 'The concept of social 'stationariness': utilitarianism and marxism', *Science and Society*, vol. 38 (1974), pp. 3–18.
23 Paul W. Blackstock and Bert F. Hoselitz (eds.), *The Russian Menace to Europe*, London, 1953, p. 40.
24 John Stuart Mill, *Dissertations and Discussions*, London, 1875, vol. 2, p. 56. Mill's fears had been stimulated by the publication of de Tocqueville's *Democracy in America* (1835); for various comments on Mill and democracy, see J. B. Schneewind (ed.), *Mill, a collection of critical essays*, London, 1969.
25 William Makepeace Thackeray, *Notes of a Journey from Cornhill to Grand Cairo*, London, 1894, p. 608.
26 V.G. Kiernan, *The Lords of Human Kind*, Harmondsworth, 1972, p. 136.
27 Within the tradition of British political economy, the analysis of despotism was important, not only for the utilitarians, but for the earlier tradition of the Scottish Enlightenment; cf. Adam Ferguson, *An Essay on the History of Civil Society*, who is discussed in W.C. Lehmann, *Adam Ferguson and the Beginning of Modern Sociology*, New York, 1930; for criticisms of Ricardo, taxation and Asia, cf. Richard Jones, *An Essay on the Distribution of Wealth and the Sources of Taxation*, London, 1831.
28 H.A.R. Gibb and H. Bowen, *Islamic Society and the West: a study of the impact of western civilisation on Moslem culture in the Near East*, London, 1950 and 1957, 2 vols.
29 ibid., pt 1, vol. 1, pp. 215–16. For additional sources on the relationship between the state and economy, H. Inalcik 'Capital formation in the Ottoman empire', *Journal of Economic History*, vol. 29 (1969), pp. 97–140 and 'Bursa and the commerce of the Levant', *Journal of the Economic and Social History of the Orient*, vol. 3 (1960), pp. 131–47.
30 S. Mardin, 'Power, civil society and culture in the Ottoman empire', *Comparative Studies in Society and History*, vol. XI (1969), pp. 258–81.
31 Roger Owen, 'The Middle East in the eighteenth century – an 'Islamic' society in deline: a critique of Gibb and Bowen's *Islamic Society and the West*', *Review of Middle East Studies*, no. 1 (1975), pp. 101–12.
32 A. Bertholet and E. Lehmann (eds.), *Lehrbuch der Religionsgeschichte*, Tübingen, 1925; G. H. Bosquet and J. Schacht (eds.), *Selected Works of C.*

Snouck Hurgronje, Leiden, 1957; C. H. Becker, *Islam-Studien*, Leipzig, 1924, 2 vols.; Julius Wellhausen, *Das arabische Reich und sein Sturz*, Berlin, 1902. These Orientalists are discussed in Jean-Jacques Waardenburg, *L'Islam dans le miroir de l'Occident: comment quelques orientalistes occidentaux se sont penchés sur l'Islam et se sont formés une image de cette religion*, The Hague, 1963.

33 The nature of that relationship was discussed in Bryan S. Turner, *Weber and Islam: a critical study*, London, 1974.

34 For additional commentary, Vatro Murvar, 'Some tentative modifications of Weber's typology: occidental versus oriental city', *Social Forces*, vol. 44 (1966), pp. 381–9.

35 General commercial and productive conditions are discussed in M. Lombard, *L'Islam dans sa première grandeur*, Paris, 1971.

36 The analytical relationship was, however, pointed out in George Lichtheim, 'Marx and the "Asiatic mode of production" ', *St Antony's Papers*, no. 14 (1963), pp. 86–112.

37 S. D. Goitein, 'The rise of the near-eastern bourgeoisie in early Islamic times', *Journal of World History*, vol. 3 (1957), pp. 583–604.

38 This is the central theme of Maxime Rodinson, *Islam et capitalisme*, Paris, 1966.

39 The issue of unity and diversity has been, of course, central not only to the Orientalist problematic, but also crucial to Islamic theology and philosophy. The problem of unity was important in the work of von Grunebaum and, for a discussion, it is important to consider Abdallah Laroui, 'For a methodology of Islamic studies', *Diogenes*, no. 83 (1973), pp. 12–39.

40 Karl Marx, *Capital*, 1970, vol. 3, p. 334.

41 Daniel Lerner, *The Passing of Traditional Society*, New York, 1958.

42 Lerner's thesis is critically discussed in Anthony D. Smith, *Theories of Nationalism*, London, 1971.

43 This internalist perspective characterized the dominant element, for example, of the contributions to *Classicisme et déclin culturel de l'histoire de l'Islam*, Bordeaux, 1956.

44 Z. Y. Hershlag, *The Economic Structure of the Middle East*, Leiden, 1975.

45 For an alternative view, Samir Khalaf, 'Adaptive modernization: the case for Lebanon', in Charles C. Cooper and Sidney S. Alexander (eds.), *Economic Development and Population Growth in the Middle East*, New York, 1972.

46 T. Stoianovich, 'The conquering Balkan orthodox merchant', *Journal of Economic History*, vol. XX (1960), pp. 234–313.

47 M. Halpern, 'Middle Eastern armies and the new middle class', in J. J. Johnson (ed.), *The Role of the Military in Underdeveloped Countries*,

Princeton, 1962, pp. 277–315.

48 E. J. Hobsbawm, *Industry and Empire*, Harmondsworth, 1969, pp. 41 ff.

49 Barry Supple, 'The state and the industrial revolution 1700–1914', in C. M. Cipolla (ed.), *The Industrial Revolution*, London, 1973, pp. 301–57.

50 W. F. Wertheim, 'Religion, bureaucracy and economic growth', *Transactions of the Fifth World Congress of Sociology*, vol. 3 (1962), pp. 73–86.

51 Roger Owen (ed.), *Essays on the Crisis in Lebanon*, London, 1976.

52 For a general discussion, Walter Elkan, *An Introduction to Development Economics*, Harmondsworth, 1973. For an Islamic illustration of entrepreneurial drive, M. Mercier, *La civilisation urbaine au Mzab*, Alger, 1922; A. Chevrillon, *Les Puritains du désert*, Paris, 1927; E. A. Alport, 'The Mzab', *Journal of the Royal Anthropological Institute*, 1954, vol. 84, pp. 34–44.

53 Paul A. Baran, *The Political Economy of Growth*, Harmondsworth, 1973, p. 385.

54 On the issue of theoretical backwardness in Middle East studies, Leonard Binder (ed.), *The Study of the Middle East*, New York, 1976.

55 A. G. Frank, *Sociology of Underdevelopment and the Underdevelopment of Sociology*, London, 1972; H. Magdoff, *The Age of Imperialism*, New York, 1969; T. Dos Santos, 'The structure of dependence', *American Economic Review*, vol. 60 (1970), pp. 231–6; C. Furtado, *Development and Underdevelopment*, California, 1964.

56 Charles Issawi, *Egypt in Revolution: an economic analysis*, London, 1963; E. R. J. Owen, *Cotton and the Egyptian Economy 1820–1914: a study in trade and development*, London, 1969; Samir Radwan, *Capital Formation in Egyptian Industry and Agriculture 1882–1967*, London, 1974.

57 Samir Amin, *The Maghreb and the Modern World*, Harmondsworth, 1970; Fred Halliday, *Arabia without Sultans*, Harmondsworth, 1974.

58 David McClelland, *The Achieving Society*, New York, 1961; A. Inkeles and David H. Smith, *Becoming Modern*, London, 1974.

59 Traditional interpretations of the Asiatic mode of production are criticized in Barry Hindess and Paul Q. Hirst, *Pre-Capitalist Modes of Production*, London, 1975, but, for an alternative viewpoint, compare Talal Asad and Harold Wolpe, 'Concepts of modes of production', *Economy and Society*, vol. 5 (1976), pp. 470–505.

60 Ervand Abrahamian, 'Oriental despotism: the case of Qajar Iran', *International Journal of Middle East Studies*, vol. 5 (1974), pp. 3–31; K. Wittfogel, *Oriental Despotism: a comparative study of total power*, New Haven, 1957; for an outline of various approaches, Gianni Sofri, *Il*

modo di produzione asiatico, Turin, 1969; and Ernest Mandel, *The Formation of the Economic Thought of Karl Marx*, London, 1971.

61 Umberto Melotti, *Marx and the Third World*, London, 1977, p. 195.

62 Immanuel Wallerstein, *The Modern World-System*, New York, 1974.

63 Caglar Keyder, The dissolution of the Asiatic mode of production', *Economy and Society*, vol. 5 (1976), pp. 178–96.

64 In addition to the research of Inalcik, cf. Bernard Lewis, 'Some reflections on the decline of the Ottoman empire', *Studia islamica*, vol. IX (1958), pp. 111–27; and A. H. Lybyer, 'The Ottoman Turks and the routes of oriental trade', *English Historical Review*, vol. XXX (1915), pp. 577–88.

65 For an application of the Asiatic mode of production to Byzantium, Hélène Antoniadis-Bibicou, 'Byzantium and the Asiatic mode of production', *Economy and Society*, vol. 6 (1977), pp. 347–76. Further aspects of the effects of Ottoman institutions on the Balkans and Yugoslavia are debated in Wayne S. Vucinich, 'The Yugoslav lands in the Ottoman period: postwar Marxist interpretations of indigenous and Ottoman institutions', *Journal of World History*, vol. 27 (1955), pp. 287–305.

66 Bryan S. Turner, *Marx and the End of Orientalism*, London, 1978.

67 The peculiarities of labour organization in colonial capitalism are discussed by Jarius Banaji, 'Backward capitalism, primitive accumulation and modes of production', *Journal of Contemporary Asia*, vol. 3 (1973), pp. 393–413; and Jairus Banaji, 'Modes of production in a materialist conception of history', *Capital and Class*, vol. 1, no. 3 (1977), pp. 1–44.

68 The revisions of Marx's analysis of Asia in neo-Marxist theories are systematically outlined in Aidan Foster-Carter, 'Neo-Marxist approaches to development and underdevelopment', in Emanuel de Kadt and Gavin Williams (eds.), *Sociology and Development*, London, 1974, pp. 67–105.

69 On the conservation of pre-capitalist modes of production, cf. Nicos Poulantzas, *Political Power and Social Classes*, London, 1973.

70 *Development in the Middle East*, MERIP Reports, (1975), no. 42; *State Capitalism in Algeria*, MERIP Reports (1975), no. 35.

71 This feature of Hodgson's view of piety has been criticized in Bryan S. Turner, 'Conscience and the construction of religion: a critique of Marshall G. S. Hodgson's, 'The Venture of Islam', *Review of Middle East Studies*, 1976, vol. 2, pp. 95–112.

72 Sami Zubaida, 'Economic and political activism in Islam', *Economy and Society*, vol. 1 (1972), pp. 308–38.

73 K. Marx and F. Engels, *Werke*, Berlin, 1963, vol. 28, p. 251.

74 For example, there is a cross-section of studies in S. N. Eisenstadt (ed.),

The Protestant Ethic and Modernization, New York, 1968; further material is examined in Syed Hussein Alatas, 'The Weber thesis and South East Asia', *Archives de sociologie des religions*, vol. 8 (1963), pp. 21–35; on particular areas or religions, Robert N. Bellah, 'Religious aspects of modernization in Turkey and Japan', *American Journal of Sociology*, vol. LXIV (1958), pp. 1–5; Robert E. Kennedy, 'The Protestant Ethic and the Parsis', *American Journal of Sociology*, vol. 68 (1962), pp. 11–20; and W. F. Wertheim, 'Religious reform movements in South and South-East Asia', *Archives de sociologie des religions*, vol. 12 (1961), pp. 53–62.

6 Politics and Society in the Middle East

Nineteenth-century social science was dominated by the nature and consequences of social change. Although there was an awareness of the negative features of industrialization – moral decay, loss of community and the threat of the 'dangerous classes' within a crowded urban environment – these theories of change were predominantly evolutionary. Industrialization, despite its destructive side-effects, brought about progress. The technological revolution provided the basis for bourgeois civil society as the cradle of individual rights, education opinion and discerning culture. From the perspective of liberal theory, Islam inevitably provided the contrast case of a society based on conformity to tradition, subservience to authoritarian laws and subjection to a despotic polity. As we have seen in earlier chapters, the absence of progressive change in Islamic societies was explained by a cluster of absences – the missing middle class, the missing city, the absence of political rights and, ultimately, the absence of the liberating revolution. These missing institutions served to explain why Islamic civilization failed to produce capitalism, to generate modern personalities or to convert itself into a secular and radical culture. Whereas in Europe the French and industrial revolutions had replaced the dormant world of feudalism, in the Orient traditional society had remained untouched by the march of history. The Orientalist argument is, therefore, that the Middle East has entered the twentieth century without the institutional apparatus – parliamentary democracy, personal rights, rational law and efficient bureaucracies – which is the necessary infrastructure of modernity.

The definition and explanation of revolution has been a key issue in political science for a considerable period; as Kautsky noted 'Few things are so ambiguous'.[1] From a common-sense point of view, revolutions involve sudden, typically violent, changes of government. Social scientists are more likely to treat these *coups d'état* as political rebellions that bring about changes in personnel of government without necessarily resulting in a transformation of the nature of society. In social science, 'revolution' normally refers to a complete change in the social structure of a society. In view of the conceptual muddle in political science discussions of revolution, the term has been ocasionally replaced by the notion of 'internal war',[2] but in practice the two terms are interchangeable. Just as there is some conceptual uncertainty, so explanations of revolution are variable. For example, in the J-curve theory, revolutions occur when, after a long period of social and economic development, there is a sudden reversal which produces an alienating sense of relative deprivation.[3] Other approaches stress the importance of military defeats, the formation of secret revolutionary organizations and the emergence of charismatic leaders as precipitants of revolution.[4] Some perspectives have analysed revolutions in terms of the stages leading up to revolution, involving mass unrest, development of strategies, collapse of legitimacy and creation of alternative organizations.[5] Despite these differences of approach and definition, there is one agreement common to all, namely, that 'palace revolutions' are not revolutions proper.

One would expect Marxist theory to produce a distinctive approach to the problem of revolutionary change; Marxist theories in many ways, however, tend to parallel more conventional social science approaches. In Marxism, the distinction between surface changes in political personnel and deeper structural changes in the mode of production is clearly crucial. Marx's view of the crisis of capitalism can be illustrated from *Capital*, where he noted that, along with the transformation of productive capital, there:

> grows the mass of misery, oppression, slavery, degradation, exploitation; but with this too grows the revolt of the working-class, a class always increasing in numbers, and disciplined, united, organised by the very mechanism of the process of capitalist production itself. The monopoly of capital becomes a fetter upon the mode of production, which has sprung up and flourished along with, and under it. Centralisation of the means of production and socialisation of labour at last reach a point where they become incompatible with their capitalist integument. This integument is burst asunder. The knell of capitalist private property sounds. The expropriators are expropriated.[6]

Marx's position looks clear enough. The contradictions within capitalist production create the conditions for working-class struggles against the economic and then the political props of capitalist dominance. However, the difficulties associated with Marx's theory of social change (as discussed in Chapter 1) are also present in the more specific theory of revolution. Although Marx at times appears to stress the inevitability of the revolutionary consequences of the contradiction between the relations and the forces of production, he also emphasized class struggle as the essential force in historical evolution. It is not entirely clear whether revolution is the effect of contradictions at the level of the mode of production, or of the antagonistic relations of classes, or of both.

Two particular difficulties are associated with Marx's analysis of class struggle as the basis of structural revolutions. In the *Manifesto* and elsewhere, it is suggested that the struggle between master and slave, lord and serf, capitalist and worker represented the crucial conflicts of social development. In each revolution, the 'expropriators are expropriated'. The class structure of European societies and the class relations that provided the background to the transition from feudalism to capitalism were very different from Marx's sketch in the *Manifesto*. For example, Marx also recognized that merchants and capitalists emerged in the interstices of the feudal class structure. Although the working class in capitalism is to expropriate the expropriators, the serfs did not replace the landlords in the transition to capitalism. A second difficulty is that in the Orient, where the Asiatic mode was dominant, there were no classes and therefore no revolutions. In formulating that argument, Marx anticipated a dominant perspective in contemporary sociological and political analyses of the Middle East.

What may be called the No Revolutions thesis states that, although many Middle East societies are extremely unstable politically and experience innumerable political coups, these political events are not manifestations of deeper structural changes. Political changes do not signify genuine revolutions; the Middle East is essentially stationary. For Shloma Avineri, the militarized Arab societies of the Middle East have not experienced social revolutions, but merely palace coups; Israel, by contrast, has undergone a profound revolution at both the social and political level.[7] In a similar fashion, Zartman commented that in the Middle East 'there have been few violent, transforming sociopolitical upheavals . . . works on "revolution" in the Middle East discuss mainly army coups and military regimes, which are not at all the same thing'.[8] Khadduri suggests that Arab populations have a preference for strong governments (if necessary, based on military takeover), rather than the uncertainties that accompany democratic politics (based necessarily on mass franchise and participation). The study which has given the most systematic statement of the No Revolutions thesis is *Revolution in the Middle East*, edited by Professor Vatikiotis.[9]The principal argument of this collection of essays is that 'struggles for independence and radical movements in the Middle East, *coup d'état*, insurrections and rebellions so far do not constitute revolutions'.[10] For Vatikiotis, a revolution is essentially political action against the status quo, based on a revolutionary ideology which presents a radical and total alternative to the existing social structure. The ingredients of this struggle include coherent political organization, subjective commitment to radical alternatives and mass political participation. Thus the revolutions of western society, Russia and China presupposed the development of a revolutionary culture and political organizations which converted oppositional sentiment into radical political action. The rebellions and political conflicts of the Middle East have been largely non-revolutionary responses of 'the educated official classes' to European intervention, rather than class struggles, equipped with indigenous political ideology and organized for the purpose of post-independence reconstruction. The alterations to Middle East social structure are brought about by the administrative intervention of states which are dominated by bureaucratic, military classes. By contrast, western society has drawn upon a revolutionary culture, having its roots in Stoicism, the 'universal humanism of Christianity' and the Natural Law tradition. Western culture incorporates a clear right of citizens to resist bad government. For Hatto, the great turning-point in the semantic history of 'revolution' was 1789, which inaugurated the modern conception of organized action to bring about 'swift, often violent changes in constitutions'.[11] Whereas Clarendon could use the term 'revolution' to describe the events of 1660, because they represented a return to old times (hence Restoration), French philosophers came to use the term in connection with massive changes in social structure brought about by the conscious intervention of human beings in the course of history. Western culture thus developed a variety of notions concerning the importance of classes or political organizations in the construction and management of revolutions.

Bernard Lewis's contribution ('Islamic concepts of revolution') is also an attempt to trace the non-revolutionary character of Middle East history and society back to the absence of an indigenous concept of revolution. Lewis considers a range of Islamic terms which have been employed to describe revolutions and political uprisings – *dawla*, *fitna*, *bid'a*, *thawra*, *bagha* – from the overthrow of the Umayyad Caliphate to the establishment of socialist regimes in Egypt, Syria and Iraq. Like Vatikiotis, Lewis comes to the conclusion that 'Western doctrine of the right to resist bad government is alien to Islamic thought. Instead, there is an Islamic doctrine of the duty to resist impious government, which in early times was of crucial significance.'[12] This right to resist sinful rulers was, however, rendered ineffectual on two counts. First, the jurists never produced any clear, practical criteria by which the impiety of governments could ever be tested and, second, no apparatus was ever constructed by which rights could be enforced against impious rulers. Instead, the duty of obedience prevailed everywhere over the right to resist, with the result that a blanket of conformity and political quietism descended on Muslim governments for centuries. Because religion and politics in Islam are 'inextricably intermingled', religious dissent inevitably posed a serious political threat to the social fabric of Dar al-Islam. In order to protect society from the double threat of *fitna* (disruptions of social order) and *bida* (departure from the Sunna), conformity was to be bought at any cost. Innumerable *hadith* were invented to legitimate blind adherence to *de facto* government. The continual threat of internal deviance and external conquest eclipsed the doctrine that 'There is no obedience in sin', thereby reinforcing the dominant conformist ethic.

Against the back-cloth of medieval conformity, the conflict and political turmoil of the nineteenth century would appear to be a turning-point for the unleashing of opposition and dissent in the Middle East and North Africa. The 'Urabi revolt of 1882, the Egyptian revolutions of 1919 and 1952, the Damascus massacre of 1860, the Syrian revolt against the French in 1925, the Lebanese revolution of 1958 – are these candidates for the term 'revolution'? Albert Hourani, in his essay 'Revolution in the Middle East', comes to the conclusion that these social movements of contemporary history 'may have been feuds rather than revolutions'.[13] One reason for this aspect of Middle East politics is that the struggle for power has been traditionally a 'Politics of Notables'.[14] The provincial centres of the Ottoman empire provided two political roles – while governing was in the hands of the Ottoman officialdom, mobilizing public support was the work of local notables. The political life-style of the notables centred on harnassing 'the active forces of society' (the support of craft guilds, mobs, religious leaders), neutralizing rivals and securing influence with the Ottoman governor. This 'Politics of Notables' sought:

> not so much to over-turn an existing order as to change it and then to restore it; not to replace the system of government by another but to change its policy and its personnel and to preserve or make stable the balance between local governor and local leaders on which provincial society depended.[15]

The political objectives of the notables were essentially conservative. With the collapse of the Ottoman empire and the eventual withdrawal of European powers, the old style of politics withered away, since the 'ruler, being no longer alien could also be leader'. In addition, the new means of communication and coercion made government through intermediaries an obsolescent political practice. In the post-independence epoch, revolution, for the first time, is on the agenda, since the new politics of bureaucrats, unlike that of notables, involves either internal support for the system, with the prospect of eventual promotion and advancement, or external opposition which seeks the total overthrow of government through the intervention of the armed forces.

Having outlined the basic features of the No Revolutions thesis, it could be objected at this stage that the thesis survives only because it is based on a restricted selection of cases. Very little consideration, if any, is given to the Palestinian resistance, the Algerian Revolution, Libya, the revolutions in North and South Yemen. It may be that the central thesis of *Revolution in the Middle East* is best answered by the examination of a more catholic selection of cases.[16] To some extent, this sort of objection might be met by the contribution of Tourneau, Flory and Duchac ('Revolution in the Maghreb') which analyses the political changes taking place in Morocco, Algeria and Tunisia. However, the political upheavals of these three societies also fail to satisfy the criteria of 'real revolution'. The Algerian Revolution was the work of a 'small number of leaders', who mobilized the masses for a national struggle and 'have lulled them since independence with hopes, slogans and formal demonstrations'.[17] The socialism of these regimes assumes a diluted character, since it denies the centrality of class conflict and class interest in favour of ethical and religious conceptions of communal harmony and evolution without violent confrontation. The socialism of the Maghreb represents a link with the past, since 'the altruistic qualities which the building of socialism demands from its citizens are the very qualities of Islam'.[18] So the No Revolutions thesis remains intact. The 'revolutions' of pre-colonial times were in fact merely feuds conducted between notables for the sake of pelf; the 'revolutions' of post-colonial times have been failures in which the notables have been replaced by soldiers turned bureaucrats.

My criticisms of the No Revolutions thesis will be in three sections. In the first, I shall attempt to demolish the argument within its own terms of reference. Even if we accept the theoretical and epistemological framework of these essays, there is little empirical justification for their argument. The second section elaborates the defects of their basic position by showing that this collection of essays belongs to a particular species of political writing which is fundamentally an 'Oriental Despotism' tradition. Lurking behind these essays is a Kiplingesque theme by which the West is perceived as dynamic and progressive, whereas the East has been locked within a stationary, stagnant culture. Finally, it will be important to examine some alternative approaches to the theory of revolution by which the Vatikiotis-Lewis position might be undermined in an alternative epistemological terrain. I shall come to the pessimistic conclusion that criticism of the Orientalist tradition, as illustrated by *Revolutions in the Middle East*, is not as forceful as one would wish, because much of the conventional Marxist alternative also contains unresolved analytic problems.

These essays are based on the belief that there is a uniform and unchanging tradition which we can identify as 'the western doctrine of the right to resist bad government', which is absent in the case of Islam. It is difficult to know what Lewis can mean by this assertion. If he means a Christian tradition, then there would appear to be little to distinguish Christian theology of political rights from the Islamic injunction 'There is no obedience in sin'. Indeed, the notion of 'rendering unto Caesar' would suggest a parallel Christian quietism to the alleged Muslim fear of dissent. At best, the medieval period could be said to include two contradictory principles – a populist (ascending) theme, in which the king held power as a representative of the community, and a theocratic (descending) principle, by which the king received power from God. From the Merovingian period (500–750), the descending principle was dominant and the tradition of German sacral kingship was combined with the Christian concept of charismatic rulership to produce a fully-fledged doctrine of the divine right of kings. The notions that 'the king can do no wrong' or 'no writ runs against the king' are hardly promising sources for Lewis's view of a western right of resistance. Even Reformation theology was only too aware of the dangers to political order implied by the Lutheran doctrine of the priesthood of all believers. In Calvinism, any right to resist sinful, secular government was carefully hedged around with restraining conditions so that the obligation to defend the faith could be undertaken only on the decision of properly instituted religious authorities. Calvin came to see that the Church and the secular government has a common aim, namely to preserve 'a well-regulated polity, which excludes all confusion, incivility, obstinacy, clamours and dissensions'.[19] Christian limitations on the right to resist can be traced historically through the authoritarianism of the Puritans to such oppositional religious movements as Methodism. It is worth recalling that Jabez Bunting, a nineteenth-century president of the Wesleyan conference, once asserted that Methodists are 'as much opposed to *democracy* as to *sin*'.

By 'the western doctrine', therefore, Lewis might be referring to the European political theory of the social contract from Hobbes, Rousseau and the utilitarians. But this tradition is also notorious for the limitations it imposed upon the individual right of resistance. Hobbes's state of nature, in which there is absolute personal freedom, was a strategic device for Hobbes's argument for despotism; the choice was between anarchy with liberty and security without freedom. The implication was that rational men would relinquish their rights in favour of a social contract which would keep them out of a state of nature. Most other social-contract doctrines contain a similar authoritarian theme. Rousseau's contract was an attempt to free men from all personal dependence ('Each, in giving himself to all, gives himself to no one'), but the condition of this freedom was that men would voluntarily surrender their individual rights. We need not delay too long over liberalism; it was based, at least in the case of James Mill and J. S. Mill, on a bourgeois fear of working-class dominance within a reformed parliament. The conclusion must be that there is no such animal as 'the western doctrine'. In addition, the right to resist was an ideological right, not against 'bad government', but against illegitimate government, and the problems of defining 'illegitimate' are no more or less difficult than those associated with the notion of 'impious government'.

The No Revolutions thesis invites us to consider the absence of revolutions in the Middle East and thereby obscures the real kernel of the argument, namely, that there have indeed been revolutions in the West. Revolutions are treated as the crucial ingredients of western modernization, which release the sluice-gates of technological progress under the control of democratic government. Unfortunately, most of the western revolutions referred to by these essays do not quite fit the bill. While the French Revolution certainly did destroy the *ancien régime*, it did have the peculiar effect of increasing the political role of the peasantry by providing peasants with a legal right to smallholdings as private property. The peculiar post-revolutionary structure of rural France and the political significance of the peasantry had the effect of delaying capitalist development throughout the first half of the nineteenth century. This aspect of French society led writers like Marx to the conclusion that the Revolution was precocious – a series of violent political uprisings which failed to galvinize the economic and social structure of France. Following Hegel's dictum that historical events always occur twice, Marx regarded the Revolution of 1789 as a tragedy and the Revolution of 1848 as a farce.

The case of Germany is also problematic for the Vatikiotis-Lewis argument. Germany was unified from above by a state apparatus which remained largely in the hands of a feudal Junker class and excluded the industrial bourgeoisie from political power in exchange for favourable tariff systems. The Nazi regime and the defeat of the German working class prior to fascism are hardly events which support the No Revolutions thesis as an attempt to contrast western democratic revolutions with Oriental stagnation.

Furthermore, the 'peculiarities of the English' case is a notorious stumbling-block for the type of thesis suggested by Lewis.[20] The enclosures, destruction of the peasantry and the capitalization of ground rent created a capitalist land-owning class in the countryside before the emergence of an industrial bourgeois class, so that in Britain the emergence of a capitalist mode of production was not accompanied by a class struggle between the aristocracy and the capitalist class. Indeed, the bourgeoisie did not gain control of the state apparatus until after 1850. It can be said, therefore, that Britain experienced an industrial revolution without an accompanying bourgeois revolution; 'gradualism' has consequently been the hallmark of British political development, rather than violent revolutionary change.

The point of these comments is that there is no *necessary* connection between violent revolutionary change, on the one hand, and capitalist development, on the other. In Lewis's terms, there is no *necessary* relationship between a democratic tradition and industrial growth. On the contrary, the dictatorships of Nazi Germany, Mussolini's Italy or Franco's Spain greatly facilitated the triumph of capitalism by accelerating the concentration of industrial capital and the penetration of agriculture by capitalist relations of production.[21] As the revolutions of China, Russia, Cuba and Mexico demonstrate, revolution is most likely to occur on the periphery of the capitalist world, where usually through direct imperialism, the capitalist mode of production (CMP) is rapidly and violently inserted into a society where some other mode (slave, primitive, feudal) has been dominant.[22] It is this insertion which leads to uneven development as a condition for a revolutionary context, rather than the internal maturation of the capitalist mode of production, which itself creates revolutionary class forces. However, to pose the issue of revolutionary potential within this conceptual scheme is to break with the assumptions of the No Revolutions thesis.

The arguments of Hatto, Vatikiotis and Lewis hark back to the old tradition of western political philosophy which regards Oriental societies as dominated by stagnant and repressive despotism. The causes of this social stationariness have been sought in a variety of factors.[23] For Montesquieu, despotism resulted from the absence of juridical restraints, the dominance of religion and the absence of hereditary nobility. In Weber's sociology of civilizations, stagnation in the East results from the integration of politics and religion, the absence of free cities and thereby the failure of an autonomous, ascetically motivated bourgeoisie. According to Mill, 'Chinese stationariness' results from a stultifying culture which inhibits the creative individualism of the educated élite. In contemporary sociology of development, 'cultural factors' are frequently paraded as the ultimate causes of low productivity, backward-sloping effort curves, irrational investment programmes or labour immobility. In Lewis and Vatikiotis, we find a similar appeal to the causal significance of 'national culture', so that the problem of the non-revolutionary quality of Middle East history is located in the superstructure, that is, in the doctrine of the right to resist. The absence of revolutions is not sought in the particular historical development of the Middle East, its economic basis, its class structure or in the international network of capitalist relations, but simply in the Islamic ideology of conformity to *de facto* government.

The superstructural features of this version of the 'Oriental despotism' tradition are amply illustrated by the wholly political criteria by which Lewis, Vatikiotis, Hatto and Hourani identify revolutions. Hourani is content to accept a dictionary definition of revolution as a 'complete overthrow of the established government in any country or state by those who were previously subject to it' (*Shorter Oxford English Dictionary*). On these grounds, as we have already suggested, it would be difficult to exclude Algeria or South Yemen from the category of 'political revolutions', unless a number of implicit riders are built into Hourani's argument. Le Tourneau, Flory and Duchac are aware of the serious limitations of a purely political notion of revolution. They argue that, with the development of socialism, 'a revolution has much more importance if it is also an economic and social revolution.[24] The 'also' is crucial, however, since in their argument they refer to the 'economic and social' as if it were merely tacked on to 'a deep transformation of the political system'. The so-called revolutions of the Maghreb are consequences of the failure of post-colonial governments to carry out the socialist aims to which they were initially committed. This interpretation adheres to the view that the primary location of revolution is in 'the political system', so that changes in social and economic conditions are largely effects of government intervention or failure to intervene. Despite judicious references to 'Marxist analyses', their treatment of revolutions is divorced from any consideration of, for example, the causal determination of political life by changes in modes of production. The 'Oriental Despotism' tradition, therefore reasserts itself with the view that the political history of the Middle East is essentially a matter of governments, constitutions and powerful élites, without reference to the nature of the economic base – soldiers and notables become the Oriental parallel of Pareto's lions and foxes. Until the Middle East can turn away from government by soldier-bureaucrats 'the very political categories essential to a revolution will be lacking'.[25] This 'fact' of political life suggests a further global contrast which is consistent with the Orientalist tradition. The modernization of the West was the work of an autonomous bourgeoisie which established the foundations of rational law, democratic politics and free enterprise, but the development of such a class of entrepreneurs was inhibited by the structure and culture of Ottoman society. Whether the military in the Middle East can provide a functional alternative to the western bourgeoisie or whether the military prevent democracy developing has become a typical Orientalist debate.[26]

The No Revolutions thesis can be criticized for: (1) presenting an entirely superficial view of the nature of revolutions as simply changes in government or constitution brought about by unspecified 'subordinates'; (2) locating the problem of revolutions simply at the level of superstructural phenomena; and (3) rehearsing in a different garb the ideology of 'Oriental Despotism'. By criticizing these essays in these terms, I am obviously appealing to Marxism to provide us with an alternative theory of revolution. It is possible, however, to argue that Marx's interpretation of Oriental society and history in terms of the Asiatic mode of production (AMP) is no alternative to the bourgeois tradition of 'Oriental Despotism'. If the Asiatic mode of production is characterized by the state as the real landlord, self-contained village communities, state slavery, the tax/rent couple, then there could be no structural transformation of society via the mechanism of revolutionary class struggle. Hence Asia has 'no history at all', but rather periodic rotations of state personnel. On this reading of Marx, the Asiatic mode of production can be put to good ideological use, since it follows that the only source of social transformation in Asia is the introduction of capitalism, which destroys the economic base of Oriental societies. Shlomo Avineri, for example, employs Marx's conception of the Asiatic mode of production to justify the state of Israel as a dynamic capitalist force in a sea of Arab backwardness.[27]

The ideological implications and theoretical problems of the Asiatic mode of production have given rise to an acrimonious debate as to whether or not Marx really believed in the existence of this particular mode.[28] Some of the conceptual fog surrounding this issue has been recently dissipated by the publication of *Pre-Capitalist Modes of Production*.[29] In this text, Hindess and Hirst argue that the journalism from which the AMP is normally derived is marginal to the scientific interests of Marx's mature writing. The central issue is not whether Marx did or did not believe in the AMP, but rather, whether this mode is theoretically coherent. Furthermore, since modes of production are purely theoretical constructions, they can have no specific geographical designation – there is nothing Asiatic about the forces and relations of production denoted by the AMP. Hindess and Hirst argue that because the AMP is theoretically incoherent and ideologically vicious, the AMP should be eliminated. Although there is obviously much to commend this argument, I am not convinced that the remaining modes of production of conventional Marxism (slave, feudal, capitalist) are particularly adequate in the case of Middle East societies. Unfortunately, the categories of conventional sociology (semi-feudal, prebendal, patrimonial, hydraulic, centralized empires) are also problematic.

Of course, it could be argued that the status of the AMP is not relevant to the problem of presenting an alternative to the No Revolutions thesis of traditional Orientalism. The real objection to that tradition is that it fails to see that the class struggle is the material mechanism of revolutions. 'The history of all hitherto existing society is the history of class struggles', culminating in either 'the revolutionary reconstruction of society at large' or in the 'common ruin of the contending classes'. The presence, absence or failure of Middle East revolutions would not be causally explained by reference to the superstructure (religious traditions, rights to resist, national character), but by reference to features of class structure. This type of Marxist position could presumably go on to assert that we already possess adequate analyses of the class struggle in the Middle East.[30] I do not, however, find an unelaborated class struggle explanation of revolutions particularly convincing, and I would suggest that, in order to come to terms with the issues raised by the No Revolutions thesis, we need a much more theoretically radical solution. Rather than treating revolutions as direct outcomes of confrontations between classes, we need to regard revolutions as political effects of complex combinations and transformations of modes of production within given social formations. Furthermore, revolutions are not immediate, direct or necessary consequences of transformations of modes. Uprisings, protests, *coups d'etat* – these political phenomena are contingent outcomes not of the elementary confrontation of two classes in a social formation, but of the contradictions within modes of production.

It is possible to indicate the nature of my argument by an exaggeration – Marxists have to make a theoretical choice between 'class analysis' (as in *The Communist Manifesto*), by which 'classes' are the ultimate causes of the reproduction and transformation of social relations, or 'mode of production analysis' (as in *Captial*), whereby 'classes' are effects of changes in modes. If we opt for the second alternative, then the manner in which we think out the problem of revolutions will be fundamentally transformed. The 'mode of production analysis' has been closely connected with the work of Louis Althusser, Nicos Poulantzas and Charles Bettelheim.[31] For Poulantzas, a mode of production is an 'articulated combination' of instances or levels (the economic, political ideological) in which the economic (relations and forces of production) *determine* which of the three structures will be *dominant*. For example, in the feudal mode of production (FMP), the economic (relations of production in which the peasantry were not separated from the forces of production) determined that extra-economic conditions (ideology in a religious form) would be dominant. This formulation of the relationship between economics, politics and ideology is an attempt to resolve some of the difficulties associated with the conventional base/superstructure distinction. Social classes are to be seen as *effects* of the complex operation of these instances (structures) of modes of production and not the primary causes of transformations of modes. Whereas modes of production are theoretical models, social formations ('societies') are 'real concrete objects'. Thus, for Poulantzas, Marx's *Capital* is not a study of a capitalist society (namely Britain), but a theoretical analysis of the CMP which is illustrated by reference to concrete social formations. Social formations are conceptualized as combinations of modes; social formations present a particular combination, a specific overlapping of several pure modes of production. In any given social formation, one mode is always dominant (except, obviously, in periods of transition), and the social class corresponding to that mode is the ruling, but not necessarily governing, class. Thus, in a capitalist social formation the CMP is the dominant mode and the capitalist class exercises hegemony over the power bloc. Given these basic concepts, it follows that the class structure of any social formation can never be a two-class system – a variety of classes and class fractions will exist as effects of the presence of different modes in combination. A revolution, the replacement of one class by another as the class exercising political hegemony, would therefore be an index at the political level of the shifting dominance of modes within a social formation. However, transformations of modes do not bring about immediate, 'overnight' displacement of dominant classes; periods of transition may be characterized by class conflict, class alliance or situations in which no single class is hegemonic. In general, Poulantzas regards fascism as a deep crisis of the power bloc without a dominant class. By way of further illustration, the dominance of the CMP in Britain did not result in an immediate dissolution of the FMP so that the British class structure contained or conserved feudal classes. In France, the CMP conserved feudal peasants and workers, feudal lords and capitalists. Revolutions in this perspective are the outcomes of complex contradictions in the 'imperialist chain' linking social formations (especially 'weak links'), contradictions within social formations between modes, and finally contradictions between capital and labour. This class struggle can, however, never be reduced to a simple conflict between bourgeoisie and proletariat, lords and serfs. From this standpoint, we have to reject what Althusser has called 'the "beautiful" contradiction between Capital and Labour', if we are to avoid the theoretical trap of regarding all revolutionary failures (1849, 1871, the German social democratic failure) as somehow exceptional. There is no warrant in the Marxist theory of modes of production for the belief that revolution is a necessary, inevitable outcome of class struggle or for the belief that there is a necessary historical sequence of modes (from feudalism to capitalism to socialism).

A number of criticisms can be raised against Poulantzas's formulation of the theory of modes; Poulantzas can also be regarded as a 'revisionist' who has watered down the conventional Marxist view of the centrality of the class struggle.[32] With regard to the theoretical status of the concept of 'revolution', however, Poulantzas's theory can be regarded as consistent with the approach Marx employs in *Capital*. Although Marx as a political activist was obviously interested in the proletarian struggles of the nineteenth century, Marx pays relatively little attention to the question of political revolutions in his mature work. What Marx does provide is a theory of the general crisis of the CMP, namely, the contradictions between the labour and valorization process. He also indicates a range of strategies by which capitalists may compensate for the tendency of profits to decline (by increasing exploitation, for example). There are a number of possible outcomes of the general crisis of the CMP – temporary containment of crisis, the emergence of a monopoly phase of the CMP, transition, replacement of the dominance of the CMP by some other mode. The constant restructuring of the CMP has its effects in the form of class struggles, the major location of which is the struggle for the control of the state apparatus. It follows from this discussion that the question posed by the No Revolutions thesis is a false question. The real object of study which is obscured by this thesis is the nature of modes of production in Middle East social formations, their restructuring and transitions. However, the conventional Marxist question – 'are Middle East social formations characterized by the AMP?' – also needs refinement. The issue is more precisely the nature of the combinations of overlapping modes and their shifting dominance in social formations.

The major transformation of European society was the result of a shift in the dominance of the FMP to that of the CMP in the nineteenth century. The effect of this replacement did not bring about an automatic and instant destruction of all feudal elements of European society, but often their conservation. Similarly, the transformation did not result everywhere in class struggles leading to revolutionary events at the political level. Hourani's dictionary definition of revolution, whereby a subordinate class replaces a dominant class in order to change the government, is obviously false in the British case. British capitalism was not created by peasants in opposition to feudal landlords! The Civil War, the Restoration, the Glorious Revolution – these were not just the consequence of the 'beautiful' contradiction of classes. Similarly, the contradictions within the social structures of Germany, Italy and Spain resulted in the defeat of the working class and fascism. In these terms, the political history of western Europe and the Middle East may not be as radically dissimilar as Lewis suggests. The difference is not a matter of pluralism versus despotism or successful revolutions in the West and revolutionary failure in the Middle East.

In the twentieth century, the Middle East has undergone a massive transformation, namely, incorporation within the capitalist world via colonialism. This incorporation has involved profound changes in pre-capitalist modes of production in these societies. Changes in these pre-capitalist modes have had effects at the political level in the form of revolutions, riots, uprisings and confrontations. It would be naive to expect these political phenomena to be exact replicas of the political struggles of European capitalism, since there are basic differences in the combination of modes between European and Middle East social formations. Thus, the primary contrast between west European and Middle East social formations could not be discovered by merely concentrating on political differences; it can only be discovered at the level of modes of production.

First, whereas the transition of European social formations was from a relatively homogenous feudalism to competitive capitalism, the transformation of the Middle East to a region within the capitalist world was brought about on the basis of a far more complex heterogeneity of pre-capitalist modes (primitive, slave, pastoral-nomadic, feudal and Asiatic).[33] As yet we do not possess any precise theory of how the articulated combination of these modes had their effects at the level of ideology and politics. Theoretical appreciation of these analytic issues has gone little further than repetitive disquisitions on Ibn Khaldun's notions concerning the circulation of tribal élites or commentaries on the 'patrimonial structure' of Ottomanism.

Second, capitalism arose in Europe as a consequence of the internal maturation of contradictions in feudalism, but the restructuring of modes in Middle East social formations was largely a consequence of the insertion of exogenous capitalism via colonialism. The problem of revolution in the Middle East is a function of the specific crises of transition of modes under the dominance of foreign capital. Thus, there have been massive transformations of modes-in-dominance, but these have rarely been accompanied by simple ('beautiful') class struggles between indigenous working class and bourgeoisie resulting in decisive and permanent revolutionary situations.

Third, one common characteristic of this transition of modes under the dominance of foreign capital has been to retard, distort or crush the emergence of indigenous capitalism, resulting in alliances between the compradorial bourgeoisie and traditional landlords. In Poulantzian terms, conservation effects have perhaps been more significant than the dissolution of existing modes and their attendant classes by the CMP – for example, the conservation of traditional landlords or tribal sheikhs in the Gulf, of the Saudi regime in the Peninsula, of Islam and the religious hierarchy in Morocco, of Berber culture after the *Dahir Berbere*, of landowners in Iran. Although Marx wrote about bourgeois capitalism sweeping away 'all fixed, fast-frozen relations, with their train of ancient and venerable prejudices', the effect of colonial capitalism on peripheral regions may in the first instance be, as Halliday observes, 'to fossilize and insulate' pre-capitalist modes.[34]

The point of these comments is to note that the impact of revolutionary western capitalism may not have the automatic progressive and transformative consequences which Vatikiotis, Lewis and Hourani implicitly associate with the spread of European industrialism and its imputed liberal, pluralist culture. However, André Gunder Frank's analyses of capitalist underdevelopment are also sufficient warning against those Marxists and neo-Hegelians (like Shlomo Avineri) who adhere to an optimistic teleological view of social change, whereby capitalism necessarily brings ultimate liberation.

Revolution in the Middle East is a work of ideology in the specific, neutral sense that it fails to break with the common-sense assumptions of everyday discourse. It does not, for example, attempt to go beyond the etymology of the concept of 'revolution' in Islam and Europe. Dictionaries cannot produce a theory of revolution, since they are themselves systematizations of common usage. The majority of these essays, as a consequence, merely reproduce the established wisdom of political philosophy from Machiavelli to Weber, in which the East is the homeland of stagnating despotisms or revolutions *manqué*. The response of conventional Marxism to this ideological tradition has been to argue that revolutions cannot be explained by reference to values, to rising expectations or to political structure, but only by reference to the class struggle. In this paper, I have attempted to suggest some theoretical weaknesses which result from treating 'social classes' as *explicans* of political revolutions. To criticize the No Revolutions thesis in these terms is to remain within the same epistemological terrain as the thesis itself – it is to take 'revolutions' for granted as a 'natural' empirical phenomenon requiring explanation. Revolutions are not necessary consequences (given the right conditions of class consciousness, class organization, a revolutionary ideology, a militant party) of class struggles; they are, instead, along with a wide range of other political manifestations of strikes, riots and take-overs, *contingent* consequences of transitions of modes – their restructuring, dissolution and replacement. To pursue the question 'why no revolutions?' by providing counter-instances of 'empirical' revolutions in Algeria, Yemen and the Gulf can only lead to false results. The question about revolutions serves to mask the real issue of the analysis of modes. It is unfortunately precisely at this point that a Marxist alternative to Orientalism is weakened by the failure to develop a set of theoretically coherent 'modes of production'. The perennial and often sterile debate about the AMP is an index of the infancy of a scientific analysis of Middle East social structure.

Notes

1 K. Kautsky, *The Social Revolution*, Chicago, 1902, p. 5.
2 H. Eckstein, 'On the etiology of internal wars', *History and Theory*, vol. 4 (1965), pp. 133–63.
3 J. C. Davies, 'Toward a theory of revolution', *American Sociological Review*, vol. 27 (1962), pp. 1–19.
4 C. Johnson, *Revolution and the Social System*, Stanford, 1964; L. Stone, 'Theories of revolution', *World Politics*, vol. 18 (1965), pp. 159–76.
5 C. Brinton, *The Anatomy of Revolution*, New York, 1965; R. D. Hopper, 'The revolutionary process', *Social Forces*, vol. 28 (1950), pp. 270–79.
6 K. Marx, *Capital*, London, 1974, vol. 1, p. 715.
7 S. Avineri, 'Modernisation and Arab society: some reflections', in I. Howe and C. Gershman (eds), *Israel, the Arabs and the Middle East*, New York, 1972, pp. 300–11. This issue is discussed at greater length in Chapter 7.
8 I. W. Zartman, 'Political science', in L. Binder (ed.), *The Study of the Middle East*, New York, 1976, p. 284.
9 P. J. Vatikiotis (ed.), *Revolution in the Middle East and other case studies*, London, 1972.
10 ibid., pp. 12–13.
11 ibid., p. 28.
12 ibid., p. 33.
13 ibid., p. 67.

14 Cf. also Albert Hourani, 'Ottoman reform and the politics of notables', in W.P. Polk and R.C. Chambers (eds), *The Beginnings of Modernization in the Middle East*, Chicago, 1968.
15 ibid., p. 67.
16 For example, Ruth First, *Libya: The Elusive Revolution*, Harmondsworth, 1974; Gerard Chaliand, *The Palestinian Resistance*, Harmondsworth, 1972; Fred Halliday, *Arabia without Sultans*, 1974; Nathan Weinstock, *Le Mouvement Révolutionaire Arabe* Paris, 1970.
17 Vatikiotis, *Revolution in the Middle East*, p. 97.
18 ibid., p. 109.
19 John Calvin, *The Institutes of the Christian Religion*, Philadelphia, n.d., Vol. 2, p. 477, quoted in Sheldon S. Wolin, *Politics and Vision*, London, 1961, p. 171.
20 Cf. Perry Anderson, 'The origins of the present crisis', *New Left Review*, no. 23 (1964); E.P. Thompson, 'The peculiarities of the English', *Socialist Register*, 1965.
21 Cf. Nicos Poulantzas, *Fascism and Dictatorship*, London, 1974; R. Miliband, *The State in Capitalist Society*, London, 1973.
22 Louis Althusser, *For Marx*, Harmondsworth, 1969; M. Mann, *Consciousness and Action among the Western Working Class*, London, 1973.
23 Cf. Perry Anderson, *Lineages of the Absolutist State*, London, 1974.
24 Vatikiotis, *Revolution in the Middle East*, p. 81.
25 ibid., p. 13.
26 M. Halpern, 'Middle Eastern armies and the new middle class', in J.J. Johnson (ed.), *The Role of the Military in Underdeveloped Countries*, Princeton, 1962; the debate between Amos Perlmutter and Manfred Halpern, in *Comparative Studies in Society and History*, vol. 11 (1969) and vol. 12 (1970).
27 Shlomo Avineri, 'The Palestinians and Israel', *Commentary*, vol. 49 (1970), 'A note on Hegel's views on Jewish emancipation', *Jewish Social Studies*, vol. 25 (1963); *Karl Marx on Colonialism and Modernization*, New York, 1968; 'Israel and the New Left', *Transaction*, vol. 7, (1970).
28 Cf. Gianni Sofri, *Il modo di produzione asiatico*, Turin, 1969.
29 Barry Hindess and Paul Q. Hirst, *Pre-Capitalist Modes of Production*, London and Boston, 1975.
30 Such as Mahmoud Hussein, *La lutte de classes en Egypte de 1945 à 1968*, Paris, 1969.
31 Louis Althusser, *Reading Capital*, London, 1970; Nicos Poulantzas, *Political Power and Social Classes*, London, 1973; Charles Bettelheim, *Economic Calculation and Forms of Property*, London, 1976.
32 Poulantzas, *Political Power and Social Classes*, p. 15. For criticism of Poulantzas, cf. Hindess and Hirst, *Pre-Capitalist Modes of Production*;

Ernesto Laclau, 'The specificity of the political: the Poulantzas–Miliband debate', *Economy and Society*, vol. 4 (1975).

33 On the 'pastoral-nomadic mode', cf. Anderson's discussion of Marx's *Grundrisse* in *Lineages of the Absolutist State*, and *Passages from Antiquity to Feudalism*, London, 1974.

34 Halliday, *Arabia without Sultans*, p. 18. For a critical comment on this aspect of Halliday's argument, cf. Maxime Rodinson, 'A Marxist view of Arabia', *New Left Review*, vol. 95 (1976).

7 Marx's Theory of Colonialism: Israel

Shlomo Avineri has made an important contribution to the contemporary understanding of the thought of Karl Marx by drawing attention to certain alleged continuities between Hegel and Marx. By extension, such an interpretation of Marx also entails the assertion of definite thematic continuity in Marx's work itself.[1] Avineri has been, therefore, a prominent critic of those writers who claim to detect a decisive epistemological break in Marx's theoretical development. In addition, Avineri is well known for his edition of Marx's journalistic writing on British colonialism which, in the sociology of development and social change, has achieved something of a classical status.[2] Through his commentary on Marx's view of colonialism, Avineri has established himself as an advocate of the theoretical significance of 'the Asiatic mode of production'.

Because of Avineri's importance in the field of Marxist exegesis, his 'occasional' writings on Israel, and more specifically his view of the relationship between Israeli modernity and Arab backwardness, have not received the critical attention they merit. This neglect is unfortunate, since Avineri's attempt to utilize the Hegelian interpretation of Marx in order to explain the apparent stagnation of Arab society is important for both intellectual and political reasons.

In this critical assessment of Avineri, I shall argue that Avineri undermines Marx's true stature by presenting Marx as merely the amanuensis of Hegel. Avineri attempts to show that Marx simply elaborated Hegel's master-conceptions of transcendence, universality and consciousness as the critical features of modern Occidental society which distinguish it from the particularism and stagnation of Oriental society. Avineri employs this interpretation of Hegel and Marx to explain the dynamic modernity of Israel and the particularism of Arab society. He attempts by use of an analogy to show that the Israeli presence is both necessary and inevitable, in the same way that British colonialism in India in the nineteenth century was inevitable, given the logic of the capitalist mode of production. It is through this analogy that Avineri's explanation also ends up as a justification. In true Hegelian fashion, Avineri is able to reconcile ethics and economics, or to quote Hegel, 'to recognize the rose in the cross of the present'.[3] In presenting Avineri's sociology, I shall concentrate first on his view of Marx's theory of colonialism, and second on his interpretation of Hegel. This, I believe, will enable us to explain Avineri's conception of Israeli development. In presenting my criticism of Avineri, I shall attempt to question his theoretical understanding of Marx and his empirical understanding of colonialism in the Middle East.

Avineri's *Karl Marx on Colonialism and Modernization* is basically a collection of quotations from Marx and Engels's contributions to the *New York Daily Tribune* for the period 1852–62. These 487 *Tribune* articles covered British domestic politics and British foreign policy, especially in India and China. It is primarily from the latter that Avineri derives Marx's view of colonialism. For Marx, the limitations of the home market compel capitalist society to seek ever-increasing foreign markets for its commodities and for capital investment. This dynamic within the capitalist mode of production eventually creates a world capitalist market. As Marx and Engels comment in *The Communist Manifesto*, bourgeois capitalism 'creates a world after its own image'. This 'cosmopolitanism' of capitalism enables Avineri to associate the growth of the world market with the Hegelian theme of universalism, which challenges the narrow conceptions of the Oriental world. Avineri writes:

> Capitalist society is universalistic in its urges, and it will not be able to change internally unless it encompasses the whole world; it is this that determines Marx's and Engels' attitude to the concrete cases of nineteenth-century European expansion in India, China, North Africa, etc.[4]

Elsewhere Avineri notes:

> As Marx sees it, it was the universal nature of modern industry which turned history into world-history, *Weltgeschichte*. Only where man consciously changes the world is there history. As capitalism means the constant transformation of the whole world, there is now, for the first time, only one, universal history.[5]

Avineri connects this Marxian theme of human history and universalism generated by the economic dialectic of the capitalist economy with Hegel's view of universalism generated by the contradictions of civil society, as elaborated in his *Philosophy of History* and *Philosophy of Right*. For Hegel, the contradictions of civil society drive it 'to push beyond its own limits and seek markets, and so the necessary means of subsistence, in other lands which are either deficient in the goods it has overproduced, or else generally backward in industry'.[6] For Hegel and Marx, as Avineri interprets them, there is no 'inner dialectic in civil society' in Asiatic societies; therefore these societies have no inner conflicts and hence no history. Having commented on the dynamic element in capitalist society, Avineri turns to Marx's interpretation of the stagnation of Asia and thence to Marx's model of 'the Asiatic mode of production'.

Avineri notes that Marx treats western history in terms of a series of historical epochs - slavery, feudalism and capitalism. Just as feudalism emerges out of slavery, so capitalism emerges out of the disintegrating womb of feudalism. Here Avineri refers to the Hegelian concept of transcendence (*Aufhebung*) to suggest that capitalism transcends feudalism only when the feudal mode of production has achieved full maturity of 'overripeness'. As Marx argues in the Preface of the 1859 *Critique*:

> No social order is ever destroyed before all the productive forces for which it is sufficient have been developed, and new superior relations of production never replace older ones before the material conditions of their existence have matured within the framework of the old society.[7]

The Asiatic mode therefore seems to present a problem, since it is apparently a merely geographic designation, rather than an analytic and historical one. It also appears to be isolated, so to speak, since it neither grows out of nor matures into an alternative mode of production. Avineri argues that the theory of social development (slavery, feudalism, capitalism) is restricted to western societies and this creates problems for the Marxist understanding of Oriental society. Hence the theoretical importance of the Asiatic mode.

It will be sufficient here to sketch the main theoretical ingredients of Marx's explanation of the Asiatic mode of productions.[8] Marx notes that 'climate and territorial conditions' in arid lands stretching from the Sahara to China created a need for large-scale irrigation works, canals and waterworks which could only be maintained by a centralized state apparatus.[9] Through the monopoly of land, the state was the 'only real landlord', leaving the general population in a condition of 'general (state) slavery', which was very different from the private slavery of classical Europe. The dominance of the state went hand in hand with self-sufficient, autonomous village units that combined manufacture and agriculture. No economic surplus could escape from these narrow social confines. Where there was no private property in land, there could be no classes; where there are no classes, there cannot be conflicts based on social contradictions. Where there are no structurally induced conflicts, there can be no history of class struggles. As Mark expressed the problem in 'The future results of British rule in India' (1853), Asia 'has no history at all, at least no known history. What we call its history, is but the history of successive intruders who founded their empires on the passive basis of that unresisting and unchanging society.'[10]

Although there were periodic changes of personnel (that is, dynastic changes), Asiatic society was characterized by massive continuity in structural arrangements. Avineri likens Marx's view of Asiatic structural stagnation to Hegel's conception that the individual cannot come to self-consciousness in the Oriental empires, because the individual is lost within the totality:

> The glory of Oriental conception is the One Individual as the substantial being to which all belongs, so that no other individual has a separate existence.... On the one side we see duration, stability – Empires belonging to mere space, as it were... unhistorical History... The States in question, without undergoing any change in themselves, or in the principle of their existence, are constantly changing their position towards each other.... This History, too, is, for the most part, really *unhistorical*, for it is only the repetition of the same majestic ruin.[11]

It follows that Asiatic society can be changed only by the direct intervention of western capitalism, which, unlike all previous empires, does not simply become absorbed into the existing, stagnating dynastic set-up, because capitalism destroys the Asiatic mode of production by the creation of private property in land.

For Avineri, Marx's understanding of socialism as the product of the universalism of capitalist society leads Marx inevitably to 'the position of having to endorse European colonial expansion as a brutal but necessary step towards the victory of socialism... the horrors of colonialism are dialectically necessary for the world revolution of the proletariat'.[12] Just as capitalism contains within itself the seeds of its own destruction, so colonialism digs its own grave by revolutionizing Asiatic society. In India, for example, Marx notes that the British, by creating private property, by providing a new political unity through a modern army, by establishing a modern civil service, unwittingly laid the basis of Indian independence and social development. Again, Avineri links Marx's grasp of the unanticipated consequences of British rule to Hegel's doctrine of the 'Cunning of Reason', in which history operates through agents who do not comprehend the ultimate significance of their actions. Similarly, Marx's notion that the European economy will ultimately become dependent on its colonies is, for Avineri, merely an application of Hegel's dialectical analysis of the master-slave relationship. What Avineri calls 'the sophistication of Hegelian dialectics' enables Marx to perceive the complex interplay between colonialism, classes and colonies. For example, Marx arrived at the conclusion that the economic rewards which the British economy as a whole derived from its Indian colony were less than the expenditure for military control, administration and defence. The real beneficiaries of British rule in India were the bondholders of the East India Company and those employed in the British administration, who creamed off bloated salaries. British colonies, therefore, represented a tax on the British people as a whole for the benefit of a cross-section of the ruling class.

Despite the brutality of British rule (which involved 'dragging individuals and peoples through blood and dirt') and despite the system of financing colonialism through an indirect tax on the British working class, Avineri tells us that Marx is committed to the view that colonial penetration of Asiatic society is necessary and inevitable. Avineri draws a corollary from this position: 'Marx would have to welcome European penetration in direct proportion to its intensity: the more direct the European control of any society in Asia, the greater the chances for the overhauling of its structure and its ultimate incorporation into bourgeois, and hence later into socialist society'.[13] Direct rule in India promised to bring about rapid and irreversible structural changes, whereas indirect rule in China threatened to leave much of the existing system of production intact. Those pockets of the globe where capitalism has not penetrated to the root represent a drag on historical development and a threat to socialism since, in Avineri's interpretation, socialism can only emerge on the back of a universal capitalist economy.

This comment on the importance of the paradoxical connection between the intensity of colonialism and the speed of the modernization process more or less concludes Avineri's introductory essay dealing with Marx on colonialism. In passing, suffice it to say that Avineri appears to accept this theory of colonialism and its consequences as an empirically valid statement of the nature and impact of capitalist colonialism in the nineteenth century. The chief criticism of this 'Hegelian Marx' voiced by Avineri is that 'Marx's sole criteria for judging the social revolution imposed on Asia are those of European, bourgeois society itself'.[14] Avineri also argues that Marx failed to incorporate the Asiatic mode (which is basically a geographical designation) into the dialectic of slavery–feudalism–capitalism. My reason for claiming that Avineri appears to accept this account as 'empirically valid' is that he uses this theory to explain Arab backwardness. Before coming to Avineri's application of the Asiatic mode to the Middle East, it is important to look more closely at his other writings on Hegel.

At first sight, it would appear that Hegel would be an unlikely candidate not only as the basis for a theory of revolution, but also as a theoretical source of Zionism. It is important to realize, therefore, that much of Avineri's recent theoretical work has been concerned to rescue Hegel from those critics who charge him with anti-Semitism, militarism and reaction. What Avineri seeks to achieve is a rehabilitation of Hegel as a progressive thinker, and he does this by concentrating once again on the universalistic/particularistic dimension.

The standard criticism of Judaism in the nineteenth century and earlier was that Jewish legalism, its separation from the community on religious and ethnic grounds, and its particularistic ethics made Judaism incompatible with the needs of a modern, industrializing society. The Jewish problem would be solved when Jews gave up their specifically Jewish identity. Those who criticized Judaism on these grounds also tended to be reluctant to grant Jews emancipation in political and social terms. Hegel stands out as different from this current of political criticism for, as Avineri attempts to demonstrate. Hegel both condemned Judaism and advocated Jewish emancipation.

It is easy to see why Hegel would want to criticize Judaism. Judaism is a formal religion which, by enslaving the individual in 'the performance of a countless mass of senseless and meaningless actions', prevents the emergence of true, subjective consciousness. Furthermore, the separate identity of the Jews and their isolation in civil society is for Hegel an embodiment of particular interests and consciousness, against which Hegel consistently argues. However, to refuse emancipation to Jews would be to limit the scope of legal rights and hence to commit law itself to a particularistic basis. The philosophical basis for this commitment is Hegel's argument that:

> It is part of education, of thinking as the consciousness of the single in the form of universality, that the ego comes to be apprehended as a universal person in which all are identical. A man counts as a man in virtue of his manhood alone, not because he is a Jew, Catholic, Protestant, German, Italian, etc.[15]

Hegel also detects a self-fulfilling prophecy in those laws which deny Jewish emancipation. The Jews are condemned because they lead a separate and isolated life within the community; laws are then passed which force the Jews to live in isolation. The best method of destroying Jewish isolation is to give Jews equality under a law granting universal emancipation.

Avineri then attempts to show the continuity between Hegel and Marx in terms of their interpretation of the relationship between bureaucracy and the state. In Hegel's political philosophy, the state transcends the egoism of individuals and families operating in civil society by setting up a system of universal norms and goals. Similarly, the bureaucracy is a universal order (*der allgemeine Stand*) which transcends the particular interests and limited objectives of private individuals in society. In the bureaucracy, Hegel says, 'individuals are not appointed to office on account of their birth or native personal gifts. The *objective* factor in their appointment is knowledge and the proof of ability.'[16]

Marx turns Hegel's formula on its head by showing that the state in capitalist society merely represents the particular interests of the bourgeoisie. While Marx is quite clearly critical of Hegel's conclusions, Avineri argues that Marx remained faithful to Hegel's method. For Marx, social change occurs when a rising class can identify its interests with the universal interests of society as a whole. Marx transforms Hegel's dialectics so that 'the Hegelian idea of a "universal class", stripped of its hypostasis, becomes, for Marx, a vehicle for historical explanation'.[17] In developed capitalism, the rising class is the proletariat, which is the only class capable of identifying its interests with the general interests of society. Hegel's static view of the bureaucracy as a universal order is changed into Marx's dynamic view of the embodiment of universality in class transformations, but the kernel of Hegel's dialectic is still clearly present.

Turning to Hegel's view of international relations, with special reference to the problem of war, Avineri wishes to rescue Hegel from any imputation that his philosophy is militaristic or totalitarian. Hegel makes a distinction between the concept of war and the actual concrete instance of war. The concept of war may have an ethical justification in Hegel's view because war serves as an ethical *memento mori*. Avineri tells us: 'According to Hegel, there lies in war an ethical (*sittlich*) element inasmuch as it exposes the accidental, the arbitrary, and the finite in life. It prevents the particular interest from becoming the master of the universe.'[18] Concrete instances of war, however, can have no ethical justification since 'concrete war is always a conflict between accidental–particular desires which contain nothing necessary, and thus no philosophical justification can be given to that or any other war'.[19] In line with this argument, Hegel makes a number of recommendations about the conduct of wars. Since war should not be an intrinsic part of civil society, wars should be conducted by professional armies, rather than by a national *levée en masse*. The military should always be under the firm control of the civil authority and the existence of military states such as praetorian Rome is always an inversion of the normal order of things. Avineri's attitude to this aspect of Hegel's philosophy is that, although Hegel's position may appear naive from the perspective of modern warfare, his treatment of war is not morally objectionable. Hegel did not, Avineri tells us, 'supply arguments from which the nationalistic case for war could be sustained'.[20]

The point of this somewhat lengthy commentary on Avineri's interpretation of the Hegelianism of Marx's theoretical ideas on colonialism, the state and social class is to show the intellectual ingredients of Avineri's view of Israel. It is to this problem which we now turn. The nub of Avineri's understanding of the Arab–Israeli conflict and the problem of the 'backwardness' of the Arab societies is contained in the following quotation from an article that was first published in 1969:

> Whatever the sins of imperialism, it did, after all (as has been pointed out very perceptively by Marx) put an end to the old, traditional society... The colonial power, whatever its own motivation, became the prime mover in the modernization of the non-European world.... None of this happened in the Arab countries.... Whether it

> was called protectorate or mandate, the system ensured the overall paramountcy of the Western power without involving it in direct administration – without, therefore, basically affecting the socio-economic infrastructure of Arab society.[21]

The system of indirect administration permitted (if it did not encourage) pre-capitalist, Asiatic elements to survive into the modern period of colonial capitalism. Instead of smashing the existing social structure, indirect colonialism merely emphasized aspects of the pre-modern élite, especially the military. Islam, according to Avineri, was a religion of conquest which gave particularly high evaluation to military prowess and military virtues.

Since the thirteenth century, the Arab lands were ruled by Turks, Seljuks and Mamelukes, so that the military society swept aside by the British and French was not an Arabic society as such. This predominance of centralized military power (whether Arabic or Turk) gave the existing social structure a relatively undifferentiated, 'lopsided' character. The apex of the status system was occupied by the warrior and craft, trading and merchant occupations were held in disdain by the élite.[22] Trade was controlled by Greeks and Jews. European colonialism reinforced this pattern by pampering the military élite. The mandate authorities 'did little to encourage industrial growth in the Arab world, or to promote literacy, or to lay the foundation for a truly Western type of constitutional state; but they modernized the Arab armies and thus reinforced the most traditional trait in Arab society'.[23] Once the western powers withdrew from the area, Arab society very easily reverted to traditional systems of authority, organization and legitimacy. An authoritarian and undemocratic military power, equipped with the apparatus of a modern army, sat atop a pre-modern and stagnant society. The only exception was Algeria, where a modern state was brought into being by a revolutionary struggle against colonialism.

This view of Arab backwardness follows directly from Avineri's understanding of Marx, since Avineri claims that colonialism is the only way by which non-European societies can be dragged into real history and hence into the modern, capitalist world. The greater the intensity of colonialism, the greater the modernity. Apart from Algeria, the Arab world resembles China in terms of the experience of partial and indirect colonization. The Arab world is consequently a hindrance to the full development of modern forces. For Avineri, the growth of Israel is very different; by contrast with Arab stagnation, Israel represents a dynamic, modern force in the area. The tragedy of Israeli–Arab relationships is that it is a conflict between two movements of national liberation, where only Jewish nationalism is truly radical and modern. Faced by the same enemies – British and Turkish – in the first half of the twentieth century:

> the two movements took separate paths, and it is in this divergence that

> one can locate the Arab nationalism. For while it is possible to maintain that the Jewish national movement succeeded in combining a national revolution with a social one, the Arabic movement remained almost exclusively political – an Arab social revolution, indeed, has yet to be undertaken.[24]

The combination of a nationalist and socialist revolution gave Zionism its special dynamic and progressive features. The creation of a Jewish national home in Palestine transformed the Diaspora social structure in which no proletariat could develop into a society of workers and peasants. It was for this reason, namely, the refusal to base the new Jewish home on the exploitation of Arab labour, that the Jewish migration was 'the only intentionally downwardly mobile social movement ever experienced in the history of immigration'.[25] By contrast, Arab nationalism remained locked within the traditional, militaristic social structure of the old Ottoman empire, in which no significant Arab commercial class could emerge. Arab nationalism lacked a genuinely modern social analysis of its problems, because it was forever looking over its shoulder to a glorious past before the rise of European colonialism. In any case, the original leaders of Arab nationalism were themselves members of the traditional élite who were not sympathetic to radical social change. The result was that the military regimes of Egypt, Syria, Iraq and Libya were not regimes produced by revolutionary struggle against a colonial power; they were merely restatements of pre-colonial social forms.

The policy prescriptions which follow from this analysis are fairly obvious. The Israeli government should cease believing that a settlement between Israel and the Arab states will provide a solution, since the real problem is the relationship between the Israeli and Palestinian national movements. Furthermore, Israel should cease giving tacit support to such Arab states as Jordan and Lebanon. A reconciliation with the Palestinians is obviously problematic, given what Avineri calls their 'maximalist policies'. Furthermore, one cannot expect the Palestinians to come to social maturity through a revolutionary conflict with Israel taking the form of a guerrilla war along Vietnamese lines. Because the terrain provides no extensive swampland, large forests, jungles or inaccessible mountainous regions, 'the Arab guerrilla effort has characteristically fallen back on personal and indiscriminate terrorism'.[26] This terrorist activity is a substitute for a real, revolutionary war.[27] Writing before Black September, Avineri looked outside Israel to Jordan, where he hoped a Palestinian force might topple Hussein's kingdom. The fall of Jordan to the guerrillas would have removed a sense of 'homelessness' among the Palestinians and produced a more realistic attitude towards the Israeli state. Inside Israel, Avineri believes that a moderate middle class has begun to emerge among the Palestinians of the West Bank, and to some extent in Gaza, which is prepared to negotiate with the Israelis. The first priority is simply the mutual recognition of the validity of each other's nationalist movements for self-determination in the area.

Israel has played the role of the 'inadvertent midwife' in a number of different ways. For example, Israeli occupation has cut the political connection between the Palestinian Arabs and their own ruling class.[28] Although the Israeli presence is itself coercive, it provides a paternalist political framework within which the occupied Arabs receive the benefits of Israel's own political democracy. In addition, the Israelis have raised standards of living through the provision of modernized agricultural technology, electrical power grids, improved sewerage systems and other public utilities. The overall impact of occupation is to provide Arabs with at least the rudiments of experience in trade union politics and democracy, a new consciousness of urban conditions separated from traditional feudal arrangements, and an expertise in modernized agriculture and urban occupations. In terms of the Arab class structure, Israel has inadvertently created the first modern urban proletariat in the area and the beginnings of a progressive Arab bourgeoisie. Although the implications of these changes are explosive in political terms, the urbanization of the Arabs at least holds out the promise that the Arab and Israeli working class will come to share common economic interests which will transform the political deadlock.

Apart from four quotations from Marx's 'theoretical writings' – *The Poverty of Philosophy, The Communist Manifesto, The Critique of Political Economy* and *Capital* – Avineri's interpretation of Marx rests almost exclusively on Marx's journalism, that is, on Marx and Engels's contributions to the *New York Daily Tribune*. It is important to ask how significant this journalism is and whether it is a reliable source of Marx's theory of capitalist colonialism. Marx's own view of that journalism was certainly not very high. In October 1853, Marx wrote:

> The continual newspaper muck annoys me. It takes a lot of time, disperses my efforts and in the final analysis is nothing. However independent one wishes to be, one is still dependent on the paper and its public especially if, as I do, one receives cash payment. Purely scientific works are something completely different. . . .[29]

In considering Marx's views on colonialism, it is important to bear in mind that Marx was writing for an American liberal bourgeois audience, which was mainly interested in Marx's criticism of British foreign policy, rather than in Marx's theoretical interpretations of the essence of capitalist colonialism and the nature of Asian society. Marx regarded the assumptions of the *Tribune* policy as mere 'socialistic humbug' disguising the protectionist interests of the American bourgeoisie. Marx's attitude here does not render his commentary on colonialism void, but it does mean that his journalistic work must be treated with caution.

Avineri's selection from the journalism of Marx is, however, odd in another direction; he fails to provide any indication of Marx's commentary on British colonialism in Ireland, which is very different from his view of colonialism in India and China.[30] Marx believed that Ireland 'has been stunted in its development by the English invasion and thrown centuries back.... By consistent oppression [the Irish] have been artificially converted into an utterly impoverished nation.'[31] In Ireland colonial capitalism stunted the growth of society, a fact which clearly contradicts Avineri's view that colonialism, especially direct and intense colonialism, must necessarily modernize a backward society. Even where Avineri does concentrate on Marx's Asiatic studies, I am not convinced that he provides the full meaning of Marx. For Marx does not claim that colonization means modernization; he merely asserts that colonization provides some of the initial conditions for structural change. He says that the people of India:

> will not reap the fruits of the new elements of society scattered among them by the British bourgeoisie, till in Great Britain itself the now ruling classes shall have been supplanted by the industrial proletariat, or till the Hindus themselves shall have grown strong enough to throw off the English yoke altogether.[32]

The developmental potential of 'the new elements in society' – private property, railways, political unity, the army, etc. – is contingent upon the occurrence of a class revolution either in the capitalist society itself or within the colonized dependencies. Colonialism only indirectly produces modernization via revolutions at home or abroad.

One of the textual limitations of Avineri's book is that it makes no reference to the *Grundrisse*, in which a slightly different picture of social forms and historical periodization emerges. For Avineri, the 'Asiatic mode of production' is analytically 'odd', because it is essentially geographical and stands outside the dialectic of slavery–feudalism–capitalism. In the *Grundrisse*, Marx argues that early social forms are routes out of the primitive communal system, and these routes include the Oriental, the ancient, the Germanic and the Slavonic. In this scheme, Marx, to quote Hobsbawm, is not:

> referring to chronological succession, or even to the evolution of one system out of its predecessor (though this is obviously the case with capitalism and feudalism), but to evolution in a more general sense.... Marx distinguishes four analytical, though not chronological, stages in this evolution.[33]

In this way, the regional designation 'Asiatic' refers to an analytic category, namely, a system based upon 'the self-sustaining unity of manufacture and agriculture', which locks surplus production within the village commune.

For this reason, the Asiatic mode is not as theoretically problematic as Avineri suggests.

A further theoretical objection to Avineri's interpretation is that it exaggerates the Hegelianism of Marx's sociology. This is obviously a very large issue which can only be touched upon here, because it would involve a discussion of the problem of the early and late Marx. Instead of going into these issues, it will suffice to make three comments on Avineri's Hegelian version of Marx. The first observation is relatively minor. According to Avineri, Marx's view of the differences between European dynamism and Asiatic stagnation follows directly from Hegel's lectures on *The Philosophy of History*. Yet, if one wanted to find immediate intellectual sources for Marx's approach, one would be better employed studying the writing of British utilitarians on India. The utilitarians thought that Asiatic society was stagnant because of the dead hand of custom, tradition and priestcraft. Mill wrote that Asia had 'no history' because of the 'despotism of custom', and his greatest fear was 'not too rapid change, but... Chinese stationariness'.[34] It was the utilitarians and the House of Commons reports that provided Marx and Engels with their immediate empirical evidence.

At a more general level, we have already noted that Avineri fails to distinguish adequately between Marx's journalistically popular comments on colonialism and the 'purely scientific' problems raised in the *Critique, Grundrisse* and *Capital*. Expressing this somewhat differently, Avineri fails to distinguish between Marx's theoretical model of the capitalist mode of production (and, by extension, his theoretical views of colonialism) and Marx's illustration of that theory by empirical examples from concrete instances. Avineri persistently conflates Marx's theoretical understanding of the universalistic consequences of capitalist expansion with Marx's empirical illustrations. As we shall see shortly, this conflation enables Avinri to jump from one example of imperialism in British India to another empirical example in the Middle East mandates, while assuming that he is dealing with the theoretical properties of the capitalist mode of production. Avineri fails to recognize that the capitalist mode of production is never completely dominant within social formations and that any real-concrete society must be conceptualized as 'a particular combination, a specific overlapping of several "pure" modes of production'.[35] He thus fails to draw a necessary distinction between the capitalist mode of production as a theoretical, abstract construction and actual capitalist societies within which the capitalist mode of production is only more or less dominant, operating alongside other modes.

This conceptual muddle in Avineri's approach creates difficulties for the analogy he attempts to draw between nineteenth-century imperialism in India and twentieth-century imperialism in the Middle East. There is an ambiguity here because the 'blame' for the backwardness of Arab society is ascribed to the indirect colonial methods of Britain and France. The existence of Israel in the Middle East is not itself regarded as colonial; therefore the emergence of the Israeli state is not an example of western colonialism, but merely of downwardly mobile migration. Nevertheless, Avineri does intend to draw an analogy between the progressive impact of Israel in historical Palestine and Britain in India. Marx's contrast between the dynamic capitalism of the West and the stagnation of the Asiatic mode becomes Avineri's contrast between the social revolution going on inside Israel and the continuity of militaristic traditionalism in neighbouring Arab states. In order to make this sort of analogy Avineri would have to prove not only parallels in empirical illustrations, but also major similarities between the social structures of India, China and the Middle East. Avineri fails even to perceive such a problem. In addition to criticizing Avineri on these grounds, it is also instructive to assume Avineri's hypotheses and then ask whether Israel is a bourgeois society with a dominant capitalist mode of production developing along the lines indicated by Marx's *theoretical* model.

The third observation is equally crucial. In comparison with their comprehensive analysis of the internal structure of the capitalist mode, Marx and Engels did not develop a theory of the economics of colonialism; nor did they spell out the social consequences of colonialism or the nature of the class struggle in colonial societies. It is true that, in order to understand the dynamics of capitalism, Marx found it necessary to elaborate some minimal understanding of colonialism. Therefore he incorporated a set of notions (such as the high level of colonial profits, the need for external investments, etc.) into the analysis of capitalism itself, but the object of his theory was the capitalist mode of production in general, not the development of non-capitalist social formations on the periphery of the system. Hence Marxist theories of development and underdevelopment must necessarily be neo-Marxist. James O'Connor strikes just the right theoretical note when he observes that:

> Marx's relative silence on the economics of imperialism may have handicapped the development of Marxist theory or it may have been a blessing in disguise. The absence of any theoretical precedent has forced (and continues to force) Marxists back on their own experiences and intellectual resources.[36]

Avineri, on the other hand, naively and uncritically attempts to apply Hegel's armchair Orientalism to the complex problems of development in the Middle East.

The history and social structure of Israel diverge in a number of important directions from the theoretical model of the capitalist mode of production. To start at the beginning, the so-called Jewish migration was in fact very different from the classical British colonialism of the Indian empire. Israel did not so much colonize Palestine as depopulate it by creating a Palestinian Diaspora. That is, the Israelis did not establish either direct or indirect colonialism: they bought land from Arab landlords before 1948 in order to create a 'national home' which would not include Arabs or Christians. After the creation of the Israeli state, the occupations of 1948, 1956 and 1967 made possible, through land-use regulations and the kibbutz system, the depopulation of Arab villages and the settlement of Jews in place of Arabs. If one wants an analogy here, it is not that of the British in India, but of the white settlers in America, Australia or Africa. Yet, perhaps even this analogy is a weak one. In America and Australia, the Europeans, according to Paul Baran, 'entered more or less complete societal vacua, and *settled* in those areas establishing themselves as their permanent residents', whereas in Asia, the Europeans 'were faced by established societies with rich and ancient cultures, still pre-capitalist or in the embryonic state of capitalist development'.[37] Israel certainly faced an established civilization in the Middle East, but since there was no European homeland to which the economic surplus of Jews could be transferred, Israel proceeded to create an economic surplus *in situ*.

Unfortunately, even this analogy will not quite work, because the surplus value extracted from the area by Israeli colonization has never been adequate in itself to support the Israeli state, which is largely dependent upon massive foreign investments. In the period 1948–68, Israel's import surplus was in the region of 7.5 billion dollars, most of which came from the United States. This financial support was unusual in that, to quote Oscar Gass:

> only about 30 per cent came to Israel under conditions which call for a return outflow of dividends, interest or capital. This is a circumstance without parallel elsewhere, and it severely limits the significance of Israel's economic development as an example to other countries.[38]

These capital inflows have allowed Israel to sustain a rate of investment of around 20 per cent of GNP in a situation where net savings without these foreign sources were zero. Since 1967 this dependence on foreign investment has sharply increased, due to the need for increased military expenditure. In 1970, for example, military expenditure was estimated to be 24 per cent of GNP. This situation has a number of important consequences. Rather than developing tourism, the phosphate industry, oil and agriculture along truly capitalistic lines, Israel has followed a 'pseudo-capitalist' line of development.[39] Because of wartime demands, wealth and talent have been directed into the weapons industry, especially aircraft. Israel is also in the uniquely favourable position of being largely financed by foreign capital without having to pay the typical price of dependency. Unlike Britain in India, Israel does not provide an economic stimulus for an additional reason – namely, the adherence to a policy of not forming trade relations with neighbouring Arabs. The Israeli imperial and economic thrust has been into Africa, rather than into the Middle East. This is only one aspect of the problem of Avineri's theoretical analogy.

Israeli society also diverges significantly from the classical bourgeois model in terms of its class structure, which is closely associated with the foreign inflow of capital. Capital and other funds from abroad are divided among the major parties in the Knesset according to their numerical strength. In turn, these funds are distributed by the party to its own kibbutzim and Moshavim, to its own housing schemes or industries. The 'divide', as it is called, creates vertical patronage lines ensuring the loyalty of client-citizens to the party and the Histadrut. Israel did not develop along European-capitalist lines, in which the means of production were dominated by a property-owning bourgeoisie. On the contrary, the ruling class was composed of the Labour bureaucracy, divided into the Jewish Agency and Histadrut and the government. The bourgeois, private sector remained a junior partner of the ruling group. (For example, in 1960 the private sector produced only 58.5 per cent of the net product of the Israeli economy.) After the Six Day War there was a so-called 'normalization' of the economy, whereby a number of industries were turned over to the private sector, but this process has so far done little to change the character of the economy, which Ghilan appropriately calls 'syndicalist-capitalism'.[40] The class structure may be briefly described, therefore, in the following terms. The dominant class is composed of a bureaucratic officialdom (*Bitzuistim*, 'doers'), including the higher military strata, Histadrut leaders, public servants generally, and the Jewish Agency bosses. Below this group comes the private capitalist class, itself often working on government contracts. The middle class proper is composed of the middle orders of the military, state and labour bureaucracies – teachers, middle executives and union leaders. The lower middle class can be identified as the kibbutz membership, shopkeepers and white-collar workers. The working class consists simply of the new Jewish immigrants, and below them the Arab workers. The lumpenproletariat is contained within the refugee camps.

This class structure is further complicated by an ethnic division. As is well known, the early white Jewish migrants (the Ashkenazim) have gained an economic and social dominance within the class system, whereas the later Spanish, African and Asiatic Jews (the Sephardim) have gone to the bottom of the status and income ladder. These Sephardic Jewish migrants have provided the personnel for new kibbutzim settlements in frontier sectors and hence bear the brunt of new colonization projects. They also have accounted for the bulk of the wartime casualties. As a result, there is:

> in spite of increasing numbers of sabras emerging in the elite groups, a predominance of Russian- and Polish-born leaders from the third and fourth aliyot. In the main, these persons live in the large cities and,

> with the exception of the kibbutzim, the rest of the country is under-represented (in the political system).[41]

The 'divide' and class system has an important impact on class consciousness and social conflict. The 'divide' and the all-embracing nature of Histadrut institutions (in a society where one-third of the population has a membership in the Histadrut) creates a widespread patronage-dependency. Since the Histadrut provides social security, education and health benefits, there is little incentive for dissent. The result is that national interests override class interests, but this is not to say that Israel is free from social conflict. There have been a number of waves of strikes (in 1951, 1962 and 1969), but on the whole social conflicts are expressed not in class terms, but in conflicts between secular and religious Zionism, between generations, and between veterans and immigrants. These conflicts rarely lead to a new alignment of political forces or to the creation of new parties, since the 'divide' means that economic power stays in the hands of parties which already enjoy a large representation in the Knesset. The racial conflict between Sephardic Jews and Arabs within the working class ensures the loyalty of the working-class Jew who fears the competition of the low-paid Arab. For good sociological reasons, the working-class Jew who receives least from the 'hand-out' system is the most loyal Zionist.

For a number of reasons (in terms of colonization, dependence on foreign capital and the peculiarities of the class structure), Israel is a society which is very different from Marx's theoretical model of capitalism; therefore the attempt to form an analogy between the Middle East and India or between indirect Chinese rule and Middle East imperialism is not only superficial, but misleading. If one wants an analogy, it might have been more profitable to find one in Ireland and Palestine. Just as Marx noted a 'stunting effect' in Britain's relationship with Ireland, so one might find a stunted development in the Middle East under the dual impact of British and Israeli colonization. It is, of course, part of the Zionist ideology to believe that the land occupied by Jewish settlers was largely unpopulated, uncultivated and undeveloped. Within a wider historical framework, however, a rather different picture begins to emerge.

The modernization and colonization of the Middle East has been both longer in duration and more complex than is suggested by Avineri, who starts his argument first with the impact of Europe in the late nineteenth century and then with the mandate period. European and Middle East trade relations had existed for centuries before the modern colonization, and because of the imbalance of exchange, it can be argued that the dependency relationship between the two economies had already been established in the Middle Ages.[42] A cash economy had developed as early as the seventeenth century in Lebanon, with the planting of mulberries and the export of silk to Europe. The grain trade received a strong impetus in the 1840s in response to European demand, which further developed production and marketing, especially after the Crimean War. From around 1850, however, raw silk was being exported from Syria and Lebanon, particularly to France, while at the same time the home market was opened to finished goods from European societies. The importation of European commodities under concession agreements with the Ottoman empire was greatly facilitated with the construction of roads in the 1850s and railways in the 1880s. The construction of a modern communications system was also in the hands of the French and other European companies. The general effect of European intervention may be summarized by a quotation from I. M. Smilianskaya:

> Favourable conditions for the development of manufactorial production were absent in the Ottoman Empire. As a result of the Capitulations, European industrial goods were put in a better position than locally produced goods. When Syria was flooded by cheap factory-made fabrics during the second quarter of the nineteenth century, local weaving manufactories could not survive under this pressure... the number of workers on Damascus weaving looms decreased from 8,000 to 2,000 between 1820 and 1840, and those in Aleppo, from 10,000 to 1,000.[43]

The Jewish migrants of the late nineteenth century and early twentieth century were therefore entering a country which had already been severely stunted by its economic dependency.

The economic dependence of Palestine and Syria was greatly increased by the French and British mandates after the First World War, and the development of local light industries was hampered by the dominance of British commercial goods. The Palestine economy received a great stimulus during the Second World War, when the British supply routes to the Middle East, which brought manufactured commodities to the area, were broken. The British forces had to rely on local supplies and on the local economy, which they had to develop. The need for roads, airfields and buildings not only eliminated Arab unemployment, but laid the basis of a modern economic infrastructure. Whereas the Arab economy had to rely on relatively unskilled labour, the Jewish migrations from Europe brought in a labour force which was, despite a significant *petit-bourgeois* dimension, already developed in certain sectors along modern capitalist lines. The Jewish community was able to take full advantage of this war period, which became known as 'The Prosperity'. One historian writes: 'By 1942, there were six thousand Jewish industrial enterprises, employing some fifty-six thousand workers and producing at the rate of twenty million pounds a year. The level of production in 1942 was more than double that of 1939 in the food, textile, metal machinery and chemical industries.'[44] The threat that Britain would reassert its commercial dominance in the area was removed by the establishment in 1948 of an independent Israeli state, which set up various protective barriers for the Israeli economy.

Contrary to the arguments of Avineri, the creation of a modern Israeli economy has not brought significant benefits for Arab labour. Despite the employment of Arab workers, the peasantry is the dominant section within the Palestinian class structure. Aswad reports that:

> over 50 per cent of the Israeli Arabs are still rural-based, as opposed to 12 per cent of Israeli Jews. Many may have wage-labor jobs in the city but return to their homes in the villages. Thus in Israel there remains a small middle peasantry with many of its members commuting to urban jobs, but a substantial rural population which has been isolated from its elites, yet it has not completely merged into Israeli society.[45]

The Arab peasantry is therefore isolated from both the Palestinian bourgeoisie and intelligentsia, which have been widely dispersed, and from the Jewish urban working class, which is wedded to the Histadrut establishment. The possibility of progressive capitalist development under such social conditions is, needless to say, very limited.

I have criticized Avineri on a number of points. The analogy which Avineri attempts to draw between British imperialism in India and imperial relations in the Middle East fails. British and Israeli colonialism in the Middle East had a stunting effect on the Arab social structure and economy, not because it was indirect, but because it was powerful and penetrating. While I do not accept Avineri's Hegelian interpretation of Marx, it is possible to criticize Avineri on his own ground, that is, in terms of an Hegelian critique of Israeli society. The Israeli commitment to the ultimately racialist ideology of Zionism, the exclusive definition of rights on the basis of a Jewish identity, and such legal apparatus as the Law of Return have produced a particularistic society, very different from the universalism preached by Hegel. It is especially ironic that, while Avineri attempts to protect Hegel from the charge of Prussianism, Israeli society itself has undergone a thorough process of Prussianization. The Israeli army penetrates every layer of society, through the school cadet system, through the draft and through industry. Because of early military retirement, the economic posts receive a continuous inflow of army personnel, with the result that the militarism which Avineri imputes to Egypt and Syria can also be detected in the social structure and ethos of Israeli society. Avineri's failure to use his interpretation of Hegel and Marx as an instrument to explain conflicts in the development of Israeli society is indicative not only of Avineri's one-sided view of Marx, but also the inadequacy of his theory. It also underlines the 'special pleading' of Avineri's Hegelian reading of history. On a more positive note, Avineri has performed at least one valuable service – he has restated, albeit unwittingly, an important lesson, namely, that the theory of the Asiatic mode of production is fraught with dangerous ideological implications.

Notes

1 Shlomo Avineri, *The Social and Political Thought of Karl Marx* (London, 1970), ch. 1.
2 Shlomo Avineri (ed.), *Karl Marx on Colonialism and Modernization* (New York, 1968).
3 G. W. F. Hegel, *Philosophy of Right*, trans. T. M. Knox (Oxford, 1945), p. 12.
4 Avineri, *Karl Marx on Colonialism and Modernization*, p. 3.
5 Avineri, *The Social and Political Thoughts of Karl Marx*, p. 166.
6 Hegel, *Philosophy of Right*, quoted in Avineri, *Karl Marx on Colonialism and Modernization*, p. 2.
7 Karl Marx, 'Preface', *A Contribution to the Critique of Political Economy* (London, 1971), p. 21.
8 Cf. George Lichtheim, 'Marx and the Asiatic mode of production', *St. Antony's Papers*, vol. 14 (1963), pp. 86–112.
9 Cf. Karl A. Wittfogel, *Oriental Despotism* (New Haven, 1957).
10 'The future results of British rule in India', *Karl Marx and F. Engels On Colonialism* (New York, 1972), p. 14.
11 G. W. F. Hegel, *The Philosophy of History* (New York, 1956), pp. 105–6.
12 Avineri, *Karl Marx on Colonialism and Modernization*, p. 12.
13 Ibid., p. 18.
14 Ibid., p. 24.
15 Shlomo Avineri, 'A note on Hegel's views on Jewish emancipation', *Jewish Social Studies*, vol. XXV (2) (1963), p. 146.
16 Shlomo Avineri, 'The Hegelian origins of Marx's political thought', *The Review of Metaphysics*, vol. XXI, no. 1 (1967), p. 38.
17 Avineri, *The Social and Political Thought of Karl Marx*, p. 58.
18 Shlomo Avineri, 'The problem of war in Hegel's social thought', *Journal for the History of Ideas*, vol. XXII (1961), p. 466.
19 Ibid., p. 472.
20 Ibid., p. 474.
21 Shlomo Avineri, 'Modernization and Arab society: some reflections', in Irving Howe and Cari Gershman (eds), *Israel, the Arabs and the Middle East* (New York, 1972).
22 T. Stoianovitch, 'The conquering Balkan orthodox merchant', *Journal of Economic History*, vol. 20 (1960), pp. 234–313.
23 Avineri, 'Modernization and Arab society,' p. 304.

24 Shlomo Avineri, 'The Palestinians and Israel', *Commentary*, Vol. 49 (1970), p. 341.
25 Ibid., p. 35.
26 Ibid., p. 37.
27 Avineri rejects any attempt to draw a parallel between Vietnamese and Palestinian liberation movements on the grounds that the struggle is not an imperialist conflict between states. Cf. Shlomo Avineri, 'Israel and the New Left', *Transaction*, vol. 7 (1970), pp. 79–83.
28 B. Shaicovitch, 'Dialectical paternalism: Marx on the West Bank', *New Middle East*, no. 55 (1973), p. 22, elaborates some of Avineri's basic assumptions.
29 Quoted in David McLellan, *Karl Marx, His Life and Thought* (London, 1973), p. 284. For further commentary, Henry M. Christman, *The American Journalism of Marx and Engels* (New York, 1966).
30 A number of the issues involved in Marx's approach to colonial capitalism in relation to this problem are raised in Aidan Foster-Carter, 'Neo-Marxist approaches to development and underdevelopment', in Emanuel de Kadt and Gavin Williams (eds), *Sociology and Development* (London, 1974), pp. 67–105.
31 K. Marx and F. Engels, *On Ireland* (London, 1968), p. 319.
32 K. Marx, 'The future results of British rule in India', p. 85.
33 E.J. Hobsbawm (ed), *Karl Marx. Pre-Capitalist Economic Formations* (London, 1964), pp. 36–7.
34 For a discussion, cf. Bryan S. Turner, 'The concept of social stationariness: utilitarianism and marxism', *Science and Society*, vol. XXXVIII, no. 1 (1974), pp. 3–18; see also Chapter 2 above.
35 Nicos Poulantzas, *Political Power and Social Classes* (London, 1973), p. 15.
36 James O'Connor, 'The meaning of economic imperialism', in R. Rhodes (ed.), *Imperialism and Underdevelopment* (New York and London, 1970), p. 107.
37 Paul Baran, *The Political Economy of Growth* (New York, 1973), pp. 273–4.
38 *Journal of Economic Literature* (Dec. 1969), p. 1177, quoted in Arie Bober (ed.) *The Other Israel* (Garden City, 1972), p. 94.
39 Maxim Ghilan, *How Israel Lost Its Soul* (New York, 1974), p. 212.
40 Ibid., p. 208.
41 David Lazar, 'Israel's political structure and social issues', *Jewish Journal of Sociology*, vol. XV (1973), p. 32.
42 E. Ashtor, 'L'évolution des prix dans le proche-Orient à la basse-époque,' *Journal of the Economic and Social History of the Orient*, vol. IV (1961), pp. 15–46.
43 M. Smilianskaya, 'The disintegration of feudal relations', in C. Issawi

(ed.), *The Economic History of the Middle East* (Chicago and London, 1966), p. 245.

44 Bober, *The Other Israel*, p. 45.

45 Barbara C. Aswad, 'The involvement of peasants in social movements and its relation to the Palestine revolution', in Naseer Aruri (ed.), *The Palestinian Resistance to Israel* (Wilamette, Illinois, 1970), p. 22.

8 Religion and Citizenship: Israel*

There has been a revival of interest in nationalism among sociologists and political scientists in recent years.[1] Within a broader historical framework, however, nationalism remains an enigma. The assumption of an earlier tradition of writing on nationalism was that it was incompatible with the long-term development of capitalism, which, given the importance of foreign markets and the development of multinational corporations, would require cosmopolitanism as a life-style and internationalism as an ideology. The paradox is well known in Marxism.[2] For Marxists like Rosa Luxemburg, nationalism was a bourgeois ideology which diminished working-class consciousness, whereas for Lenin nationalism was an important part of the revolutionary strategy. With the development of anti-colonial struggles under the banner of national resistance, Marxism has shown a greater sensitivity to the importance of nationalism, but it remains difficult to find a convenient place for nationalism within conventional Marxist theory; in particular, how do national differences relate to economic classes? A similar range of problems confronts sociology, because it is difficult to grapple with nationalist particularism within the model of liberal, pluralist democracy. Industrial societies *ought* to develop open, competitive political systems which depend on secular ideologies, legitimating the diversity of civil society. Nationalism within this perspective appears to be atavistic. Although various attempts have been made to account for the persistence of traditional nationalist movements and for the growth of regional nationalism in Europe,[3] 'nationalism' remains an unsettled dispute in social science and Marxist theory.

One influential theory of nationalism is that of Gellner,[4] who treats nationalism as a response to the uneven development of industrial society; national differences are constructed and emphasised to protect different groups of workers as a form of social closure and to provide a platform for alienated intellectuals. Nationalism, however, has to work on certain differences, of which language is the principal component. Religious differences are also seen to be crucial in marking out national cultures. The assumption is, however, that religion may be important in the origins of nationalism, but it is quickly overtaken by secular ideologies. The 'normal' model of

* *Aspects of this chapter are based on Elizabeth Miller's doctoral thesis (in progress) on Hebrew Christianity in Israel, department of sociology, University of Aberdeen.*

nationalist development is from sacred symbolism to secular values and institutions, especially socialism.[5] It is thus common to make a contrast between Arab nationalism and Israeli nationalism. The former is defective because it has not emerged from its religious chrysalis; the latter is the 'normal' type because Zionism, for example, is a clear expression of a secular world-view of political reality. This contrast is well known in the work of Kedourie[6] and Avineri,[7] but it is most clearly expressed in an article by Smith on the religious genesis of nationalism amongst Jews and Arabs,[8] and also in his theoretical treatment of the nature of nationalist movements in general.[9]

What nationalists have in common is a sense of 'distinctiveness' in relation to their oppressors, or at least to the majority amongst whom they happen to be embedded. The notion of cultural distinctiveness is complex, but it is possible to conceive of a nationalist continuum from ethnic to territorial movements. At the ethnic end, nationalists are bound together by a sense of common ethnic identity, and at the territorial end there is an aspiration for a territorial/political basis for nationalist membership. Zionism, in Smith's view, represents a solution to the problem of the ethnic diaspora, that is, of small communities scattered across larger political units within which they are, in some sense, alien entities and subject to social oppression. These communities are unable to achieve self-rule within the existing context of the hostile political area.

> The only mode of ensuring the survival of the culture and its bearers is through evacuation of the communities to a territory outside the hostile areas – preferably to one able to attract a zeal for self-regeneration. Both conditions are best fulfilled by an 'ancestral homeland', with its memories, its promise of security through an historic right, and the historical delimitation of its identity.[10]

The foundation of the state of Israel and the ingathering of the Jews were thus ideally suited to maximise zeal and national regeneration against a background of Nazi oppression and Arab hostility. The binding of communal ties at the level of civil society almost required such external threats as a constant reminder of 'the promise of security'.

Although this typology of 'varieties of nationalism' is a useful introduction to the analysis of Zionism, it has, in the Jewish case, to be set within the broader historical framework of the so-called 'Jewish Question' which first came to prominence in nineteenth-century social thought. The issue of Jewish distinctiveness is, of course, very ancient – some would argue that it is in fact coeval with the Jewish religion itself. In Weber's argument,[11] the distinctiveness of Jewish communalism resided in the Ark of the Covenant whereby the Israelite tribes were bound together by a religious alliance to Yahwe, the one God who punished transgression and protected the People from their enemies in return for their loyalty to the 'social contract'. This theme – the land, the people, the book – provided a distinctiveness which often had the appearance of nationalism, a nationalism that was precocious and primitive. To use the term 'religious nationalism' in this context is, however, to render the term vacuous by over-extension. Nationalism, in its modern meaning, is essentially a nineteenth-century conception of political identification, which presupposes the existence of the nation-state, equipped with a bureaucratic apparatus that is able to bring about the identity of citizens within a secular state. Within the diaspora situation, the Jews did, however, retain a strong sense of particularity and separateness, which was partly enforced by ghetto status and partly self-imposed by the need for ritual purity.

The essence of the Jewish Question was the preservation of cultural particularity within the developing sense of political universality, which lay at the centre of the European notion of modernity. For example, although Hegel condemned Judaism for its adherence to statutory obligations which were formal and particularistic, he advocated equal rights of citizenship for Jews as a necessary aspect of the modern institutionalisation of politics. For Hegel, legal norms were necessarily universal in their application within a rational scheme of justice and hence the particularity of Judaism would be dissolved in the universality of rights within a rational state.[12] Marx criticised Hegelians such as Bruno Bauer by suggesting that the political emancipation of the Jews would not bring about genuine freedom without a corresponding social and economic transformation of capitalist society; the political emancipation of Jews would still leave the social enslavement of humanity unresolved.[13] Paradoxically, Marx's views provided one root, however remote, of Zionism through the theories of Borochov.[14] For Borochov, every nation was organised in terms of a system of social stratification, which was shaped like a pyramid. At the top, there was a small stratum of property owners, supported by professional occupations, and at the bottom a broad band of workers and peasants. The peculiarity of Jewish history was that the Jewish Diaspora was based on an inverted pyramid. The concentration of Jews in professional and merchant roles had meant that Jewry was largely devoid of workers. The solution to the Jewish Question had to involve proletarianisation, and this could only be achieved through a territorial solution, whereby Jews could become workers of the land. Zionism was not, however, colonialism, since, for Borochov, the 'natives of Palestine' had no genuine culture or nationality of their own.

A number of rather distinctive answers to the Jewish Question can thus be detected. In principle, these include: (1) religious assimilation through conversion to the Christian Church, largely by inducement; (2) political assimilation through the development of citizenship rights within the nation-state; (3) proletarianisation through membership of the radical working class; (4) proletarianisation through evacuation to a 'homeland'; (5)

a process of ritual involution which rejects any solution by emphasising the messianic aspiration for the restoration of Zion by a supernatural agency. The first three solutions entail the loss, or at least diminution, of any specific Jewish identity, which becomes submerged within Christian culture or within the state or within a class. The last two solutions – Zionism and messianism – offer the possibility of combining a Jewish identity with the continuity of the community in a manner which does not have the negative connotations of liberal assimilation. The conventional view of Zionism was that it represented a proletarian and territorial solution to the diaspora problem of ethnic distinctiveness. Zionism was secular because it sought to create a nation-state with territorial hegemony, and it was proletarian because it involved the downward mobility of the Shtetl population into workers of the land.[15]

The secularity of Zionism remains problematic on two counts. First, it is difficult historically to separate ethnic/cultural distinctiveness from religious/ritualistic distinctiveness; religion was the seed-bed which nurtured Jewishness. Second, the religious theme of exile–return–restoration has been transposed into the nationalist theme of ingathering and state-building. That national distinctiveness draws its political strength from traditional religious symbolism is not uncommon in nationalist development, but it is normally claimed that Zionism has made a successful transition from traditional religion to secular politics via the intermediary stage of religious reform. Arab nationalism, by contrast, has not emerged as a viable form of secular politics. Thus,

> While in logic nationalism stands opposed to religion, in practice both may uneasily coexist for periods as rival principles of group cohesion. Alternatively, circumstances may encourage one principle to exclude or supplant the other as the definer of identity and source of action. In the case of the Jews, nationalism has on the whole supplanted religion, and this is particularly marked in Israel, despite the survival there of a vocal orthodox minority.[16]

By contrast, the majority of educated Arabs still cling, according to Smith, to 'Arab Islam'. This view, which was published in 1973, has not exactly been confirmed by the recent history of Israel. We argue that there are particular reasons, in part connected with the nature of the Israeli polity, why the religious parties have recently gained cultural dominance, but there are also more general causes which explain why it is that religious orthodoxy, Jewish identity and nationalism cannot be easily separated. It is the continuity of the problem of Jewish identity, not its step-like resolution in Zionism, which is the striking feature of contemporary Israeli politics.[17]

It is arguable that Smith's view of Jewish nationalism as undergoing a successful transformation from a religious to a secular basis could be substantiated at least until 1973, when the article was published. Since then, much has been written on the nature of post-1973 Israeli society, its increasing complexity, ambiguity and search for identity.[18] Israel has often been characterised in terms of political disillusionment and spiritual malaise. Politically, the failure of labour Zionism to create a socialist society has been a major source of political disenchantment; economically, although the standard of living has increased overall, inflation has continued to weaken the economy, an economy heavily dependent on American support;[19] socially, the widening gap between Oriental and European Jewry, reflected in education, housing and occupations, has been a constant reminder that the search for a common Jewish identity is far from being realised; militarily, the Yom Kippur War of 1973 led to further increases in the occupied territories, giving rise to the inevitable problem of control and containment of an unwilling population; and as a direct result of occupation, the Jewish state was faced, and continues to be faced, with a whole set of difficult ethical questions regarding its coexistence with non-Jewish minorities.

However, the argument that Israel has only had to face these issues in any depth since 1973 is misleading. It would be more accurate to suggest that the problem of political unity had always existed from the earliest days of the state, only reaching a critical conjuncture in more recent times. It is therefore incorrect to suggest that pre-1973 Israeli society was a society working towards some resolution of the 'Jewish Question' by transforming its religiously-based identity into a secularised concept of Jewish nationhood. It can be suggested that the tension between the religious and the secular has always existed for the Jewish community, although some writers would question the usefulness of the terms 'religious' and 'secular' for this kind of analysis. In conventional terms, there has always been a desire to escape from the demands of the Law and thus to be released from the burden of divine election. The importance of political emancipation in nineteenth-century Europe was that it created in principle the foundation for the separation of Judaism and Jewishness. It can be argued that the establishment of the state of Israel in 1948 represented an institutionalisation of this separation. For the first time in its history, the Jewish community formally dissassociated itself from its religious contract to the Ark of the Covenant; state and society were formally uncoupled.

In his study of modern Israel, Segre[20] has outlined the various movements and trends of thought which preceded the development of late-nineteenth-century Zionism, by which the concepts of Return and Eretz Israel (the land of Israel) were transformed into instruments for political change. In this discussion, our concern is to examine critically this transformation from religious symbolism to political utility, the claims that are made about it, and its bearing on the issue of religion and citizenship. This transformation was part of the Diaspora experience, part of the movement towards a renewal of Jewish national consciousness, but it must be stressed that it was largely a minority concern and one which brought much criticism from within the Jewish community.[21]

The effect of Napoleonic legal reforms was to bring about a partial emancipation of the Jewish communities in Europe, granting them comparable citizenship rights under the law with the wider Gentile community. Jacob Katz,[22] in his study of Jewish–Gentile relations, has observed that during the period leading up to emancipation, when the Jewish Sanhedrin, convened by Napoleon in 1807, and the French authorities were in consultation:

> a profound change had occurred in the alignment of Jews in the Gentile world. Instead of being faced, as before, with Christianity as such, Judaism was now confronted with the secular State, which had absorbed Christianity into its framework as a complementary factor and was similarly prepared to absorb Judaism, provided it adapted its teachings and precepts to the interests of the State.[23]

In this period, many future problems were anticipated and many echoed the ambivalent apprehension expressed by one Rabbi who declared, on hearing of Napoleon's success, 'If Napoleon loses, I fear for the Jews; if he wins, I fear for Judaism.' Emancipation provided Jews with an opportunity to solve the 'problem' of their Jewish identity. The choice was now institutionally available: assimilation with the wider Gentile society. Many followed this course, especially among the educated classes who came under the influence of the Haskalah, the Jewish Enlightenment. However, the concept of 'assimilation' covers an immense variety of different levels and expressions of accommodation to the host society. Assimilation did not, in practice, offer a clear-cut choice. Most Jews had the dual ambition of acceptance within Gentile society while also remaining Jewish. Some, however, tried to make the transformation from Jew to non-Jew as complete as possible, especially in the fashionable intellectual circles of Paris and Berlin, where exponents of liberal society expressed their complete rejection of Zionist aspirations.

The intellectual climate of nineteenth-century Europe had a very significant effect on the process of assimilation. The mood of the time was undoubtedly optimistic, being convinced of the inevitability of progress. Intellectual development, in an atmosphere of rational free thought, would enhance the quality of life, allowing emancipated individuals to free themselves from constricting and non-rational beliefs. This emerging secular society would be freed from the shackles imposed by religious thought: new principles of action were developing, based upon concepts of rationality and scientific advancement. If in the past religion had divided people, reason would now unite individuals emancipated from their particular, restricting cultures. In this secularised, rational and progressive society, Jew and Gentile, freed from the divisive effects of their religious traditions, would freely coexist.[24]

In principle, the argument that nineteenth-century emancipation provided the basis for the separation of Judaism and Jewishness, though still accurate, must be seen against the wider and more complex relationship between religion and ethnic identity. The process of separation had in fact started much earlier, under the influence of the Haskalah and the subsequent impact of ideas in the Gentile world. Incipient secularisation in Europe was eventually to transform the Jewish world in terms of the separation of religion from everyday life. As a result of its separation from the wider Christian society, Jewish culture was left largely untouched by the earlier secularising influences in the Christian world, until the middle of the eighteenth century.[25] In comparison with the Christian milieu,

> Intellectual effort in the Jewish community remained devoted to the interpretation of the Talmud and its commentaries, and there was no equivalent drawing apart of the world-views of the intellectual elite and other strata. There was a growing interest in mathematical and scientific knowledge among a few rabbis in the first half of the eighteenth century, but it was only in the second half of the eighteenth century, with the emergence of the Jewish Enlightenment movement, the *Haskalah*, that the intellectual changes in the wider society can be seen to have made a significant impression on Jewish thought. The movement of the Jews out of the separate Jewish sub-society was the crucial factor; as Jews entered gentile society, their religion lost its dominant position in explaining and interpreting the world.[26]

In the nineteenth century, Jewish culture experienced a growing awareness and accommodation to Gentile beliefs and practices, although this social accommodation developed at many different levels.

By the end of the nineteenth century, however, evidence of anti-Semitism in the liberalised societies of western Europe and violent expressions of anti-Semitism in Russia and eastern Europe forced many Jews to re-evaluate the alleged benefits of assimilation. The conclusions reached by Moses Hess, who clearly appreciated the paradox of being a Jew, were confirmed. There was an irreducible linkage between race, culture and history, however hard Jews tried to escape from this ensemble by entering Gentile society. The Gentile world itself would not permit any resolution of the Jewish paradox: a Jew was a Jew. In reality, the emancipation the Christian world granted to the Jews was a form of 'Gentilisation', involving equality in Christian terms, but paradoxically these conditions of social emancipation were never adequate to cancel out inherent Jewishness.

Zionism as the secular, national and territorial solution to the Jewish Question thus gained momentum. Theodore Herzl, the arch-secularist of the Jewish community, provided direction and leadership of the alienated Jewish community. An Austrian journalist, he was converted to Zionism while covering the trial of Alfred Dreyfus, who had been unfairly accused of betraying military secrets to the German forces. The so-called Dreyfus Affair[27] of 1895 revealed a major reservoir of anti-Jewish sentiment in French public life. Found guilty and sentenced to penal servitude, it was not until 1905, a year after Herzl's death, that Dreyfus was cleared of all charges and reinstated into the French army with the rank of major.

In its formative years, Zionism was far from being homogeneous. The official declaration of Zionist aims was expressed at the first Zionist Congress at Basle in 1897. The previous year Herzl had outlined his concept of the Jewish state in his *Der Judenstaat*. Orthodox Jewry was strongly opposed to Herzl's secularism, their conception of the Restoration of Zion being entirely dependent on the coming of the Messiah. As the secular aims of political Zionism became more clearly defined in subsequent Zionist Congresses, the religious opposition also became sharper and more precisely formulated. The division between religious and secular views of the Jewish state persisted into the twentieth century without definitive resolution. Jewish nationalism was to be characterised by diversity, producing many political leaders and intellectuals, reflecting a wide range of contradictory philosophical positions.[28]

The creation of the state of Israel had the consequence of raising the critical issue of Jewish identity to a new level and a variety of political crises magnified the traditional Jewish Question. There was an urgent need for national unity, if the society was to survive Arab opposition and European indifference. Ben-Gurion imposed on all parties a purely pragmatic policy of avoiding any decision-making about the fundamental principles upon which the society was to be founded. There were no specific national borders and no particular ideological character for the state. This policy of avoidance in policy formation on the basis of principles was dictated by the military situation and by party interest. Only by not deciding on issues could Mapai, a social democratic party with a third of the seats in Parliament, act as a national party. This pragmatic attitude limited the growth of internal dissension in the political system. Military victories in 1967 radically changed this situation and opened up the arena of political debate. However, despite significant military success and territorial expansion, Israel has never enjoyed that climate of economic and political security which could tolerate the luxury of ideological dissent on a large scale.

Thus to assume that Zionism was an unambiguous secular expression of Jewish national feeling would be a mistake, for reasons we have already suggested, since secular Zionism cannot be separated from its religious roots. The ambiguity was clearly present in Herzl, who observed that what was required in order to realise Zionist objectives was a revival in Judaism.[29] Yet Herzl's thought, and the direction it gave the Zionist movement, resulted in the first Jewish community to separate itself on principle from its religious foundations. Political emancipation provided the basis for the formal separation of Judaism from Jewishness, to which the state of Israel gave institutional expression. The religious controversy and opposition surrounding the First Zionist Congress illustrated the gulf between religious and secular elements, which had never been fully resolved and which was to characterise many crucial political issues in Israel after 1948.

In this chapter we will examine the relationship between 'the religious' and 'the secular' under three broad headings, namely, law, politics and civil society. Contrary to the conventional view in the sociology of religion, we argue that, far from being in tension, religious and secular institutions actually require each other in modern Israel - although the nature of this requirement is often contradictory. Indeed, our discussion suggests that, at least in Israeli society, the identification of any sharp differentiation between the secular and the religious (or sacred and profane) is necessarily misconstrued. This discussion has, therefore, important implications for some modern theories of nationalism.

Although the overriding conviction of the Zionist movement, under the direction of David Ben-Gurion, was the establishment of a secular Jewish state, recognition had to be given to the demands of the Orthodox, and eventually some accommodation to these demands secured. In the early stages, these religious elements were reluctant to seek direct control over the state, and some completely disassociated themselves from secular power. However, they also wanted to secure their influence over the religious and cultural values of Israeli civil society. The state of Israel was created in a situation of military and political crisis, and some compromise between the contending groups in the Jewish community was necessary to ensure the survival of the state. This compromise can be illustrated in a number of ways. The absence of a written constitution is itself evidence of the problem of achieving compromise between social groups with irreconcilable interpretations of the nature of Jewish society. Although Israel has no written constitution it does have certain Foundation Laws, which are equivalent to constitutional laws. Of particular importance in the determination of the nature of the state are the Law of Return, laws relating to marriage and divorce, and regulations concerning religious observance (Sabbath). These laws define what it is to be a Jew.[30] In particular, political membership of the state is dependent on a set of criteria which necessarily include religious conceptions of membership within the Jewish community. In Avineri's terms, the universal categories of the state necessarily hinge upon the particular criteria of the community.

The Israeli Proclamation of Independence published by the Provisional State Council in Tel Aviv on 14 May 1948 is equally ambivalent with respect to the conjunction of the religious and the secular. Following an introductory preamble outlining the suffering of the Jewish people in modern Europe and asserting an historic claim to the land of Palestine as a national home, the document asserts certain basic principles of liberty and justice, promising to 'uphold the full social and political rights of all its citizens, without distinction of religion, race, or sex'.[31] However, the Proclamation opens and closes with certain religious claims which provide the framework within which these pluralistic propositions are couched. It was in the land of Israel that the 'spiritual, religious and national identity' was established, and the Proclamation concludes by placing its 'trust in the Rock of Israel'. The principles of liberty and equality of citizens asserted by the Proclamation of Independence thus presupposes that the political equality of citizenship rests on a prior equality of religion, or more precisely, that Jewish identity, following the Law of Return, has pre-eminence in the definition of political membership. The Proclamation can be considered as a social contract which creates a state. In conventional theories of social contract, the contract creates citizenship, but in the Israeli case all Jews, by virtue of their Jewishness, have rights of membership. Since Jewishness is inescapably bound up with a religious identity, the political reality of Israeli society is shaped by the history of the Jewish community, a history shot through with religious significance.

Ultimately, it is religion which legitimates Jewish occupation of the land of Palestine via the existence of the state which exerts a legitimate monopoly of force within the territory. More specifically, it is the particularity of Jewish identity as a religious identity which guarantees the rights of citizenship as a universal and apparently secular category. The argument can be presented diagrammatically:

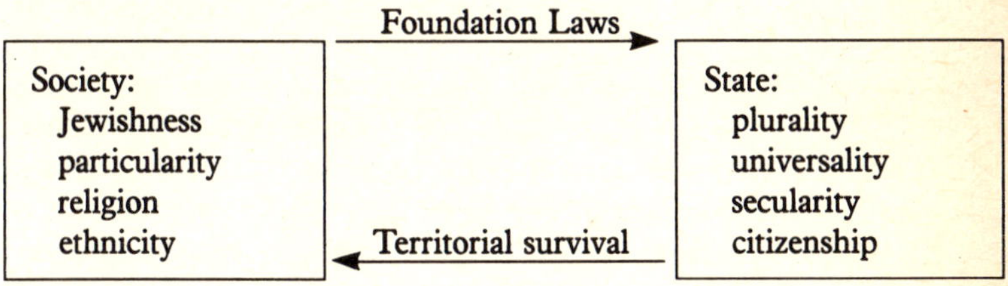

The state, which is formally characterised by its neutrality, pluralism, universalism and secularity, is based upon a society determined by its Jewishness, particularity and religious history. State and society exist upon mutual exchanges. The Jewish community world-wide provides the members of the state through the complex network of constitutional law. In return, the state, through its monopoly of force, guarantees the territorial survival of the community. This exchange of legitimation and force is subject to periodic crises. Any failure on the part of the state to guarantee through military means the integrity of the community brings into question the legitimacy of the state. Within the civil society, any shift in the nature of

Jewish identity (for example, a process of secularisation) necessarily changes the nature of the political basis of the state. It is for this reason, as we shall show later, that Christian missionary activity inside the civil society is a direct and potent threat to the basis of the state.

The state/society relationship is characterised by a number of structural contradictions. Following Habermas,[32] it can be argued that in capitalist society the state is at least partly legitimated by certain 'welfare pay-offs'. In return for political legitimation via the electoral system, the state counteracts the effects of capitalist production by the distribution of welfare, employment, education, health and other benefits of citizenship.[33] The legitimacy of particular governments is thus brought into question by chronic economic failure. The Israeli state operates on a different set of criteria. Its primary source of political legitimacy is the security of its citizens from permanent external threat and through the provision of internal stability. The Israeli economy, which is characterised by permanent rising inflation, is in any case largely dependent on American support. The crucial question therefore for any Israeli government, regardless of its political complexion, is the achievement of military security. One aspect of this security, at least in principle, is territorial annexation. Territorial annexation entails two dilemmas. First, it dilutes the Jewish nature of civil society by incorporating populations (namely, Christians and Muslims) within the geographical boundaries of the state. Second, it undermines the notion of civil liberties, which is basic to citizenship in Israeli society, because annexation brings with it an inevitable extension of 'the repressive apparatus of the state'.[34]

These two dilemmas are to some extent mitigated by religious culture. For secular Zionists, especially those with a commitment to the socialist tradition, territorial annexation as the basis of security is deeply problematic. For example, annexation creates the possibility of employing Arab labour to create an economic surplus which is realised primarily by Jewish citizens. Similarly, for certain groups in Orthodox Jewry, such as the Neturei Karta, annexation is unacceptable on the grounds that the establishment of the state of Israel, let alone its growth, must await the coming of the Messiah. However, some Orthodox groups, in particular the Gush Emunim (Block of the Faithful), find a policy of secular annexation largely compatible with their religious views of a Greater Israel.[35] Although there is evidence that many Israelis do not wholly support policies of annexation, some branches of Orthodox Jewry provide a religious legitimation, however minimal, of the growth of the state. It is partly for this reason that in the last decade the secular state has come to depend increasingly on the support of religious groups, who provide a relatively coherent justification for territorial expansion as the principal means of security. The unintended consequence of the secular requirement for political security is the resurgence of religious orthodoxy as the only unambiguous definition of Jewish identity. Given this complex exchange between state and society, it is crucial that the social cohesion of the Jewish community should be maintained in detail. The preservation of this social unity depends increasingly on the preservation of the Jewish religious identity. A number of institutions function to consolidate the Jewish religious social identity.

With the foundation of Israel in 1948, the polity of Israeli society was predominantly secular. From the point of view of certain Orthodox groups, the state had not been constituted by principles which were regarded as religiously legitimate. From the conception of the state, there was a deep-seated contradiction between democracy and theocracy – a contradiction which has yet to be resolved. Certain religious groups, in particular Agudat Israel, would only recognise a 'Torah state' embodying the full tenets of Halacha (Jewish religious law). Convinced of their right to the land, they were not prepared to accept a *de facto* situation, in which a secular state had brought about some degree of security and a territorial basis for the people of Israel. These religious groups had to exist in a society where the dominant political force in the Knesset was exercised by the Israeli Labour Party, Mapai. However, given the nature of the Israeli political system (a system based upon proportional representation), the achievement of a political consensus requires compromise and co-operation between parties of very different political persuasion. Though not recognising the authority of the state of Israel, these religious groups were paradoxically drawn into the political process and were able to achieve certain religious objectives, despite the fact that their electoral support was insignificant. Religious parties and religious institutions enjoy a prominence within Israeli public life which is not wholly reflected in the social support given to religious values by the population at large.

Opinion surveys of the Israeli public indicate a very complex set of attitudes towards the influence of religion both in politics and society. For example, when asked 'Should the government see to it that public life be conducted in accord with Jewish tradition?' 23 per cent replied 'definitely' and 20 per cent 'probably'.[36] Other evidence suggests strong, but nowhere near universal, support for religious tradition and practice. In response to the question 'Do you observe the Jewish religious law?' in a survey conducted in 1969, only 26 per cent claimed not to observe it at all. To the question concerning synagogue attendance, only 27 per cent said they never attended. In addition, the religious state schools have a considerable importance in Israeli life; 29 per cent of Israeli parents send their children to such institutions, and 7 per cent send their children to the schools of the Agudat Israel.[37] Although many authors have quoted the well-known fact that only 12½ per cent of the electorate vote for religious parties and only 22 per cent of the adult population declare themselves religiously committed,[38] religious groups have considerable political importance within the complex political coalitions that characterise the workings of the Knesset and, more importantly, 'religious sentiments are more widespread than straight electoral patterns show'.[39] Indeed, the prominence of the Orthodox in the Likud coalition government of Begin has been achieved despite a decline from twelve to six in the number of seats held by the National Religious Party.

The findings of opinion research, though adequately reflecting individual belief, underestimate the importance of religious ritual, symbolism and institutions in the formation and transmission of the national culture. The Rabbinate, the synagogues and the yeshivas play a critical part in the maintenance of national awareness, specifically Jewish awareness. Irrespective of individual belief, these collective practices are fundamental, as Durkheim recognised, in the organisation of the *conscience collective*, a consciousness which is not simply the summation of private opinion. Although some authors may wish to argue that Israel, despite the influence of the religious leadership, is experiencing a process of secularisation, it is important to realise that secularisation is not simply the decline of religion, but may involve the transposition of beliefs and practices from a religious to a secular context. In Israel,

> the religious festivals are now celebrated by many Israelis as national holidays with little reference to the divine; there is a re-emphasis on their relationship to the changing agricultural seasons and their commemoration of historical events in the past struggles of Israel. A new festival, commemorating Israel's Day of Independence, has its own secular ceremonies, and although special synagogue services are held as part of the celebrations, the majority have not accepted the day as a religious festival.[40]

Although some would wish to identify these practices as part of a 'new civil religion'[41] that is a secularised Judaism, it is difficult to conceive such a civil religion surviving without the synagogue, the Rabbinate and the Halacha. Unlike many national religions, the Judaism of Israel is remarkably coherent and unified. For example, in the 1970s of the 6,000 synagogues in Israel only 22 were non-Orthodox. The Orthodox Rabbinate has an official monopoly over the interpretation and administration of the Halacha, which has prohibited the modernisation of Judaism in Israel. The coherence of the national religion does not, however, rule out conflicts within the Rabbinate itself. A recent report points to the conflict between the Sephardic and the Ashkenazi Orthodox. Each community has its own rabbis who frequently find themselves in bitter disagreement. Regardless of these internal conflicts, the Rabbinate as a whole appears to be developing in an increasingly anti-secular direction. Whereas traditionally the Rabbi was an expert in both secular and religious knowledge, the modern Rabbi:

> is expected to limit his studies wholly to Talmud, Midrash, the Codes and the Talmudic commentaries, and the possession of a university degree would almost certainly bar him from being recommended by the religious authorities for any position.[42]

In many Christian industrial societies, the priesthood has been to the forefront in proclaiming the death of God, but the Orthodox Rabbinate of modern Israel is developing a particularly rigorous position on traditional belief and practice. They have thus played an important part in preventing the modernisation of Judaism and the secularisation of society.

No Israeli government has been able to establish a working majority in the Knesset without the co-operation of the religious parties. Therefore, the history of Israeli politics has been a history of compromise and adjustment between the coalition partners: Israel's Labour Party formed successive governments until its downfall at the 1977 elections, when Menachem Begin's Likud Party came to power. However, the incoming Begin government was faced with the same task of forming a stable government on the basis of support from the religious parties, and their support inevitably depended on certain concessions. Over a longer time-span, the first concessions to religious demands were made by Ben Gurion. Thus, the religious elements have always held a critical advantage in politics which has far outweighed their numerical strength in the electorate. When the state was established, there was no written constitution, because no satisfactory agreement could be reached within the Assembly concerning the place of Judaic Law in Israeli legislation. For the Orthodox, their paramount concern was to create a Jewish nation rooted in adherence to Jewish law and tradition, namely, in a 'Torah state'. The goal of the secular wing of Zionism was to create a secure national home for a people with a common historical identity and a dominant sense of nationhood. In the absence of a constitutional agreement, the Orthodox used their strategic political position to pass legislation which fully embraced Judaic religious norms. The state of Israel, under successive Labour governments, failed to make any clear statement of its relationship to the reconciliation of secular laws and the Halacha.

This reluctance or inability to clarify the question of the Jewish nature of the state, however pragmatic politically, meant that with the increase in the Arab population, following the Six Day War of 1967, the Israeli government had no set of coherent principles by which to tackle the pressing problem of citizenship. Critics were able to suggest plausibly that the Palestinian conception of a secular, pluralistic democratic society was more consistent with the original Declaration of Independence than the existing state of affairs. These political developments demonstrated that the perennial 'Jewish Question' was far from definitely resolved.

The separation of Church and State, common to western concepts of the democratic state, does not exist in Israel. The state maintains an Orthodox Rabbinate and a system of rabbinical courts, which are invested with an exclusive claim to religious authority and which do not acknowledge the authority of other branches of Judaism. There is no civil marriage or divorce, and religious schools are part of the state educational system. Orthodox religious practices, dealing with such matters as the Sabbath and dietary rules (kashrut), are observed on state facilities. These regulations on behaviour in state premises were among the first concessions won by the Orthodox in the early days of the state from Prime Minister Ben-Gurion, who has often been regarded subsequently as responsible for this 'unholy alliance'.

The tension between religious and secular interpretations of events can sporadically erupt into violence. There have been incidents of stone-throwing by ultra-Orthodox elements in Jerusalem on the Sabbath at vehicles passing near the Orthodox areas. Violent scenes erupted over an archaeological dig in 1981 on the ancient site of the City of David beside the present walls of the Old City of Jerusalem. The Supreme Rabbinical Council, declarings its opposition to the dig on the grounds that it was the site of a late-medieval Jewish cemetery, asserted that 'The Jewish *halacha* is external and not subordinate to any secular authority with regard to the State of Israel, in which our rights are based on the Tora. The *halacha* is what governs our lives, and no power on earth will replace it.'[43] More recently, the Agudat Israel secured a commitment from the government to end flights of the national airline, El Al, on the Sabbath. This, and similar rulings on religious practice, inevitably implies that, in order for public services to function on religious days, Israeli society would be forced to rely increasingly on the labour of *shabbas goyim* (Gentiles). Massive difficulties would be incurred, should Israel observe the year of *shmita* when the land must rest every seventh year, following religious law. These rulings pin-point an important difference between Conservative and Orthodox Judaism, in that the former recognises that *halacha* must be interpreted to meet modern requirements. Behind these theological struggles, there also lies a political conflict as religious groups seek political support from the faithful by increasingly rigorous interpretations of religious tradition.[44] Both the religious and the political conflicts are periodically highlighted by such events as the City of David dig and the re-interment of human remains, believed to be those of the 'Bar-Kochba' warriors.[45] Although these archaeological finds are important for the symbolic unity of the state and for the historic claim to the land, they also bring to the foreground the potential conflicts between modern secular culture and traditional religious values. Despite the initial disengagement of the religious leadership from the Israeli state in 1948, the Rabbinate has come to see itself as the bastion of Jewish values and, by implication, of Israeli society. This situation is qualified by the fact that the Agudat Israel do not recognise the Rabbinate as authoritative in Jewish affairs. The Rabbinate has identified a number of social processes which in their view threaten the cultural basis of the Jewish state. These are inter-marriage, assimilation and conversion. To guard against these developments, the religious leadership has created a situation in which inter-marriage is only possible where the non-Jewish partner converts to Judaism. A number of recent developments in Israeli law have had the effect of restricting missionary activity on the part of Christian churches in Israel, a limitation which conflicts with the principle of freedom of conscience on the part of the individual. Much controversy surrounds this legislation,[46] but it is evident that the possibility of missionary conversion and the development of Hebrew Christianity[47] are regarded as fundamentally threatening to the socio-religious consensus that pervades modern Israel. Anxieties about the dilution of the Jewish identity by inter-marriage or conversion have to be located within the wider problem of the Sephardic/Ashkenazi relationship and of Levantization. The original Israeli leadership was overwhelmingly recruited from eastern Europe and Russia, as was the Zionist settler population. Through Mapai, this group exercised a stable leadership in Israeli society, but since the 1970s the Sephardic (Oriental) section of the population has grown in numbers and influence.[48] Public debate about the Black Panthers, the social problems of the Sephardic population and the lack of political representation of Oriental Jews were illustrations of a deep-seated inequality between European and Oriental Jews. With the growth of the Oriental Jewish population, the Israeli political system is in the 1980s beginning to reflect their influence.[49] The religious system was also affected and there was evidence of tension as a division developed between the Ashkenazi and Sephardic Rabbis. Being excluded from social influence, the Sephardic religious leadership was forced to compete in the political arena by demonstrating its orthodox credentials. With the establishment of the Begin government, however, the Sephardic leadership have a firmer social footing, and ultimately some reconciliation within the Rabbinical leadership is likely to occur.

The conventional assumption has been that, with the development of the modern state, religious legitimations of political power would give way to overtly secular systems of civil values. In other words, state-building would be accompanied by a definite process of secularisation. In the modern state, the most prevalent form of civic culture would involve some potent element of secular nationalism, as the basis for mobilising populations. Since, in practice, it has been found that religion, especially in the Middle East, shows a remarkable persistence in the transition to an industrial society, some critics[50] have suggested that there can be no general theory of nationalism. There is no unitary process of industrial development and the effects of industrialisation on cultural systems are very diverse. In the Israeli case, we have shown that, prior to 1948, there were evident tensions between religious and secular Zionism and that, during the dominance of Mapai, the secular remained prominent, despite compromise with religious groups over issues of, for example, public observance. Increasingly since the Six Day War, the religious dimension of the civil society has become more pronounced, to such an extent that it can be argued that the preservation of the state depends on the active support of the religious system as the guardian of social unity.

There are two levels of explanation – the particular and the general – which account for this symbiosis between the religious and the political system in Israel in the 1980s. First, there are a number of conjunctural circumstances[51] that explain the prominence of religious personnel in government circles, the social influence of the Rabbinate, the political significance of the Religious Party and the symbolic functions of religious ceremonial for national life. These conjunctural conditions are closely related to the political record of Mapai and its failure to resolve certain key social and constitutional issues. There has been rising dissatisfaction with Labour politics, a loss of political credibility, accusations of corruption and mismanagement and, finally, a failure to solve deep-seated economic issues (relating to inflation, military expenditure, the use of Arab labour and dependence on foreign funding). There are, secondly, more permanent causes of the prominence of religion in national life; these operate irrespective of the particular circumstances of the Israeli political system, which requires, through proportional representation, some alliance between the religious and the secular. These general conditions are that it is, in practice, difficult to separate Jewish political identity from Jewish religious identity. The so-called 'Jewish Question' has not been resolved by the emergence of a Jewish state, because religious values are a powerful component in the definition of Jewishness. Furthermore, the traditional theological *motif* of exile–return–restoration provides a convenient and potent theory of the character of Israeli political life and, in large measure, the theme of the land – the people – the book offers one of the main ideological bases for Jewish claims to the land of Palestine. The theological view of Jewish land rights can thus be combined with the more practical and mundane need for military security. It is unlikely, given the secular view of Zionism as a socialist movement, that a pure theocracy will ever become entirely dominant in Israel, but it is the case that religious nationalism will give Israel certain peculiar and particular features, which cannot be easily incorporated within the 'Gentile' model of state-formation and social development.

Notes

1 In particular, Ernest Gellner, *Thought and Change*, London, 1964; G. Poggi, *The Development of the Modern State*, London, 1978; Anthony

D. Smith, *Theories of Nationalism*, London, 1971; Karl W. Deutsch, *Nationalism and Social Communication, an inquiry into the foundations of nationality*, Cambridge, 1953.

2 Tom Bottomore and Patrick Goode (eds), *Austro-Marxism*, Oxford, 1978; H. B. Davis, 'Nations, colonies and classes: the position of Marx and Engels', *Science and Society*, vol. 29 (1965), pp. 26–43; E. Kamenka (ed.), *Nationalism: the nature and evolution of an idea*, London, 1976; Leszek Kolakowski, 'Marxist philosophy and national reality: natural communities and universal brotherhood', *Round Table*, no. 253 (1974), pp. 43–55.

3 Michael Hechter, *Internal Colonialism, the Celtic fringe in British national development, 1536–1966*, London, 1975; Tom Nairn, *The Break-Up of Britain, crisis and neo-nationalism*, London, 1977; J. E. S. Hayward and R. N. Berki (eds), *State and Society in Contemporary Europe*, Oxford, 1979; E. A. G. Robinson (ed.), *Backward Areas in Advanced Countries*, London, 1969; S. Holland *Capital versus the Regions*, London, 1976.

4 For a discussion of the place of the theory of nationalism in Gellner's thought as a whole, John A. Hall, *Diagnosis of Our Time, six views of our social condition*, London, 1981.

5 Peter Worsley, *The Third World*, London, 1964; E. J. Hobsbawm, *Primitive Rebels*, London, 1959.

6 Elie Kedourie, *Nationalism*, London, 1960; Elie Kedourie, *Afghani and Abduh: an essay on religious unbelief and political activism in modern Islam*, London, 1966; Elie Kedourie (ed.), *Nationalism in Asia and Africa*, London, 1970. For a discussion of Kedourie, see Bryan S. Turner, *Marx and the End of Orientalism*, London, 1974.

7 Schlomo Avineri (ed.), *Israel and the Palestinians*, New York, 1968; Shlomo Avineri, 'Political and social aspects of Israeli and Arab nationalism', in Kamenka, *Nationalism*, pp. 101–22.

8 Anthony D. Smith, 'Nationalism and religion, the role of religious reform in the genesis of Arab and Jewish nationalism', *Archives de Sciences Sociales des Religions*, vol. 35 (1973), pp. 23–43.

9 Smith, *Theories of Nationalism*. On some general aspects of religion in relation to political organisation, political conflict and the state, David Martin, *A General Theory of Secularization*, Oxford, 1978.

10 Smith, *Theories of Nationalism*, p. 222. This observation might be compared with the 'diaspora' of Muslims in, for example, Canada; see Harold Coward and Leslie Kawamura (eds), *Religion and Ethnicity*, Ontario, 1978.

11 Max Weber, *Ancient Judaism*, New York, 1952. For a discussion of Weber, I. Schiper, 'Max Weber on the sociological basis of the Jewish religion', *Jewish Journal of Sociology*, vol. 1 (1959), pp. 250–60.

12 On Hegel's analysis, Shlomo Avineri, 'Hegel and nationalism', *Review of Politics*, vol. 24 (1962), pp. 461–84; Shlomo Avineri, 'A note on Hegel's views on Jewish emancipation', *Jewish Social Studies*, vol. 25 (1963), pp. 145–51.

13 On Marx and the Jewish Question, Soloman F. Bloom, 'Karl Marx and the Jews', *Jewish Social Studies*, vol. 4, (1942), pp. 3–16; on the biographical problem of Marx's own Jewish identity, cf. David McLellan, *Karl Marx, his life and thought*, London, 1973.

14 Ber Borochov, *Nationalism and the Class Struggle, a Marxian approach to the Jewish problem*, New York, 1937.

15 Shlomo Avineri, 'Modernization and Arab society: some reflections', in Irving Howe and Carl Gershman (eds), *Israel, the Arabs and the Middle East*, New York, 1972, pp. 300–11.

16 Smith, 'Nationalism and religion', pp. 27–8.

17 For a contemporary commentary on the Jewish identity problem, Daniel Bell, *Sociological Journeys*, London, 1982.

18 For example, D. V. Segre, *Israel, a society in transition*, London, 1971; D. V. Segre, *A Crisis of Identity: Israel and Zionism*, Oxford, 1980.

19 Uri Davis, *Israel: Utopia Incorporated*, London, 1977.

20 Segre, *A Crisis of Identity*. For further studies, Arthur Hertzberg (ed.), *The Zionist Idea: historical analysis and reader*, New York, 1959; Jacob Katz, *Out of the Ghetto: the social background of Jewish emancipation 1770–1870*, Harvard, 1973; Alan Arian, *Ideological Change in Israel*, Cleveland, 1968.

21 Segre, *Israel* and also *A Crisis of Identity*. In addition, David Vital, *Zionism: the formative years*, Oxford, 1982.

22 Jacob Katz, *Exclusiveness and Tolerance, Jewish-Gentile relations in medieval and modern times*, New York, 1962.

23 ibid., p. 187.

24 For a general discussion of religious tolerance and economic change, Lucien Goldmann, *The Philosophy of the Enlightenment*, London, 1973. For an illustration of tolerance of Jews in the context of Dutch commercialism, George L. Smith, *Religion and Trade in New Netherland*, Ithaca and London, 1973.

25 This claim was true of the Jewish community in western Europe, but not of east European Jewry, which remained largely untouched by many aspects of these developments. More precisely, the impact of these developments was very uneven across the Jewish community. On Jewry in eastern Europe, Mark Zborowski and Elizabeth Herzog, *Life is with People, the culture of the Shtetl*, New York, 1952.

26 Stephen Sharot, *Judaism, a sociology*, Newton Abbot, Devon, 1976.

27 On the case, see G. Chapman, *The Dreyfus Case*, London, 1955; and D. Johnson, *France and the Dreyfus Affair*, London, 1966.

28 For a fuller discussion, Norman L. Zucker, *The Coming Crisis in Israel, private faith and public policy*, Massachusetts and London, 1973; and David Vital, *The Origins of Zionism*, Oxford, 1981.
29 See I. Cohen, *The Zionist Movement*, London, 1912; W. Laqueur, *History of Zionism*, London, 1972; Alex Bein, *Theodor Herzl: a biography*, London, 1957.
30 Nira Yuval-Davis, 'The bearers of the collective – women and religious legislation in Israel', British Sociological Conference, 1979, mimeo.
31 State of Israel Proclamation of Independence, 1948, in Walter Laqueur (ed.), *The Israel–Arab Reader*, Harmondsworth, 1970, p. 161.
32 Jurgen Habermas, *Legitimation Crisis*, London, 1976, p. 5.
33 On the growth of rights of political membership, T. H. Marshall, *Class, Citizenship and Social Development*, Chicago and London, 1977.
34 On the distinction between ideological and repressive state apparatus, see Louis Althusser, *Lenin and Philosophy and Other Essays*, London, 1971.
35 The Gush Emunim is a group of religious Jews claiming a right to settle in all parts of the biblical land of Israel, who protested against the Camp David settlement, especially with reference to Sinai. Some features of the religious system in Israel have been discussed in Leonard Weller, *Sociology in Israel*, Wesport, Conn., 1974.
36 Zucker, *The Coming Crisis in Israel*, p. 59.
37 Sharot, *Judaism, a sociology*, p. 181; Zucker, *The Coming Crisis in Israel.*
38 Yuval-Davis, 'The bearers of the collective'.
39 Zucker, *The Coming Crisis in Israel*, p. 59.
40 Sharot, *Judaism, a sociology*, p. 188.
41 On the civil religion problem, Roland Robertson, *Meaning and Change, explorations in the cultural sociology of modern societies*, Oxford, 1978.
42 Rabbi Louis Rabinowitz, 'The irony of Israel's rabbinate', *Jewish Chronicle*, 13 July 1979, p. 21.
43 See *Jerusalem Post*, 24 September 1981.
44 See Moshe Kol letter to the *Jerusalem Post*, 6–12 June 1982.
45 *Jewish Chronicle*, 14 May 1982.
46 *Religious Liberty and the Law*, Proceedings of the Symposium at Hebrew Union College, Jerusalem, 1980; Israel Shahak, *Civil Rights in Israel Today*, London, n.d.
47 B. Z. Sobel, *Hebrew Christianity: the thirteenth tribe*, New York, 1974.
48 S. N. Eisenstadt, *Israeli Society*, London, 1967; S. N. Eisenstadt, 'The Oriental Jews in Israel', *Jewish Social Studies*, vol. 12 (1950), pp. 199–222; Maxime Rodinson, *Israel: a colonial-settler state?* New York, 1973.
49 As recent migrants, the Sephardic community tends to become politi-

cally significant in settlement areas, where they exercise considerable local political influence. Much of their social protest has been expressed through the 'Tami' Party. On the political system in Israel, cf. Leonard Fein, *Politics in Israel*, Boston, 1967; E. Gutmann, *Politics and Parties in Israel*, Jerusalem, 1961.

50 S. Zubaida 'Theories of nationalism' in G. Littlejohn *et al.* (eds), *Power and the State*, London, 1978, pp. 52–71. For a general criticism of the relationship between ideology and capitalism, Nicholas Abercrombie, Stephen Hill and Bryan S. Turner, *The Dominant Ideology Thesis*, London, 1980.

51 Louis Althusser, *For Marx*, Harmondsworth, 1969.

9 Capitalism and Feudalism: Iran

With the fall of Muhammad Reza Pahlavi on 16 January 1979, Iran has experienced a violent political transformation in which previously covert divisions within the religious opposition have become increasingly overt and tragic. It is now obvious that what Ayatollah Khomeyni sought to achieve was the re-establishment of the authority of the *ulama* over society, a return to the dominance of the religious law, the reassertion of the traditional role of women and the preservation of the authority of the religious leadership in matters of everyday life. In pursuit of these traditional ends, the followers of Khomeyni have crushed the radical movement in Iran which has been centred around intellectuals like Dr Ali Shariati, and whose main support came from students and middle-class professionals. Whether Khomeyni's government can survive inflation, war and internal opposition remains an open question. This chapter on Iranian society was written in 1978, in the prelude to the Shah's fall, before Khomeyni's return and the outbreak of the war with Iraq. In terms of contemporary Iranian politics, this chapter does not discuss the political changes which have taken place since January 1979. The existing analysis does, however, provide a detailed study of the social structure of Iran as the necessary basis for any comprehension of modern Iranian politics. In particular, this chapter is concerned with the historical development of capitalism in Iran as the background both to the fall of the Pahlavi dynasty and to the political crisis of modern Iran.

In the opening passage of 'The Eighteenth Brumaire of Louis Bonaparte', Karl Marx made the famous aphoristic observation that human beings make their own history, but not as an act of free will unrestrained by given conditions. Men make history 'not under circumstances they themselves have chosen but under the given and inherited circumstances with which they are directly confronted' (Marx 1973: 146). In this discussion of Iran, I want to examine the historically 'given and inherited circumstances' which provide the conjunctural constraints on the so-called Islamic Revolution which brought down the regime of Muhammad Reza Shah in the early months of 1979. To understand these given circumstances, however, we have to confront a number of critical analytical issues relating to problems of the classification of pre-capitalist modes of production, the constitution of the state and the emergence of social classes. In particular, the perspective of the western observer who wants to comprehend modern Iran is, in my view, limited not so much by the paucity of empirical evidence, but by the inadequacies of theoretical refinement in social science. In these introductory comments, I want to suggest that our attempts to understand Iran (or any other non-western, Islamic, developing society) are bedevilled by an established tradition of historical and sociological analyses to which I shall attach the general label of 'Orientalist' (Turner 1978; Said 1978).

The critique of the Orientalist problematic has been difficult and largely ineffectual precisely because sociology and Marxist analyses have themselves contained significant elements of an Orientalist perspective. In Hegel's philosophy of history and in Marx's journalistic observations on India and China, we find the development of the concept of the Asiatic mode of production (hereafter, AMP) in which all the lands stretching from 'the Sahara, through Arabia, Persia, India and Tartary, to the most elevated Asiatic highlands' (Marx and Engels 1972: 37) were socially stagnant and politically despotic. There is in sociology equally a traditional analysis of Oriental Depotism, which provides a theoretical link between Max Weber's analysis of patrimonial empires and the investigations of political scientists such as S. N. Eisenstadt into 'centralized empires' (Eisenstadt 1962). In these sociological models the centralized bureaucracies of Asia are contrasted with the 'parcellized sovereignties' of the differentiated feudal systems of Europe (Anderson 1974). The Orientalist problematic, which in terms of the specific notion of 'Oriental Despotism' can be traced back to the political writing of Machiavelli and Montesquieu (Stelling-Michaud 1960–1; Koebner 1951), attempts to make a fundamental distinction between Oriental stationariness and Occidental dynamism (Turner 1974). The principal argument of this paper is that prior to the land reforms of the 'White Revolution' Iran was a predominantly feudal society and that Iranian feudalism was not *in essence* different from, for example, European feudalism or the feudalism of a society like Egypt.

The Orientalist problematic can also be related to two further theoretical issues in contemporary social science. In the sociology of development, we can make a distinction between internalist and externalist models. Internalist development theories attempt to provide explanations of social change in terms of causes which are internal and specific to given societies considered as isolated, autonomous social units. The American structural-functionalist school has typically treated development as an endogenous process of structural differentiation and cultural integration (Hoselitz and Moore, eds 1963). Similarly, development theories which stress the importance of values and attitudes as key determinants of modernization (McClelland 1961) have selected the family and the school as primary agencies of social change. The Orientalist tradition as a whole has focused on the alleged absence of a middle class, rational entrepreneurship and commercial law as an explanation of Asiatic economic stagnation (Turner 1979). In response to these internalist theories, Marxist and neo-Marxist writers like E. J. Hobsbawm, T. Dos Santos and A. G. Frank have created various dependency models which attempt to show that the apparent underdevelopment of Third World societies is the result of their historical and spatial location within the global division of labour. In the centre–periphery model of Frank (1971), the underdevelopment and de-industrialization of South American societies are specific effects of the extraction of an economic surplus by a commercial network linking peripheral regions to the capitalist core states.

Whereas the internalist model naively assumes that it is possible to write the history of development without a theory of imperialist relationships, the neo-Marxist externalist treatment of global capitalism commits the mirror-image mistake of assuming that the internal class relationships of a society are simply internal effects of an external, capitalist cause (Melotti 1977). By equating capitalist relations of production with commercial relations of commodity circulation, Frank fails to provide a satisfactory analysis of class forces and relations of economic domination within peripheral societies. A complete theory of economic dependency would have to provide an account of the logic of modes of production within social formations and the articulation of these modes of production with the set of constraints which emerge historically out of the growth of a global capitalist system. The recent research of Immanual Wallerstein (1974) points us in the correct theoretical direction by showing how the internal logic of production is related to the development of world-empires and world-economies. In my view, the analysis of Iran cannot start from either the view that external imperialism is the principal cause of economic retardation or from the argument that the internal structure of the prebendal state slowed down the autonomous emergence of an industrial bourgeoisie. The analysis of the Iranian economy and society must be premised on a view of the mutual, interpenetrating causality of the internal logic of Iranian feudalism and the external impact of colonial capitalism.

The final theoretical issue to which I want to draw attention in these prefatory remarks is the problem of what may be called the 'correspondence theory'. In Marx's commentary on the impact of British colonialism in India, Marx appears to suggest that the introduction of private property in land, railway system and a modernized army will produce an almost automatic reorganization of the whole social formation. A radical change in the economic base will produce a corresponding change in the legal and political superstructure. We need not enter here into the debate over the 'base/superstructure' metaphor which has dominated Marxism from Engels's letter to Bloch in 1890 to Althusser's reformulation of the 'dominance/determinance' relation in 1968. At this stage, I am merely claiming that Marx's analysis of colonialism has been interpreted (Avineri, ed. 1968) as showing that the introduction of capitalist relations via colonialism necessarily has corresponding effects throughout the rest of the social formation and that furthermore capitalism is progressive in destroying all pre-capitalist relationships. A similar view is common in sociology, where the advent of industrial society is seen to correspond with equivalent changes in religion, the family and the community. For Parsons (1943), there is a functional fit or correspondence between the isolated nuclear family and the labour requirements of industrial society; for Weber, there is 'an elective affinity' between universal, abstract law and capitalism.

One important theme of neo-Marxist analysis of colonialism has been to deny any simple correspondence between colonial capitalism and the progressive demolition of pre-capitalist economic and social relations. Starting with Trotsky's *History of the Russian Revolution*, it can be argued that capitalism does not have uniform, functional consequences, but rather, that the introduction of capitalism typically has uneven and combined developmental effects. Development is uneven and unequal in that the growth of certain economic and social sectors is always at the expense of other sectors. Development is combined in that there is a combination of inequalities which are structured and intensified by the transfer of resources from underdeveloped to developed regions. Halliday (1974) argues, for example, that the development of the oil industry in Saudi Arabia has not transformed the pre-capitalist structures of that society, but has, on the contrary, produced a profoundly unequal and combined social underdevelopment. In two articles on India, Jairus Banaji (1972; 1973) attempts to show that the extension of capitalism into underdeveloped regions may result in the intensification of pre-capitalist relations of exploitation, namely, the reproduction of slavery and serfdom. In Banaji's view, various forms of 'archaic' labour organization (slavery, serfdom, indentured labour) are historically compatible with the growth of the capitalist mode of production. In short, there is no necessary correspondence between the growth of colonial capitalism and the disappearance of formally unfree labour.

In defence of Marx's analysis of colonialism, it can be shown that Marx did not uniformly assume that British imperialism had always had progressive consequences in terms of liquidating all pre-capitalist economic and social arrangements. Although Marx, in his article 'The British Rule in India', refers to British intervention producing 'the greatest, and, to speak the truth, the only *social* revolution ever heard of in Asia' (Marx and Engels 1972: 40), Marx's analysis of the effects of British colonialism in Ireland has an entirely different conclusion. With reference to Ireland, Marx notes that it 'has been stunted in its development by the English invasion and thrown centuries back' (Marx and Engels 1968: 319). These passages in Marx can be identified (Foster-Carter 1974) as a starting-point for the theory that, in certain circumstances, Marx thinks that capitalist colonialism may stunt a society's economic development by setting off a process of de-industrialization and underdevelopment, resulting in a non-correspondence between the capitalist relations and its socio-economic environment.

Another version of this perspective on uneven development can be found in the economic analysis of imperialism by Michael Barrat Brown (1974) and Gunnar Myrdal (1954). Against the background of neo-classical Manchester economics (Lewis 1954), which assumes that backward societies can develop as capital investments expand by employing the 'unlimited' surplus labour from the subsistence sector, Myrdal has pointed to the uneven 'backwash' effects of capitalism, which concentrates essential commercial, industrial and financial services in given regions. Similarly, Brown argues that capitalist development has produced a permanent economic dualism between high-wage, capital-intensive, high-productivity sectors and low-wage, labour-intensive, low-productivity centres.

The general trend of much contemporary Marxism and sociology is to stress the uneven, contradictory nature of capitalist development, the continuities rather than discontinuities between feudalism and capitalism, the conservation rather than dissolution effects of the capitalist mode of production (Poulantzas 1973) and the prevalence of 'archaic' institutions and labour forms in colonial capitalism in dependent, peripheral societies. In short, to deny the correspondence between base and superstructure has been a general feature of the rejection of mechanical causal models in either structural functionalism or vulgar economism. How can we give a more precise theoretical formulation of this denial of functional correspondence? The answer to these difficulties lies in the distinction between 'mode of production' as a model of concrete societies (Hindess and Hirst 1975). The logic of the mode of production is never perfectly reproduced and never perfectly corresponds to the contingent realities of the social formation. At the social, empirical level, the contingent struggle between social classes does not produce any necessary or uniform effects. As Marx and Engels point out in the *Communist Manifesto*, the class struggle is a contingent process resulting 'either in a revolutionary reconstitution of society at large, or in the common ruin of the contending classes' (Marx and Engels 1973: 68). There is consequently no general theory of the 'royal road' to capitalism or socialism, since the particular circumstances of class formations and the particular historical and global circumstances of the social formation have their own particular consequences for the development of the forces and relations of production. The 'peculiarities' of English capitalism are a pertinent illustration of this issue and Iran may well be another. We cannot assume that the introduction of land reform or the production relations of oil have resulted in or will inevitably lead to a dismantling of feudal, archaic economic and social relations. We cannot assume in sociological terms that the 'modernization' of land tenure corresponds with the development of parliamentary democracy or that fascist politics is somehow an unusual consequence of the development of agrarian capitalism (Poulantzas 1974).

In summary, my argument is that our understanding of Iran must be prefaced by a critique of certain theoretical positions in social science. Traditional approaches to Asian development are vitiated by the presence of an Orientalist problematic, an internalist version of development and by a correspondence theory. In order to arrive at a more satisfactory perspective on Iran, it is important to get a more detailed account of Orientalism as a preamble to the debate about pre-capitalist modes of production.

The Orientalist tradition seeks to define 'Islamic Society' as a series of absences. Both Montesquieu (*L'Esprit des Lois*, 1748) and Benigne-Bossuet (*Politique tirée des propres paroles de l'Ecriture Sainte a Monseigneur le Dauphin*, 1709) established the tradition that the key to the constitution of Oriental Despotism was the absence of private property in land. It was this absence of property that gave the Orient both its stagnatory and despotic condition by reducing all citizens to an anonymous mass of undifferentiated individuals. For Marx and Engels, the absence of real property in land, in a situation where the state became the only genuine landlord, meant that with Asiatic conditions of production there could be no social classes. The Orient consequently lacked the dynamism of class struggle as the solvent of all traditional modes of production. Asiatic society does not, therefore, have a clearly defined class structure, but instead presents itself as a complex mosaic of separate tribes, religious sects, ethnic groups and distinct communities. We are told (Coon 1951: 2) that the most important anthropological fact about Middle East society is that 'in each country the population consists of a mosaic of peoples'. The mosaic diversity of the social structure provides the environment within which the despotic overlord can divide and rule without organized, coherent opposition.

Just as 'Islamic Society' is characterized by the absence of property, so also it lacks an urban environment of genuine, autonomous cities. Weber was impressed by the historical significance of the autonomous, internally integrated Occidental city with its own militia, political assemblies and legal charters. By contrast, the Oriental city developed as an urban community in which Christianity had eroded magical and ethnic ties. Islamic cities lacked autonomy because they did not possess a legal character and they lacked internal coherence. This situation arose because 'Islam never overcame the rural ties of Arabic tribal and clan associations but remained the religion of a conquering arm structured in terms of tribes and clans' (Weber 1958: 100). In similar fashion, Marx (1973: 479) commented that 'Asiatic history is a kind of indifferent unity of town and countryside (the really large cities must be regarded here merely as royal camps, as works of artifice erected over the economic construction proper)'. In the absence of autonomous cities, the conditions for the development of the urban burgher, urban piety and asceticism were absent. In short, Islam lacked the typical features of a 'civil society' (Al-Azmeh 1976).

In the Orientalist model, these social characteristics are the prelude to the notion that 'Islamic Society' did not enjoy those conditions of stability of economic and political arrangements which were so significant for the development of European feudalism. In particular, there was the absence of a system of formal rational law as the institutional guarantee of property. The absence of formal rational law in Islam was of especial interest to Weber, who claimed that Islamic Holy Law was fixed by revelation and could not systematically adapt to changes in economic and social conditions. The gaps between legal norms and social practice were filled by arbitrary legal devices (*fetwa*). Furthermore, the arbitrary power of centralized patrimonial empires was well served by the *ad hoc* law-making of *qadi* justice. Over this issue, there has been little substantive difference between Marxist legal theory (such as Karl Renner and E. V. Pashukanis) and Weber's sociology to the effect that in capitalism the form of law is that of a gapless system of abstract, universal, formal law. It was Engels who originally observed that 'Turkish, like any other oriental domination, is incompatible with a capitalist economy; the surplus value extorted is not safe from the hands of greedy satraps and pashas. The first basic condition of bourgeois acquisition is lacking; the security of the person and the property of the trader' (Marx and Engels 1953: 40).

Because in the 'Islamic Society' there are no cities in which the rational, entrepreneurial bourgeoisie can develop free from state intervention, there was in Islam no theory of individual rights and the legitimacy of political opposition to despotic government. Bernard Lewis (1972: 33) claims that 'the Western doctrine of the right to resist bad government is alien to Islamic thought' and that Islamic opposition to impious government was rendered ineffectual because no apparatus was ever institutionalized by which this doctrine could be put into practice. Similarly, P. J. Vatikiotis (1972) argues that the modern history of the Middle East exhibits frequent *coups d'état*, military take-overs and rebellions, but there have been no genuine and radical revolutions producing fundamental changes in social structure. This No Revolutions thesis is the modern representative of the classical Orientalist position that the Orient has no history (Turner 1978). In searching for the historical conditions for human self-consciousness, Hegel had come to the conclusion that Islam 'has long vanished from the stage of history at large, and has retreated into Oriental ease and repose' (1956: 360). The irony is that, although it is often claimed that Marx systematically rejected Hegel's metaphysic of the Spirit (Althusser 1969), in the theory of the AMP Marx largely reproduced Hegel's doctrine of Oriental stationariness. It was Marx who wrote that 'Indian society has no history at all, at least no known history. What we call its history, is but the successive intruders who founded their empires on the passive basis of that unresisting and unchanging society' (Marx and Engels 1972: 81) and that the village system made Asian society 'resistant to disintegration and economic evolution, until wrecked by the external force of capitalism' (Marx 1964: 38).

In recent years there have been a variety of attempts to criticize these Orientalist assumptions about 'Islamic Society'. Said (1978) draws the obvious connection between the Orientalist view of Islam as stagnant and the growth of western imperialism. He argues that Orientalism changed from a scholarly inquiry into exotic language into a theory of political practice 'because the Oriental–European relationship was determined by an unstoppable European expansion in search of markets, resources, and colonies, and, finally, because Orientalism had accomplished its self-metamorphosis from a scholarly discourse to an imperial institution' (Said 1978: 95). That the Orientalist view of Asian stagnation is a thinly disguised justification for imperialist policies is particularly evident in Shlomo Avineri's employment of the AMP as an analysis of the development of Israeli society. Avineri (1971; 1976) draws the implication from Marx's writing on colonialism that the greater the degree of imperialist penetration, the greater the potential for eventual social transformation. In Avineri's view, the backwardness of the Arab Middle East is a consequence of the indirect method of political control which the French and British exercised through the system of mandates. This indirect imperial rule permitted the traditional Arab military élite to continue in power long after the formal withdrawal of Anglo-French control. Whereas Arab society has had a political without a social revolution, Israel was formed by a social revolution in which petty-bourgeois European Jews became a socially conscious Israeli citizenry through the process of downward social mobility.

Against the Orientalist view of the necessarily beneficial effect of western capitalist colonialism, we need to assert (Turner 1976; 1978) that, in the periphery, capitalism had a stunting rather than progressive effect, by destroying the nascent indigenous bourgeoisie as a result of undermining native capitalist enterprise and petty commodity production by the system of capitulations, special economic arrangements and concessions. Marx's view of the stunting of Irish development by British dominance is therefore far more relevant for the analysis of Asia and the Middle East than is the journalistic commentary on India and China. Secondly, we need to avoid over-simplified contrasts between Occident and Orient, between a dynamic West and a stagnant Asia, by recognizing the specificity of social structures and economic processes which took place historically in the various societies and regions to which we give the misleading label of 'Middle East' or 'Asia' or 'Orient'. Although very few serious scholars would want to employ the reified concept of 'Christendom' to describe the history and structure of western Europe over a period of nearly two thousand years, Orientalists are prone to treat the term 'Islamic Society' or 'Islamdom' as if that term had a unified object of analysis. On the one hand, it is necessary to argue for the specificity of the history of Egypt or Syria or Iran and, on the other hand, to be aware of the continuities between the socio-economic characteristics of certain European societies and certain Middle East and Asian societies. In short, whereas Orientalism concentrates on the *discontinuities* between Islamic and western history, I shall try to focus on the structural *continuities*.

These preliminary comments on the Orientalist problematic can be summarized by the argument that we can have no satisfactory *general* theory of capitalist development which would provide an account of why capitalism developed initially in the Occident rather than the Orient. In a recent paper on nationalism, Sami Zubaida (1978) has attempted to show that we can have no general theory of the rise of nationalism as a concomitant of such processes as 'industrialization' or 'modernization' or 'capitalist development'. This claim follows from his view that there are no general, universal or necessary social consequences flowing from the installation of the capitalist mode of production (hereafter, CMP) in a given society. Thus, 'while "capitalism" can be thus specified and its world-wide spread and expansion established, its consequences for particular countries must be examined in the specificity of the particular conjuncture' (Zubaida 1978: 59). For example, the incorporation of a society within the global system of capitalist relations does not necessarily result in the dominance of capitalist relations or the commodity form. This argument can be extended to criticize both general, timeless models of 'the Orient' and general theories about the spread of colonial capitalism and the correspondence between the CMP and other structural or superstructural features of law, politics and religion.

The problem of providing an effective critique of Orientalism is connected with the fact that both Marxism and sociology have themselves contained various Orientalist assumptions about the structure and history of pre-capitalist Middle East and Asian societies. It is for this reason that I have pointed to certain thematic parallels between the analyses of Marx, Weber and Orientalist historians. At the centre of this issue is the debate over the general relevance of Marx's theory of pre-capitalist modes of production and the particular status of the AMP. Before attempting to give an account of the specific structures of Iranian society, it is important to turn to a brief consideration of the critique of Marx's AMP.

In British sociology the most coherent attack on the scientific status of the AMP has been undertaken by Barry Hindess and Paul Q. Hirst in *Pre-Capitalist Modes of Production* (1975). By adopting Althusser's concept of an 'epistemological break' in the development of Marx's thought, Hindess and Hirst argue that most of Marx's comments on Asia which appeared in the *New York Daily Tribune* occurred prior to the development of Marx's mature, scientific writing. These journalistic comments cannot, therefore, provide the basis for a rigorous theory of pre-capitalist modes of production. The only appropriate location for a theory of pre-capitalist modes of production is to be found in Marx's *Capital*. In Marx's mature work, Marx argued that in Asia, where the state is the landlord, 'rent and taxes coincide, or rather, there exists no tax which differs from this form of ground rent' (*Capital* III: 771). Hindess and Hirst then assert that no distinct and theoretically coherent mode of production corresponds to the 'tax/rent couple'. This form of surplus-product appropriation in this form of taxation 'is no different in this respect from the total social product, the level of which is politically determined, and which is the means of maintenance of the state' (Hindess and Hirst 1975: 192). There is nothing, then, peculiarly Asiatic about the tax/rent couple as a form of surplus appropriation. However, this fact alone does not provide any theoretical warrant for assuming that an analytically coherent mode of production corresponds to the tax/rent couple. One particular weakness of the AMP is that it cannot provide an explanation of the condition of the state. For example, if there are no economically defined social classes in the AMP as a consequence of the absence of property, then it is not possible to give an account of the state as the product of class struggle. The 'tax/rent couple' presupposes the state, but cannot explain its presence.

The implication of Hindess and Hirst's position is that if the AMP is theoretically inadequate, then the principal mode of production which was dominant historically in Asia and the Middle East was the feudal mode of production (FMP) in one of its variant forms. One problem with such a position is that it encourages us to consider the history of all pre-capitalist societies as the history of the dissolution of feudalism; in short, it drives us dangerously close to the 'impasse of a quasi-universal feudalism' (Anderson 1974: 484). Those writers who have been reluctant to subsume all the economic variations of the Middle East into the restricting straight-jacket of 'feudalism' as a category have often gone to the other extreme of denying the relevance of existing concepts of pre-capitalist modes of production to Middle East societies. For example, El Kodsy (El Kodsy and Lobel 1970) divides the Arab world into three regions (Al Maghreb, Al Mashraq and the societies of the Nile) and argues that these regions were not determined by their rural and feudal characteristics, but by urban and commercial factors. Egypt, as a 'peasant civilization' based on the extraction of a surplus from peasant cultivators, was the principal exception to this rule. Given the aridity of the climate and the low level of development of forces of production, the economic surplus was never sufficiently large in other Arab regions to support a dominant class of landlords. Instead, the Arabic dominant class depended on commercial profits from the trade between Asia and Europe – 'an income derived, in the last analysis, from the surplus extracted by the ruling classes of other civilizations from their own peasantries' (El Kodsy and Lobel 1970: 6). A similar argument is presented in Samir Amin's *The Arab Nation*, which argues that 'the pre-colonial Arab world was not feudal, that it constituted a constellation of social formations articulated around a tributary mode of production. The latter was relatively prosperous in Egypt and relatively poor elsewhere . . . due to the weak development of the agricultural forces of production in this semi-arid area' (Amin 1978: 7). Because surplus extraction via ground rent was relatively weak, the main character of Arab social formations was determined by the extraction of a surplus from other societies through long-distance trade.

There are a number of problems with this rejection of feudalism as an adequate model for Middle East societies. First, it is not possible to specify a distinct mode of production in terms of intercontinental trade, since the existence of trade and merchants is compatible with any form of surplus extraction. Merchants may be present under any mode of production; because merchants operate in the sphere of circulation, we cannot deduce anything about the relations of production. Secondly, by concentrating on climatic conditions and the weak forces of production, El Kodsy and Amin are in danger of accepting some form of simple technological determinism. The size of the surplus to be extracted from peasant cultivators does not provide the means for defining a mode of production.

It has been argued that the AMP is not a satisfactory concept of a distinct mode of production. Once this situation is accepted, we need to avoid the trap of defining all pre-capitalist modes of production as feudal and of rejecting the FMP as a concept which is never applicable in the Middle East, with the possible exception of Egypt. Having considered some of these general issues, we can now take up the issue of the application of Marxist categories of 'mode of production' to the case of Iran. As a starting-point, we can deal critically with those authors who have attempted to preserve some notion of the AMP in order to provide an analysis of pre-capitalist Iranian society.

The Qajar dynasty (1779–1925) of Iran has been categorized as an Oriental Despotism by Ervand Abrahamian (1974; 1975), but Abrahamian argues that the most adequate aspect of Marx's AMP as a perspective on Iran is not the sections on the state as landlord as the real basis of Oriental Despotism. In *Capital* Marx had referred to the 'blending of agriculture and handicrafts', 'the unalterable division of labour' and the 'self-sufficing communities that constantly reproduce themselves' as the 'key to the secret of the unchangingness of Asiatic societies' (Marx 1965, vol. 1: 338). Abrahamian contrasts the model of the AMP as a centralized bureaucracy with this 'fragmentation thesis' in order to demonstrate the relevance of this latter perspective on the 'unchangingness' of Iranian social structure. Whereas in Europe the feudal estates had been 'viable collectives', in Iranian society the *tabaqat* ('orders' or 'strata') were internally fragmented and antagonistic. For example:

> the landed class was split into feuding families, antagonistic chiefs, and rival nobles. The *ulama* were splintered into local sects, legal schools, and differing doctrines. And the general population, both urban and rural, was fragmented into conflicting groups – into warring tribes, villages, and even town wards. (Abrahamian 1975: 138)

In Europe, according to the fragmentation thesis, the various feudal estates enjoyed a high degree of social cohesion and acted to preserve their corporate liberties and legal privileges, whereas in Iran the various *tabaqat* could never be mobilized to protect themselves from external political control.

There are a number of difficulties with this thesis. Abrahamian correctly wants to avoid the conventional implications of the traditional model of Oriental Despotism, but he does retain much of the standard assumptions of the mosaic model of Iran by his emphasis on internal urban divisions and fractionalism. One aspect of this internally fissiparous structure was, for example, 'a mosaic of diverse tongues and dialects' (Abrahamian 1975: 140). Another feature of Abrahamian's argument, which again follows much of the conventional treatment of Orientalism, is the way in which climatic conditions determine social relationships. In their original formulation of the problem of the AMP, Marx and Engels emphasized the importance of climate as the explanation for bureaucratic state involvement in irrigation and defence. This concern for the causal role of irrigation in the origins of the centralized state became the whole basis for the classical statement of the 'hydraulic economy' in Karl. A. Wittfogel's *Oriental Despotism* (1957). In a similar fashion, Abrahamian declares that 'at the basis of social fragmentation was geography' (1975: 138). Apart from the general theoretical difficulties which are attached to a 'technicist' or 'reductionist' position in general, the specific problem with this thesis is that very different social forms may correspond to the need for irrigation works in arid or semi-arid conditions. In other words, aridity does not necessarily correspond to a managerial-bureaucratic state over the 'hydraulic economy' (Hindess and Hirst 1975). In his study of irrigation works in Ceylon, Leach showed that irrigation works were constructed over a long period without a centralized state or a 'Department of Public Works' and that Ceylon in this period was in fact predominantly feudal, not 'Asiatic'.

Abrahamian does break with many of the traditional perspectives on the state in Asiatic societies on the question of the effectiveness of the centralized authority in Iran. Wittfogel presents a picture of the Persian state as an efficacious political system which had successfully centralized an apparatus of communication, taxation and political control. The Qajar shahs accrued a list of impressive titles; they were the Shadow of God on Earth, Guardian of the Flock, the Subduer of Climates and the King of Kings. These titles, however, are inevitably misleading as descriptors of the real power of the Qajar shahs. As Abrahamian points out, the Qajar rulers 'were despots without the instruments of despotism' (1975: 135). The Qajar despots had very little authority outside the main towns precisely because they did not have a significant standing army and they did not have the support of an effective bureaucracy:

> The standing army was no larger than a contingent of Qajar tribesmen and a body-guard of 4,000 Georgian slaves. And the bureaucracy, if it can be called that, was nothing more than a haphazard collection of hereditary *mustawfis* and *mirzas* in the central and provincial capitals. (Abrahamian 1974: 11).

The impressive ranks of officials and provincial officials were in fact the hereditary rulers or tribal chiefs who enjoyed virtual political autonomy from the Qajar shahs. These official *il-khans*, who were supposedly under the control of the shahs, were tribal chiefs who collected their own taxes and ruled their own regions with little effective external control from the shahs. The image of the powerful, centralized and despotic bureaucracy is, therefore, part of the mythology of Oriental Despotism which has been handed down from Montesquieu to Wittfogel and which can play no part in the sociological analysis of Iranian social formations.

One of the persistent errors of many standard approaches to Iranian history is the presupposition that the Iranian social formation can be characterized by one mode of production. Thus, sociological analysis has searched for an adequate account in terms of a 'tributary mode of production' (Amin 1978) or a 'hydraulic economy' (Wittfogel 1957) or an 'Asiatic mode' (Marx and Engels 1972) or 'a semi-feudal mode' (GOPF 1976). A more adequate approach would be to study the Iranian social formation as constituted by overlapping modes of production. I want to suggest in particular that Iranian history is the effect of the oscillation between prebendalism and feudalism, in which the feudal mode of production is dominant. Secondly, we need to notice that the pattern of landownership in Iran has always been mixed. Thirdly, the argument for the dominance of the FMP allows us to perceive the similarities between Iran and other forms of feudalism – both Oriental and Occidental; there is consequently no Iranian 'essence' which permits an Orientalist differentiation between western democratic and Oriental despotic history.

Although I have been critical of Weber's general history of Oriental societies, Weber's concept of 'prebendalism' does have a specific validity in the analysis of certain imperial structures. For example, unlike the notion of 'Asiatic' characteristics, Weber's 'prebendalism' has no geographical connotations. 'Prebend' was originally an ecclesiastical term signifying the stipend drawn from land granted to a canon from a cathedral estate. Weber uses this term to mean 'allowances in kind' or 'rights of use of land in return for services', where these allowances or rights are not granted on a hereditary principle. The point of prebends is that they provided a patrimonial ruler greater control over his military subordinates because unlike feudal land rights, they provided conditional rights of ownership. From the patrimonial ruler's point of view, prebendalism could be secured most adequately in a situation of territorial expansion. In a period of imperial contraction, however, when patrimonial monarchies were experiencing fiscal crises, there was political and economic pressure to convert prebendal holdings into feudal land rights. Prebendalism was consequently inherently unstable. All pre-capitalist social formations have strong tendencies of decentralization and disintegration. The feudalization of patrimonial empires thus represents a powerful disintegration of prebendal control of previously subordinate officials, chiefs or nobility.

In Weber's view the collapse of prebendal empires represented a diminution of the money economy as tax revenues were replaced by payments in kind. One of Weber's illustrations of this point concerned the conversion of Seljuk and Mameluke slave troops into feudal landlords:

> The feudalization of the economy was facilitated when the Seljuk troops and Mamelukes were assigned the tax yield of land and subjects; eventually land was transferred to them as service holdings, and they became landowners. The extraordinary legal insecurity of the tax-paying population *vis-à-vis* the arbitrariness of the troops to whom their tax capacity was mortgaged could paralyze commerce and hence the money economy; indeed since the period of the Seljuks (ca. 1050–1150) the oriental market economy declined or stagnated. (Weber 1968, vol. 3: 1016)

Weber argued that the development of patrimonial rulership away from prebendalism towards feudalism strengthened traditional attitudes towards economic relations, limited rational calculation of leases, curtailed the money market and oriented the use of money towards consumption. Where the patrimonial state encouraged trade monopolies, these openings for profit were often left to nobles or administrative staff. Similarly, the organization of tax-farming, provision of armies and state administration provided opportunities for capitalistic development, but this was often 'diverted in the direction of political orientation' (Weber 1966: 355). Weber's standpoint on the traditional limitations on capitalism in patrimonial empires does not necessarily reproduce the full gamut of Orientalist assumptions:

(1) because Weber does not want to treat the existence of prebends or benefices as a peculiarity of Asiatic societies;

(2) Weber does not treat prebendalism as inherently static (indeed it has a built-in tendency towards change as a result of its own contradictions); and

(3) Weber does not have to treat prebendal states as powerful and efficient since they are subject to powerful decentralizing, feudal tendencies.

Weber's account of these contradictory processes in patrimonial empires has recently been put to good use in the case of the political structures of Thailand (Tambiah 1976). Weber's distinction between the 'feu' and 'prebend' can also provide an introduction to Iranian social structure which I want to treat as an oscillation between centralization and decentralization, prebendalism and feudalism, a pastoral/nomadic mode of production and a feudal mode.

The early caliphates – Umayyad (660–750), Abbasid (762–1258), the lesser Buwayid (945–83), Ghaznavid (976–1040) and Seljuk (1040–1118) dynasties – assumed a predominantly prebendal form. State lands that had been seized by conquest were allocated as military benefices by which the holder enjoyed the rights of land tax. The sources of revenue for the state included taxation on Crown land, a land tax on privately owned land, a poll tax on non-Muslims, *zakat* (alms), a tax on surface mines, customs duty, real-estate tax and royalties on minting coins. The variety of sources of taxation parallels the variety of types of landownership. These were: (1) state land (*aradi-yi-divani*); (2) private domains of the royal family (*khassa*); (3) religious land (*vaqfi* or *waqf*); and (4) private lands which were held unconditionally (*mulk, milk* or *arbabi*). *Mulk* property corresponded completely to the European feu, in that it was held unconditionally, without obligation to the state and could be sold or bequeathed without hindrance. As a general rule, there was a see-saw relation historically between state land and *mulk* property. Conquest or the rise of a new dynasty often resulted in the decline of *mulk* property and its conversion into state land. However, the general trend was away from prebendal to feudal control. Under the Umayyad and Seljuk rulers, the prebendal rights had been gradually converted into hereditary rights conditional on military service (the *iqta*), whereas under the Mongol control of the Il-Khans ('subject khan') in the thirteenth and fourteenth centuries the hereditary *iqta* and unconditional *mulk* had greatly expanded at the cost of state land, resulting in a concentration of land in the hands of feudal landlords. From this period also the peasants were bound to the land and where the landlord exploited his own land, slaves were used, since the peasantry did not provide *corvée*. The general features of Iranian feudalism can be best summarized by a lengthy quotation from I. P. Petrushevsky:

> The most typical features of specifically Iranian feudalism antedating the (Mongol) conquest survived it also. Such were the outstanding importance of irrigation; the coexistence of settled agriculture and nomadic and semi-nomadic cattle-breeding; the absence of demesne and *corvée* in the villages; the combination of large-scale feudal landownership with small-scale peasant tenants; the predominance of product rent (money and labour rent had only secondary importance); the growth of the military fief system; the close connexion between the big merchants and the caravan trade and a group of feudal lords, and even their coalescence; the absence of self-governing towns, so typical of western Europe in the Middle Ages; and the widespread use of slave labour in the crafts and agriculture (irrigation and market gardening) alongside the exploitation of the labour of dependent peasants. (Petrushevsky 1968: 514)

Although Iran retained a number of features which may have been fairly specific, we can claim that the Iranian social system had rapidly evolved from a position in the tenth century where prebendalism had been common to a situation where feudal landlordism was predominant. In particular, this transition can be marked by the decline of the non-hereditary, conditional *iqta* to the hereditary, increasingly unconditional *iqta* and by the increasing importance of *mulk* property in relation to state land. In this regard, there is little evidence to support any notion that Iran can be distinguished from European feudalism in terms of the presence of the AMP.

Although Petrushevsky made a distinction between nomadic cattle-breeding and settled agriculture, it could be argued that we need a stronger distinction between a nomadic/pastoral mode of production and a feudal mode in which the latter was dominant. The political balance of forces in Iran between the centralizing state and the local autonomy of tribal chiefs was a reflection of the balance between these two modes of production. The strength of the state under feudal conditions can be measured by its success in subordinating the local or provincial khans and their tribal power base. The symbiosis between tribal pastoralism and settled agrarianism has been, of course, a traditional theme of Middle East analysis from Ibn Khaldun's theory of tribal élite circulation to Frederik Barth's study of the sedentarization of the Basseri (Barth 1961). In Iran, the periodic penetration of nomadism into settled society in the form of invasion and conquest had catastrophic and long-term consequences. The Mongol conquest in the thirteenth century was of particular significance, resulting in depopulation, decline of agriculture, a decline in urban life and a loss of trade.

We have established that, contrary to the traditional Orientalist account of Asiatic societies, private property in land which was unconditional and secure did develop in Iran with a corresponding distinction between landlord and peasant classes. It is true that state lands were far more common in Iranian feudalism than was the case in European feudal societies. There was a general coincidence between taxes and rents. Petrushevsky (1968: 515) comments that one 'peculiarity of State ownership of land was that the State itself exploited its tenants – the village communes (*jamma at-i dih*) – by means of finance officials (*ummal*)... rent and tax coincide, and the rents or taxes (the land-tax, etc.) paid in cash and kind to the State by the tenants, were then redistributed amongst the military caste as wages, pensions, subsidies, gifts, etc.' Thus, although Petrushevsky demonstrates that pre-capitalist Iranian society was feudal, he wants to preserve some notion that Iranian feudalism was nevertheless distinctive in terms of the presence of state land, the tax/rent couple, the absence of autonomous cities and the use of slave labour in agriculture. In short, his argument involves a theory of the dominant social role of a centralized state.

Petrushevsky's view of the position of the state in thirteenth and fourteenth-century Iran has been replicated by Marshall Hodgson's study of the state in the Safavi empire (1503–1722). Hodgson describes the Safavi absolutist state in terms of the 'military patronage state'. In Safavi times, Hodgson claims that the central bureaucracy was able to gain effective control over local, peripheral regions through its civilian and military apparatus. The absolutist shahs of this period were able to concentrate wealth at the imperial centre, reduce the autonomy of the *ulama*, to bring the guilds under state supervision and to extend the influence of the state machine throughout civil society. The outcome was that 'the empire was yielding to classical dangers of agrarian absolutism' which made it 'vulnerable to internal paralysis' (Hodgson 1974, vol. 3: 56–7).

One problem with Weber's contrast between the state in European feudalism and the patrimonial rulership of Asian societies, between Hodgson's view of 'the military patronage state' and European political structures is that such ideal typical contrasts tend to suppress the issue of the absolutist state in Europe and the relationship between political absolutism and the rise of capitalism. In order to make this contrast, we need a more sophisticated analysis of the development of the state in Europe. In the thirteenth century a new political pattern emerged in Europe which gave increased autonomy to towns and strengthened their enjoyment of feudal immunity from the king. These urban franchises were defended by enlarged civil militia, fortifications and city walls. The new corporate identity of the towns was the legal expression of an increased urban division of labour in production and commercial relations which gave the urban burghers a greater sense of economic identity and coherence. The new independence of the towns was matched by the development of other assemblies to represent the interests of universities, clergy, lawyers and political groups. The growth of the system of *Ständestaat* is conventionally contrasted with the absence of legally autonomous assemblies, parliaments and towns in Asiatic society, but such a contrast ignores the fact that the *Ständestaat* system was greatly weakened by the emergence of the absolutist state in the seventeenth and eighteenth centuries.

The struggle between urban burghers, feudal landlords and monarchs had rather different outcomes in different societies. In France, the estates were successfully weakened by a dynasty which managed to build up an effective state apparatus around the centralized power of the monarchy. In England, by contrast, Parliament achieved a decisive limitation of monarchical power in a series of political struggles which spanned the seventeenth century, culminating in the constitutional settlement of 1688. In Germany:

> centralization was carried out at comparatively low levels by territorial rulers who successfully opposed attempts by higher-level forces to make the Empire itself a state. In most parts of Germany, the failure of high level centralization meant that the establishment of strong political-administrative structures was retarded at all levels. The main exception was Prussia. (Poggi 1978: 58–9)

Although there are regional variations in the development of absolutism, there are a number of important common factors. The restrictions on the power of assemblies *vis-à-vis* the bureaucratic state did not represent an outright defeat of urban assemblies by either the monarchy or the traditional feudal class. On the contrary, the expansion of centralized power was a necessary condition for the growth of the urban economy. Protection of the internal economy of the town became less important than the territorial expansion of a uniform economy under the political protection of the state. The absolutist state provided greater uniformity and reliability for economic expansion than was possible under a system of autonomous, local, town-based productive systems. This affinity of interests between the urban burghers and centralized monarchies corresponded to a decline in the economic and political power of the system of military fiefs which had been the core of European feudalism in the period between the eighth and twelfth centuries. The growth of urban commerce and the influx of bullion decreased the value of land rent, which was the main buttress of feudal power. In England, the nobility was de-militarized by the time of the Tudors and commercial groups bought their way into the aristocracy. In France, at a later stage, the richer elements within the burgher class were able to purchase offices which had been traditionally held by the nobility, giving rise to the distinction between *noblesse de robe* and *noblesse d'épée*.

The precise relationship between the absolutist state and the rise of capitalism is, of course, a controversial issue. Poggi (1978) regards the centralization of political power in the seventeenth century as a necessary condition for capitalist development. By contrast, Anderson (1974) treats the absolutist state as a response by a politically threatened feudal class to defend itself against the urban mercantile class and against the peasantry which had achieved considerable commutation of dues. However, Anderson also recognizes that, in attempting to recharge the apparatus of feudal domination, the absolutist state performed important functions for nascent capitalism in providing a new infrastructure of national taxation, codified law, a permanent bureaucracy and a unified market. My argument is that, whatever view one takes about absolutism, some degree of state intervention was crucial for capitalism and this intervention was particularly important on the continent after the capitalist mode had become dominant in England. In other words, the establishment of English capitalism precluded a policy of *laissez-faire* economics in so-called 'late developers' in Europe. In Germany, Italy, France and Russia, where the urban bourgeoisie was weak and underdeveloped, the state became the major agency for capitalist development by encouraging and providing investment, by creating a politically unified nation and economic market, by protecting new industries from foreign competition and by developing new systems of communication and education (Gerschenkron 1962). It has, for example, been frequently suggested that the slow economic development of Middle East and Asian societies can be connected with the fact that these societies lack an independent class of entrepreneurs or that these societies, in the absence of a middle class, will be forced to depend on the military as a modernizing élite (Alexander 1960; Halpern 1962; Meyer 1959; Perlmutter 1977). However, the same type of argument would fit the case of European capitalism equally well. European capitalism developed through a variety of agencies such as an alliance between agrarian capitalists and politically subordinate bourgeois industrial class (England), through the investment of banks (Italy), through state control (Germany). The idea that capitalism depends on primitive accumulation brought about by an ascetically motivated class of politically autonomous bourgeois is simply a sociological myth which found its author in Adam Smith's notion of 'previousness'.

My argument is that the contrast between the system of *Ständestaat* in Europe and the powerful, centralized bureaucracies of Asiatic society as an explanation for the absence of independent capitalism in Asia is fundamentally misconceived. There are two aspects to this criticism. The first is that it is not possible to ask questions about the failure of spontaneous capitalism in non-European societies by taking the latter as a privileged model of how capitalism develops. Following the arguments of Frank, Barratt Brown, Baran and Hobsbawm, the underdevelopment of capitalism in Asia and South America is precisely the historical effect of capitalism development in Europe. If there is such a thing as a *general* set of conditions for capitalism, then they would not apply in Asia because of the 'contaminating' effect of colonialism and neo-colonialism. I have, however, suggested that it is in any case difficult to spell out a general theory of capitalist development because the experience of capitalism in Europe took very divergent forms. One only has to think, for example, of the great differences in class formations in the societies that underwent capitalist development in the eighteenth and nineteenth centuries. If there is one common feature, it appears to be the presence of a powerful political agency, namely, the centralized state, which played a crucial role in creating the institutional framework for economic development along capitalist lines. The main contrast between Asian - in this case, Iran - and European societies is not the presence of an all-pervasive state in Asia as opposed to the innovative European bourgeoisie, but exactly the opposite. It may well have been the weakness of the Iranian state apparatus and the subordination of the Iranian state to Russian and British economic interests which inhibited economic changes. Because the Iranian state could not supersede the powerful decentralizing forces present in Iranian feudalism and pastoral nomadism, the Iranian state was not equipped to integrate the divergent class interests of merchants, bourgeois, clergy, tribal chiefs and feudal landlords which constituted the power bloc. My argument in the final section of this paper is consequently that Iran was a feudal society whose potential for independent capitalist and commercial development was stunted by the effects of European imperial interests in the nineteenth century. Although Iran in the twentieth century has undergone a process of capitalist development of agriculture and industry under the aegis of a centralized state, these developments have taken place in the context of political and economic constraints which have been set by the global requirements of capitalism.

The effects of European colonialism on Iran in large measure replicate the pattern of underdevelopment which was experienced by North Africa, Egypt and greater Syria. Petty commodity production and small-scale industry collapsed under the effect of imported finished goods from Europe, which had the advantage of concession arrangements. With the development of mono-crop exports, an unfavourable balance-of-payments situation resulted in heavy dependence on imported agricultural commodities. The fiscal crisis of the post-colonial state reinforced the degree of dependence on foreign governments. The capitalist development of certain sections of the economy produced a variety of internal social contradictions within the society and the state responded by introducing a series of political and social 'reforms' under external pressures which were aimed to forestall revolutionary tendencies within these peripheral economies. These processes in Iran can be dated from the emergence of concessionary treaties with Russia and Britain following the Iranian–Russian War (1828), the Herat expedition (1855) and the Anglo–Iranian War (1856).

These unfavourable economic relations with Russia and Britain had a number of dramatic consequences. The Iranian manufactories which had grown during the Safavid period were destroyed, European manufactured goods superseded local Iranian commodities and the export of raw materials replaced the export of manufactured goods. In the nineteenth century, industrial centres in Isfahan, Kashan, Tabriz, Yazd, Kirman and Mashhad all declined (Ashraf 1970). The principal exports from Iran became opium, tobacco, cotton, almonds and rice, and through a policy of dumping and low customs duties, the British textile industry undermined indigenous production. External economic constraints often prevented Iranian producers from achieving an economic surplus from agricultural exports. For example, the price of wheat fell from $1.5 a bushel in 1871 to 23 cents a bushel in 1894 on world markets. Although the export of wheat from Bushire expanded eight times between 1869 and 1894, the value of the wheat exported remained virtually constant (McDaniel 1971). In the same period, agricultural production was hit by a series of natural disasters. The staple silk industry was crippled by low rainfall between 1869 and 1872; the spread of silkworm disease in the 1860s reduced silk production in Gilan from 20,000 bales of silk per annum to less than 6,000 bales by the 1870s. In a situation of a loss of foreign-exchange earnings and a depreciating currency, Iranian landlords responded by increasing peasant rents, which had the consequence of stimulating the process whereby land was progressively concentrated in fewer hands. While landlords were unable to realize fully the value of agricultural production, the independent Iranian bourgeoisie was also restricted by nineteenth-century social and economic conditions. According to Ashraf (1970), the limitations on the Iranian bourgeoisie included:

(1) the penetration of foreign capitalist interests, which favoured the European bourgeoisie;

(2) the decline of indigenous industry;

(3) the failure of Persian money-dealers and traders to establish an autonomous local and national banking system;

(4) the preference of Iranian merchants to invest in land, rather than industrial production.

These circumstances contributed to the process whereby

> many prosperous Persian traders were converted into the agents of Russian and British commercial firms and lost their independence. The predominance of the two colonial banks over the Persian money market, the apathy of the Asiatic rulers toward the local bourgeois elements in a situation of decentralized patrimonialism, and the intervention of the two powers to protect the interests of their traders and

> investors, forced Persian traders to work with the foreign firms to survive. (Ashraf 1970: 326–7)

If the economic history of nineteenth-century Iran was a replay of the pattern of economic subordination taking place throughout North Africa, the Middle East and Asia, then the political history of Iran was similarly a replica of anti-colonial struggles throughout the Islamic world. Reactionary regimes and their compradorial élites were challenged by an alliance of intellectuals, *ulama* and dispossessed merchants which, in the name of a restoration of pristine, unadulterated Islam, sought to introduce some element of modernization and liberalization. A return to Islam became the principal method of simultaneously rejecting western political control and economic colonialism, while accepting western institutions of political democracy. In response to western hegemony, Muslim intellectuals discovered that the true meaning of *ijma* was democratic, public opinion, that *jihad* had to be read as the positive effort of economic man, that *maslaha* was in fact Benthamite 'utility', that *taqlid* (imitation) was inimical to Islam and that 'the gate of *ijtihad* (independent reasoning) had to be reopened. The only significant alternative to a rediscovery of Islam as an anti-colonial ideology was the rediscovery of a pre-Islamic national culture demonstrating the wealth of a golden past in contrast with contemporary decline. Iran, like Egypt, espoused both forms of anti-colonial ideology.

The political events which marked the Iranian struggle against external, colonial domination need not be documented in all their complex detail (Upton 1960). It is possible to examine the modern history of Iran in terms of five crises (Halliday 1979). The first crisis concerns two related episodes, namely, the Tobacco Uprising (1890–2) and the Constitutional Revolution (1905–11). Nasiruddin Shah (1848–96) embarked upon a number of social reforms (such as improvements in printing and distribution of newspapers), which remained somewhat superficial and which were achieved at the cost of extending concessionary arrangements to both Britain and Russia. In 1889, de Reuter was given the right to organize the Imperial Bank of Persia, which was to be a commercial bank with limited privileges for the issue of notes. In the following year, a British company was awarded a tobacco monopoly over the export and internal trade in tobacco. This monopoly had very general implications for all social classes in Persia: tobacco-growers would find themselves increasingly under foreign control, small traders would be forced out of the market and smokers would purchase their supplies from the hands of infidels who were ritually impure. In this situation, Jamaluddin Afghani, the Muslim reformer, persuaded the chief *mujtahid* to declare that to smoke tobacco under conditions of foreign monopoly was against religion. This religious ban on tobacco resulted in its virtual disappearance as a commodity and in the dismantlement of the concessionary arrangement. The importance of Afghani's intervention was that it helped to cement the alliance between the intellectuals, the tradesmen and the *Shii ulama* against the shah, whose economic policies were mortgaging Iran to foreign companies. The rift between the merchants and *ulama*, on the one side, and the shah, on the other, was further deepened in the first decade of the twentieth century, when a number of clergy and merchants sought refuge (*bast*) from the shah at the Abdul azim shrine outside Tehran in 1905. This event was followed by a series of sympathetic *bast*s in Tabriz, Rasht, Isfahan and Shiraz. The *basti*s, mainly merchants and guildsmen, called for a constitution, a national assembly, a code of law and regular courts to be a check on royal finances and administration. Following the provisions of the Belgian constitution, the opposition called for the establishment of a national assembly (*Majles*) elected on the basis of a limited franchise. The Majles sought to restrict the shah's power by curbing royal expenditure, directing taxes to the treasury rather than to the shah's personal needs and by establishing a national bank. These early attempts at constitutional reform were thwarted by resistance from the shah, tribal leaders and the Russians, but they were also swamped by the social turmoil resulting from foreign invasion during the First World War.

The second period of crisis concerned the attempts by the Pahlavis Shahs in the period before the Second World War to establish an autonomous state apparatus which would encourage industrialization and independence from colonial powers. The reign of Reza Shah (1925–41) has been compared with that of Ataturk's in Turkey. Reza Shah attempted to base his power on a modernized army by, for example, introducing conscription in 1925. Like Ataturk, Reza Shah pursued a policy of secularization by limiting the power of the *ulama* (in such areas as education and public festivals), by proscribing the veil for women and by laws designed to change traditional dress. The new regime also attempted to develop railways, industry and production by a policy of tariff protection. The new regime also represented a growth of centralized state power at the cost of the decentralizing force of tribal groups through a process of conscription, disarmament and sedentarization. At the same time, there was an extension of government control over trade and industry, following the creation of a government system of monopolies. One great weakness of Reza Shah's economic strategy was its neglect of agriculture and irrigation, which placed a severe restriction on the capacity of the government to raise internal revenues. However, in Halliday's view the 'state he created provided the context for the later capitalist development of Iran but it was incapable itself of initiating the major changes required in this direction' (Halliday 1979: 24–5).

The programme for state-directed industrial change was terminated by the third major crisis of the twentieth century, namely, the invasion of Iran in 1941 by Russian and British troops. After the collapse of Kurdistan and Azerbaijan as autonomous republics under Russian sponsorship, the

Pahlavi regime reasserted its control over the whole country, which was left with a wartime legacy of high inflation and food shortages.

The fourth major crisis involved the attempt by Dr Muhammad Musaddeq's government (1951–3) to nationalize the Iranian oil industry and to achieve some control over supply and refinery. With the exile of Reza Shah and his replacement by his son Muhammad Reza, the govenment passed into the control of the Majles. In this period, the national assembly was dominated by conservative businessmen and landlords, who rejected the radical movement towards political liberalization or towards reform of agriculture. The Majles were, however, willing to support Musaddeq's policy of preventing oil concessions going to the Soviet Union, and in 1951 they supported the decision to nationalize the British-held oil fields. Musaddeq also enjoyed the support of the *ulama*, which sought to re-establish its social position following the fall of the secularizing Reza Shah regime. Despite this popular internal support, Musaddeq's strategy of oil nationalization as the basis for national independence was quickly terminated by a combination of internal and external forces. The British oil company was able to enforce a successful blockade of Iranian oil on the world market, and production and refining of oil were affected by the loss of western technicians. Musaddeq failed to gain the support of the new Eisenhower administration, which assumed that Musaddeq was too closely associated with the Tudeh Party or that the Musaddeq government would not be able to control the spread of Communist influence. With the loss of oil revenue, it was difficult to retain the loyalty of the bourgeois elements within the national assembly. Musaddeq also lost popular support because he was forced to exercise much tighter control over the population by the extention of martial law, prohibitions on strikes and labour unrest, suspension of the senate and elections for the Majles. A combination of forces loyal to the Shah (the army, nationalist merchants and bourgeoisie with CIA backing) was able to stage a coup against Musaddeq and to drive the Tudeh Party underground. With the incarceration of Musaddeq, the Pahlavi state under Muhammad Reza Pahlavi emerged even stronger than its position before oil nationalization (Wilber 1958).

The fifth crisis in Halliday's account of the emergence of the Iranian state covers the period from the early 1950s to the fall of the Shah in the late 1970s. The White Revolution of land reform (1960–72) was largely in response to pressure from the Kennedy administration, which recognized that land reform was a suitable strategy in securing the continuing loyalty of pro-western underdeveloped or peripheral regions. Thus, the GOPF argues that 'the political and cultural superstructure of feudalism could no longer meet the economic needs of imperialism. Nor was it in its political interests to preserve such an archaic system: feudalism was a decrepit system which had outlived its usefulness, and it was dangerous to support it' (GOPF 1976:

5). The White Revolution marked a rapid advance of capitalist development in agriculture and industry; the state's control over industrialization was aided by a rise in oil revenues from around 1971. The process of capitalist industrial development was accompanied by a decisive advance of political dictatorship, a growth of repressive and ideological state apparatus, and a curbing of minority rights and regional autonomy.

The point of this description of recent Iranian political history is not to provide a chronology of the dilemmas of the Iranian élite, but to draw some sociological lessons about the political economy of capitalist development in peripheral, feudal societies. For example, it would be a mistake to assume that the Pahlavi state is simply a modern reproduction of the 'military patronage state' of Safavid times or, more generally, the survival of Oriental Despotism. In my view, Halliday is perfectly correct in stressing the profound *discontinuity* between the state in feudal Iran and the Pahlavi state under conditions of dependent capitalist development. Thus, the Pahlavi Shahs of the twentieth century:

> have ruled in a manner quite distinct from that of those who went before them, and the social classes associated with the monarchy in the nineteenth century... Moreover, whereas the monarchy had very little power over the rest of the country a century ago, it now commands a unified and highly centralized country... [The modern Iranian state] controls the whole of its national territory, whereas the other's writ did not run outside the main cities. It promotes economic development, whereas the other neglected it. It has a large standing army, whereas the other had virtually no armed force at all. It has to a considerable extent transformed socio-economic relations in the Iranian countryside, whereas the other left the countryside alone. (Halliday

In other words, the dissolution of feudal relations of production required the intervention of a relatively autonomous, centralized state which orchestrated the conversion of feudal landlords into agrarian capitalists and created an intermediate service class between wage-labour and compradorial bourgeoisie.

The history of capitalism is often written as if merchants were the principal corrosive agent of feudal production. In the case of Iran, writers like Ashraf have suggested that there were three major obstacles to capitalist development. These were:

(1) the existence of tribal power in the countryside and frequent tribal invasions;

(2) the dependence of economic initiative on the state;

(3) colonial penetration which undermined the traditional artisan bourgeoisie, creating a dependent bourgeoisie.

These circumstances meant that merchants and traders acted in a traditional manner so that the 'non-rational practice of hoarding by treasury and money-dealers, the disposition towards luxurious living and resulting corruption set strict limits to the development of rational economic activities' (Ashraf 1970: 321). This interpretation ignores the fact that merchants operating in the sphere of circulation have not historically contributed to the development of productive relations and that merchants play a largely conservative role in economic change. In this respect, Marx's view of merchants as a class has been confirmed by more recent historical analyses. Merchant capital was not used in an innovative fashion in agricultural or industrial production and the intervention of merchants did not become historically decisive until the process of feudal dissolution was well under way (Hilton 1976). The origins of English capitalism are to be found in the class struggle between landlord and peasant over the economic surplus, the collapse of feudal serfdom after 1348 when bubonic plague wiped out half the English population, the crisis of land revenues and the eventual separation of the peasantry from the means of production and their conversion into agrarian wage-labourers. The secret of primitive accumulation for Marx was not Smithian previousness or Weberian asceticism, but the draconian separation of the peasant from the land by political and economic coercion. What, however, is the secret of accumulation for peripheral capitalism, for late developers, for nascent capitalism without external colonies or for young socialist societies? The answer must be, as Evgeni Preobrazhensky recognized in the *New Economics* (1924), the endogenous production of a surplus under the primary control of the state. The importance of the Pahlavi state has been precisely its ability to organize social forces towards the dissolution of feudal relationships in the countryside and the deployment of oil revenues for industrialization. In this respect, however, Iran is not essentially different from any other society undergoing capitalist development, since I have already suggested that capitalist development in Italy, Germany and Russia also required massive state intervention. The lesson to be drawn from this is that, although the conditions for capitalism in Europe and the Middle East did differ in some respects:

> certain common factors, and certain specific factors, make investment in industry as little attractive in that region [the Middle East] as it was in the Europe of three centuries ago. Hence the important role of the state both in Europe in the age of mercantilism and in Turkey, Iran, Egypt and Japan at the start of their industrialization. (Rodinson 1977: 142)

The problem of state-directed accumulation in peripheral, dependent capitalist societies is that, as we have seen in the period from the Tobacco Uprising to the fall of the Pahlavi Shahs, the internal economic role of the state is severely circumscribed by the exigencies of the external, global structuring of the capitalist world economy.

In theory, the existence of substantial oil revenues should allow oil-exporting countries in the Third World to industrialize rapidly without massive increases in direct or indirect taxation and without running into crippling inflation problems. As the second largest oil producer with annual revenues averaging 20 billion US dollars over 1975–7, Iran has been thought to possess the greatest potential for development in the Middle East. Economic and social development on the basis of oil revenues does, however, take a peculiar form. Oil production does not necessarily stimulate widespread economic effects, since it employs a very small section of the labour force and many skilled manual and white-collar workers will be drawn into the economy from outside the host society. Oil production does not necessarily lead to manufacturing development, since in a society like Iran most of the oil will go directly for export. Oil provides the state with an income that can be regarded as a form of rent (Halliday 1979: 139), and hence we may use the term 'rentier state' (Mahdavy 1970). What becomes crucial in this situation is the social and political context of the ruling class in directing investment into manufacture or into consumption, waste and unproductive outlay of the oil surplus, on the one hand, and the state's ability to operate in a global context to shape world-market demand for raw materials, on the other.

It would be difficult to deny that Iran has experienced a period of industrialization via state-financed factories in sugar, cement, textiles and matches. Production workers have increased from 23 per cent in 1956 to 29 per cent in 1972. Heavy industry has been developed in chemicals and fertilizers by the Shahpur Chemical Company, the Iran Fertilizer Company and the Aryamehr Iron and Steel Plant. There has also been a significant increase in the construction industry and major improvements in transport. However, despite the obvious signs of industrialization and urbanization, economic growth and investment have fallen far below the economic plan of the Iranian government and below the expectation of foreign economic assessment. A series of economic explanations have been offered to account for this under-performance. These economic and technical explanations often include references to inadequate long-term economic management, shortages of appropriate skilled labour, failure to protect the informal sector of the economy, bottle-necks in supply, inflation in the costs of imported capital goods and the detrimental effect of monopolistic markets on the workshop economy (Wilson 1979).

Perhaps a more adequate explanation can be found in the notion of the rentier state as a post-colonial state apparatus (Alavi 1972). The post-colonial state inherits an overdeveloped bureaucratic–military apparatus which is required to maintain artificial territorial boundaries and to manage a power bloc constituted by landlords, a small indigenous capitalist class and the comprador bourgeoisie. Recruitment to the bureaucracy creates a client class of petty-bourgeois elements, which form the governing as opposed to the ruling class. Oil revenues are directed to the unproductive class of bureaucrats and military personnel. As with other rentier states, Iran has experienced a rapid development of the service sector from 32 per cent of GNP in 1959–60 to 39 per cent in 1974–5, while industry amounts to only 16 per cent. Military expenditure in 1974 accounted for 32 per cent of the state's budget and 31 per cent of planned expenditure in the 1973–8 Plan, or 9 per cent of GNP. Thus, the state employs around 10 per cent of the employed population. The Pahlavi state appears to have developed along classic post-colonial lines in accentuating the combined and uneven development of the social formation. The most important aspect of this uneven development is illustrated by the fate of the agricultural sector. Some measure of the problem can be obtained from the fact that, although the population (of 34 million) is increasing by approximately 3.2 per cent per annum and food consumption is increasing by 10 per cent per annum, domestic crop production is rising by a mere 2 per cent per annum. The consequence of these relationships is that Iran has switched from being a food-exporting economy to a net importer. In order to understand this transition, it is important to examine the land-reform programme of the 1960s.

As we have seen, prior to land reform the land-tenure system of Iran was a mixture of public and private feudal land. To be more precise, we can distinguish between state-owned land and villages, royal land and villages, religious (*waqf*) property, private ownership of feudal property and collective, tribal property. The majority of villages (around 72 per cent) were owned by landlords, whereas royal villages represented around 2 per cent, public domain was under 4 per cent and tribal property was less than 4 per cent. Property was, in fact, more concentrated than these percentages suggest, since, as Halliday estimates, 37 families owned 1,900 villages. Where Reza Shah had in the 1920s acquired some 2,100 villages, peasant proprietors owned a mere 5 per cent of the land they cultivated. Since the majority of landlords lived in the large cities, the village contained a number of distinct social groups – the local agents of absentee landlords, peasants and landless labourers (Askia 1979). Peasants were bound to landlords by share-cropping and tenancy arrangements. Tenancy contracts, which were arranged on a short-term basis, were paid in money or crops. Share-cropping contracts, which were regulated by local custom, were based on five factors of cultivating the land, namely, water, land, seeds, oxen and labour. Peasants who possessed four factors of production would receive four-fifths of the crop, those with only two factors would receive two-fifths of the crop, and so on. The most common situation was that the landlord possessed three factors (land, water and seed) so that the peasant share of the crop was determined by the input of oxen and labour. The peasant share was further reduced by payments to the village headman, field watcher, religious officials, blacksmith and others. Peasants were also subject to additional levies and personal service involving unpaid, compulsory work for the landlord. Below the peasants were the landless labourers who did not possess cultivation rights (*nassaq* or *wasagh*) and who were hired by peasants to perform seasonal work such as weeding and threshing. These labourers, who constituted between 30 per cent and 40 per cent of the village population, provided a pool of cheap labour for landlords; these labourers could be used to discipline peasants, because landlords could transfer *nassaq* rights from unruly peasants to previously landless workers.

Prior to the Musaddeq period and White Revolution, the land-tenure system was, therefore, a feudal institution. Peasants were subordinated by the fact that, although they had customary rights to land, the landlords owned the land, controlled the production process by their control of irrigation, and exercised political control through their local agents. Exchange was in terms of barter and the use of money was limited. Production by peasants was for subsistence, rather than for commodity exchange on the market. In this context, the land reforms of the shah were designed for a number of political objectives:

(1) to reduce the potential for agrarian unrest;

(2) to weaken the power of the large landlords in order to provide the state with a wider social base in the villages;

(3) to diminish the political power of tribal chiefs.

The economic objectives of the land reforms were to increase the purchasing power of the peasantry in order to expand the home market for industrial goods and to increase agricultural productivity to provide further labour for capitalist industry. To achieve these goals it was necessary to redistribute land and extend long-term credit through a system of rural co-operatives.

The first stage of land reform (1961) was aimed at the break-up of large-scale ownership of land and attempted to reduce landownership to the equivalent of one village (*Shesh-Dang*). The feudal landlords responded to this situation by redistributing their villages among their wives, children and relatives. Furthermore, since the landlords were able to select which village lands they intended to sell to the government, they were able to retain top-quality agricultural land for their own use. Certain clauses of the law exempted the sale of orchards, grazing land, suburban villages and mechanized farms, and these clauses provided the loop-hole for the re-definition of remote villages as 'suburban' or barren land as 'orchards'. As a result of these responses to the land-reform law, the landlords remained the major economic power in society, despite the redistribution of land to peasants through the rural co-operative and the consequent liquidation of large estates. At the village level, the co-operatives became the vehicle for the introduction of a variety of manufactured goods (such as washing powder and vegetable oil) as well as commodities (tea and sugar). However, the co-operatives had to borrow money to pay instalments on the land and to purchase commodities and because 'the societies want their money back at a certain date, the farmers often have to borrow from money-lenders and shop-keepers in the village, or even perhaps in the town, at a much higher rate of interest in order to pay back the loans' (GOPF 1976: 38). The effect of this situation has been an expansion of money relationships into the village, an extension of the social role of money-lenders and an increase in peasant indebtedness.

In a situation of growing political conflict from landlords and religious leaders, the second stage of land reform (1962) took a conservative direction by normalizing the existing situation and attempting to remove the share-cropping system. The new land-reform measures provided landowners who had been exempted under the initial legislation with a choice of five methods of settlement: to rent their lands to peasants; to sell their lands to peasants; to share their land; to form joint-stock agricultural units; to buy peasants cultivation rights and farm the land with wage-labourers. The first of these options – to rent land – proved to be the most popular so that over a million peasants were involved in this scheme. These arrangements worked to the disadvantage of the peasants, who found that their new rents were more exploitative than traditional feudal duties and land which was acquired by the peasants was often too small or too infertile to support their families.

In the third stage of land reform (1968) the five settlement options were reduced to two, namely, the sale or distribution of rented lands (in proportion to share-cropping) and the sale or distribution of lands under the joint-stock arrangements. In this stage, attempts were also made to bring religious endowments within the land-reform policy and to facilitate appropriate arrangements for the sale of orchards which were jointly owned by farmers and landlords. The object of this final stage was simply to complete the process of eradicating feudal landownership and to finalize the transformation of the agrarian class structure.

The general effects of all three stages have been brilliantly summarized by the GOPF research report (*Land Reform and its Direct Effects in Iran*) under six headings:

(1) the expansion of mechanization and agricultural investment;

(2) a growth in the class of small landlords (farmer–owners);

(3) a rapid increase of landless wage-labourers;

(4) the growth of money relationships and of a bureaucratic financial bourgeoisie;

(5) an extension of orchards; and, finally,

(6) a growth of class consciousness among villagers.

My own view is that this process of conversion of feudal agrarian production in capitalist agriculture perfectly illustrates my thesis that primitive capitalist accumulation in dependent, peripheral societies is achieved through an extension of state activity, but at the cost of distributing revenues to client classes in the service sector, on the one hand, and to the capitalist fractions, on the other.

In this paper, my concern has been to challenge the conventional Orientalist viewpoint that societies like Iran can be classified under the general rubric of Oriental Despotism or as societies dominated by the Asiatic mode of production. The point of Orientalism is to establish that Asiatic and Middle East societies were precluded from capitalist development by the absence of autonomous cities, independent guilds and merchants, rational law and *Ständestaat*. Asiatic societies contained an essential flaw – the absence of inheritable, private property and the dominance of arbitrary power in the form of the centralized state – which produced a stultifying economic order incapable of internal transformation. Against such a viewpoint, I have stressed the importance of Iranian feudal relations from early times and the general role of the state in dissolving feudal relations of production. If European capitalist development can be meaningfully contrasted with capitalist development in Iran, the important difference is not the existence of an all-pervasive Iranian state in feudalism, but precisely its opposite, namely, the weakness of the Iranian state *vis-à-vis* a civil society in which nomadic pastoralism and tribalism placed a decisive break on the building of an effective state apparatus.

I am, however, reluctant to raise this observation to the level of a general theory of capitalist development, namely, that all primitive accumulation in early capitalism requires a centralized state which is capable of autonomously reorganizing class relationships and providing the necessary infrastructure for the extraction of an economic surplus. The general, abstract laws of the capitalist mode of production operate at the level of social formations, where there are present a range of *contingent* superstructural, economic and class factors which may or may not correspond to the *logic* of the mode of production. At a very obvious level, the fact that Britain industrialized on the basis of cheap energy sources – labour-intensive surface coal mines, internal and external waterways, an expanding labour force – without the constraint of powerful competitors and with important colonial possessions produced social effects which were very different from Iran's dependence on oil revenues in a global context of neo-colonialism. It is the specificity and peculiarity of capitalist development in particular social formations which appear to dominate over uniformities and generalities. To take one pertinent illustration, there are no important relations of correspondence between legal/political superstructures and capitalist modes of production in social formations which we conventionally designate 'capitalist'. To conclude with Ernest Gellner's aphorism – if capitalism had not existed, nobody could have invented it.

In general, both Marxism and sociology have not been particularly successful in producing a theory of the relationship between religion and modes of production. The classical position of Weber, Durkheim and Marx was that capitalism was the grave-digger of Christianity and that secularization and industrialization were necessarily connected. The historical research of the French *Annales* School and the sociological analysis of English sociologists like David Martin have raised a large question mark over the assumption that Christianity was dominant in feudal society. Similarly, the centrality of religion in movements of national and regional autonomy in both Europe and Asia casts doubt on the supposed inevitability of the demise of a sacred cosmos under the impact of industrialization, urbanization and increasing mass literacy. The obvious response to this apparent disconfirmation of the secularization thesis is a reductionist argument that treats religious symbolism as the outer garment of real political and economic class interests in situations where alternative secular symbolism is either inappropriate or unavailable. The recent history of Islam in general and of Shiism in particular presents certain difficulties for simple reduction in sociology and for the Orientalist presentation of classical Islam. Rather than treat this issue at a very general level, it will be more profitable to ask the question: what is the relationship between Shiism and the state in Iran?

It has often been observed that, in the case of Islam, it is particularly difficult to draw a clear division between the religious and the political, and consequently western sociologists are in constant danger of importing misleading contrasts between distinctly secular realms and sacred phenomena. This non-separation of private religion from public politics is sometimes associated with the fact that there is a sense in which Islam has no sacerdotal clergy, no confessional, no sacramentalism and no 'church'. Other writers like Ernest Gellner have attempted to connect the distinctiveness of Islam as a social system with the fact that Christianity emerged as an apolitical, millenarian, chiliastic religion of a colonially dominated group, whereas Islam created an empire in the political vacuum between Byzantium and the

Sassanian empire. One consequence of this contrast between the origins of Christianity and Islam is that Sunni Islam has no real tradition of *religious* martyrdom. There are, as a result, broadly two interpretations of the political and the religious in Islam. Max Weber came very close to saying that Islam was not a religion at all, but a this-worldly political movement of an expanding Arab migration out of the Arabian peninsula which created no lasting inner-worldly tension between extra-empirical interests and political contingencies. The second line of interpretation has been developed by Wilfrēd Cantwell Smith and Marshall G. S. Hodgson, who make a distinction between Islam as a socio-religious system and Islam as the personal faith of the individual in relation to his Creator.

The distinction between Sunni Islam and Shiism, however, creates further difficulties. There are various ways of approaching this division in Islam. At one level, the difference between Sunnism and Shiism hinges on the question of charismatic succession. At the death of the Prophet in 632, there was no clear guide for political succession to create a leader for the new Islamic community. One custom suggested that the new leader should emerge by counsel, designation and acclamation, but another custom pointed to the importance of selection through the male line of kinship descent. The first three caliphs - Abu Bakr (632–4), Umar (634–44) and Uthman (644–56) - who emerged according to the first principle, were not acceptable to the party of Ali (Shiat Ali), who claimed that Ali was the rightful caliph as the first cousin of the Prophet, the husband of the Prophet's daughter and the father of the Prophet's male descendants, al-Hasan and al-Husayn. When Ali was assassinated in 661, Shiism emerged as an oppositional political force which rejected the legitimacy of the Sunni caliphate. Shiism was, however, also profoundly religious in that Shiism came to insist on the fact that the caliph was not simply the secular leader of the community, but the charismatic embodiment of esoteric knowledge and spiritual authority. The martyrdom of Shiite leaders was simultaneously a political and religious sacrfice. Shiism thus became an oppositional, eschatological movement, centred around the expectation of the return of the hidden *imam*. All existing political arrangements were thereby regarded as partial, inadequate and temporary.

These elementary features of Islam bear on the question of the fall of Muhammad Reza Shah in the following respects.

(1) Shiism has, as it were, a built-in oppositional ideology which can be mobilized to de-legitimize the state as the sole authority within society. I am not claiming that official Shiism is permanently oppositional, but merely that the doctrine of the hidden imamate can be readily called upon to justify opposition to the political regime. The *ulama* has, of course, had ample cause to oppose the Pahlavi regime, which has adopted a policy of

secularization and flirtation with the mythology of pre-Islamic, Persian greatness. Furthermore, since the Tudeh Party was discredited by its pro-Russian politics and its dubious role in the fall of Musaddeq, there has been no ready-made alternative oppositional ideology for the masses – at least in the short run.

(2) Islam has a greater sense of religious space than is the case for Christianity. There are two aspects to this sense of space. First, Islam has a potent sense of the geographical dimension of Islam, which is connected with the importance of pilgrimages to the holy places of Mecca and Medina, and for Shiism, the shrines of Iraq and Iran. The loss of geographical integrity has a greater religious significance for Islam than it does for Christianity. Despite the obvious counter-example of the Crusades, the loss of the Holy Land has been of greater religious signficance to Islam and Judaism than to Christianity. Secondly, this religious space has a political dimension, in that Christianity is more able to tolerate alien, irreligious political control because it can render unto Caesar the things that belong to Caesar. Because of its sense of religious space, Islam has been quickly mobilized in opposition to colonialism by the (nominally) Christian West. Opposition to concessions during the Tobacco Uprising and support for Musaddeq's policy of oil nationalization are good examples of popular religious support against infidel colonial penetration of sacred space. The opposition of Ayatollah Khomeyni to the Pahlavi regime is based solely on the fact that the Shah's policies have provided the opening for alien, non-Muslim influence inside Iran.

(3) The mullahs and ayatollahs have provided a national vehicle for opposition because the *ulama* is at once a powerful national and local organization. The local mosque, local mullahs and the Friday sermon provided a means by which discontent over rural conditions could be discussed in a relatively open fashion. The religious schools and the holy city of Qum could thus become centres of opposition of a conservative and traditional nature to the Shah's regime. The religious structure thus provided an institutionalized channel of popular opposition to the authority of the Pahlavi state.

References

Abrahamian, Ervand, 'Oriental Despotism: the case of Qajar Iran', *International Journal of Middle East Studies* (1974), vol. 5, pp. 3–31.

Abrahamian, Ervand, 'European feudalism and Middle Eastern despotism', *Science and Society* (1975), vol. 39, pp. 129–56.

Alavi, Hamza, 'The state in post-colonial societies – Pakistan and Bangladesh', *New Left Review* (1972), no. 74, pp. 59–81.

Al-Azmeh, Aziz, 'What is the Islamic city', *Review of Middle East Studies* (1976), vol. 2, pp. 1–12.

Alexander, A. D., 'Industrial entrepreneurship in Turkey: origins and growth', *Economic Development and Cultural Change* (1960), vol. 8, pp. 349–65.

Althusser, L., *For Marx*, London, 1969.

Amin, Samir, *The Arab Nation*, 1978.

Anderson, Perry, *The Lineages of the Absolutist State*, 1974.

Ashraf, Ahmad, 'Historical obstacles to the development of a bourgeoisie in Iran', in M. A. Cook (ed.), *Studies in the Economic History of the Middle East*, 1970, pp. 308–32.

Askia, Mostafa, 'The significance of agricultural development in Iran', unpublished research paper, University of Aberdeen, 1979.

Avineri, Shlomo (ed.), *Karl Marx on Colonialism and Modernization*, 1968.

Avineri, Shlomo, *Israel and the Palestinians*, 1971.

Avineri, Shlomo, 'Political and social aspects of Israeli and Arab nationalism', in E. Kamenka (ed.), *Nationalism*, 1976.

Banaji, Jairus, 'For a theory of colonial modes of production', *Economic and Political Weekly* (1972), vol. 7, pp. 298–302.

Banaji, Jairus, 'Backward capitalism, primitive accumulation and modes of production', *Journal of Contemporary Asia* (1973), vol. 3, pp. 393–413.

Barratt Brown, M., *The Economics of Imperialism*, 1974.

Barth, F., *The Nomads of South Persia*, 1961.

Coon, Carleton S., *Caravan*, 1951.

Eisenstadt, S. N., 'Religious organizations and political process in centralized empires', *Journal of Asian Studies* (1962), vol. XXI (no. 3), pp. 279–95.

El Kodsy, Ahmed and Eli Lobel, *The Arab World and Israel*, 1970.

Foster-Carter, Aidan, 'Neo-Marxist approaches to development and underdevelopment', in Emmanuel de Kadt and Gavin Williams (eds), *Sociology and Development*, 1974, pp. 67–105.

Frank, A. G., *Capitalism and Underdevelopment in Latin America*, 1971.

Gerschenkron, A., *Economic Backwardness in Historical Perspective*, 1962.

GOPF, *Land Reform and its Direct Effects in Iran*, 1976.

Halliday, Fred, *Arabia without Sultans*, 1974.

Halliday, Fred, *Iran: Dictatorship and Development*, 1979.

Halpern, M., 'Middle Eastern armies and the new middle class', in J. J. Johnson (ed.), *The Role of the Military in Underdeveloped Countries*, 1962.

Hegel, G. W. F., *The Philosophy of History*, 1956.

Hilton, R. (ed.), *The Transition from Feudalism to Capitalism*, 1976.

Hindess, Barry and Paul Q. Hirst, *Pre-Capitalist Modes of Production*, 1975.

Hodgson, Marshall G. S., *The Venture of Islam*, 1974, 3 vols.

Hoselitz, Bert F. and W. E. Moore (eds), *Industrialization and Society*, 1963.

Koebner, R., 'Despot and despotism: vicissitudes of a political term', *Journal of the Warburg and Courtauld Institutes* (1951), vol. XIV, pp. 275–302.

Lewis, A., 'Economic development with unlimited supplies of labour', *Manchester School* (1954), vol. 22.

Lewis, Bernard, 'Islamic concepts of revolution', in Vatikiotis, 1972, pp. 30–40.

Mahdavy, H., 'The patterns and problems of economic development in rentier states: the case of Iran', in Cook (ed.), 1970, pp. 428–67.

Marx, Karl, *Pre-Capitalist Economic Formations*, 1964.

Marx, Karl, *Capital*, Moscow, 1965, 3 vols.

Marx, Karl, *Surveys from Exile*, 1973a.

Marx, Karl, *Grundrisse*, 1973b.

Marx, Karl and F. Engels, *The Russian Menace to Europe*, 1953.

Marx, Karl and F. Engels, *On Ireland*, 1968.

Marx, Karl and F. Engels, *On Colonialism*, 1972.

Marx, Karl and F. Engels, *The Communist Manifesto*, 1973.

McClelland, D. *The Achieving Society*, New York, 1961.

McDaniel, Robert, 'Economic change and economic resiliency in 19th century Persia', *Iranian Studies* (1971), vol. IV, no. 1, pp. 36–49.

Melotti, Umberto, *Marx and the Third World*, 1977.

Meyer, A. J., *Middle Eastern Capitalism*, 1959.

Myrdal, Gunnar, *Economic Theory and Underdeveloped Regions*, 1954.

Parsons, Talcott, 'The kinship system of the contemporary United States', *American Anthropologist* (1943), vol. 45, pp. 22–38.

Perlmutter, Amos, *The Military and Politics in Modern Times*, 1977.

Petrushevsky, I. P., 'The socio-economic condition of Iran under the Il-Khans', in J. A. Boyle (ed.), *The Cambridge History of Iran*, 1968, Vol. 5, pp. 303–421.

Poggi, G., *The Development of the Modern State*, 1978.

Poulantzas, Nicos, *Political Power and Social Classes*, 1973.

Poulantzas, Nicos, *Fascism and Dictatorship*, 1974.

Rodinson, Maxime, *Islam and Capitalism*, 1977.

Said, Edward, *Orientalism*, 1978.

Stelling-Michaud, Sven, 'Le mythe du despotisme oriental', *Schweizer Beiträge zur Allgemein-Geschichte* (1960–1), vol. XVIII–XIV, pp. 328–46.

Tambiah, S. H., *World Conqueror and World Renouncer*, 1976.

Turner, Bryan S., 'The concept of "social stationariness": utilitarianism and Marxism', *Science and Society* (1974), vol. 38, pp. 3–18.

Turner, Bryan S. 'Avineri's view of Marx's theory of colonialism: Israel', *Science and Society*, (1976) vol. 40, pp. 385–409.

Turner, Bryan S., *Marx and the End of Orientalism*, 1978.

Turner, Bryan S., 'The middle classes and entrepreneurship', *Arab Studies Quarterly* (1979), vol. 1, no. 2, pp. 113–34.
Upton, Joseph M., *The History of Modern Iran: an Interpretation*, 1960.
Vatikiotis, P. J. (ed.), *Revolution in the Middle East and Other Case Studies*, 1972.
Wallerstein, Immanuel, *The Modern World-System*, 1974.
Weber, Max, *The City*, 1958.
Weber, Max, *The Theory of Social and Economic Organization*, 1966.
Weber, Max, *Economy and Society*, 1968.
Wilber, Donald N., *Iran, Past and Present*, 1958.
Wilson, Rodney, *The Economies of the Middle East*, 1979.
Wittfogel, Karl A., *Oriental Despotism*, 1957.
Zubaida, Sami, 'Theories of nationalism', in Gary Littlejohn *et al.* (eds), *Power and the State*, 1978, pp. 52–71.

10 Agrarian Capitalism: Bangladesh and Egypt*

Emerging out of colonial domination on two separate occasions, first under the British (1757–1947) and then under Pakistan (1947–71), Bangladesh is now regarded as one of the poorest countries of the world. However, as colonial integration means ultimate subjugation of the colonial economy to an economy dominated by a capitalist mode of production, both colonial conditions gave specificities to the capitalist transformation of the country's agriculture. The British inherited an agricultural structure which, in many respects, resembled the one introduced by the colonial regime. But it stunted the organic growth process of the contradictions of the pre-existing mode of production in the interest of colonial capitalism. For instance, British colonialism destroyed many of the elements of a pre-capitalist mode of production (such as village self-sufficiency, simple reproduction of capital and the use of extra-economic coercion for the realisation of the surplus from the actual producer), but it delayed the emergence of a full-fledged capitalism which could be antagonistically contradictory to metropolitan capitalism.[1] The Pakistani colonial regime, on the other hand, formally abolished all the vestiges of feudalism, but restricted the capitalist transformation of the agriculture by re-imposing a double edifice of class and colonial exploitation in the interest of the development of an industrial capitalism in Pakistan (West). Thus, both colonial conditions contributed to a restricted capitalist transformation of the country's agriculture, which is reinforced in the post-colonial situation by neo-colonial control. The present chapter therefore attempts to reconstruct the history of capitalist underdevelopment in Bangladesh, drawing an analogy from another country which, in many respects, experienced similar developments, namely, Egypt.

It was in Bengal that the British laid the foundation of their subsequent colonial expansion in India. Historians are now almost unanimous about the fact that eighteenth-century Bengal embodied features such as proprietary rights over land, commodity production, use of money, existence of markets, mutual exchange of goods between the town and the country, a considerable degree of social stratification among the indigenous

* *Aspects of this chapter are drawn from Dr. B. Chowdury's doctoral thesis on Bangladesh, University of Aberdeen, 1982.*

population, the organisation of commercial credit, insurance and rudimentary deposit-banking. All these features, according to Habib, remind one of the conditions of Renaissance Europe.[2]

As far as proprietary rights over land were concerned, Mughal revenue documents were quite unambiguous about the right of ownership in agricultural land by individual persons. The superior class of property holders were known as *zamindars*. There were both large and small *zamindari* estates. According to one source, some of the large landed aristocratic families, such as the Rajas of Burdwan, Rajshahi, Dinajpur, Nadia, Birbhum, Bishnapur and Jessore, controlled more than half of the land resources in Bengal just prior to the British occupation of the country.[3] These *zamindars* held their estates within the territories which were conferred by the state on condition that the holders paid a fixed revenue. Failure to pay the stipulated amount could lead to their eviction.[4] The system of evicting *zamindars* from their land for non-payment of revenue was extensively practised by the Mughal governor, Murshid Quli Khan. It is reported that Murshid Quli Khan deliberately pursued a policy of:

> rewarding those *zamindars* who were able to deliver the increased sums that he demanded, and by punishing those who were not. His rewards often took the form of opportunities for successful *zamindars* to acquire the right to more land, while his punishment usually consisted either of physical harassment and sometimes imprisonment or else removal of a *zamindar* from his *zamindari*.[5]

The provisions of reward and punishment thus opened up avenues of acquiring increased wealth through additional revenue rights, making it possible for landowners to effect a change in their official status.[6] The whole system thus represented a considerable amount of dynamism within the upper strata of the rural social hierarchy.

In addition to the *zamindars* having land within the territories under direct imperial control, there were those who held their land outside it. They were known as *Karad rajas* or frontier chiefs.[7] These *Karad rajas* retained hereditary rights over land by paying tribute to the imperial authority. The Mughal emperors never interfered with the internal affairs of the *Karad rajas* as long as they were satisfied with their loyalty.[8]

However, what distinguished the pre-colonial land-tenure pattern from the colonial one was the fact that almost all the peasants were occupancy *ryots*. Their holdings were hereditary and they had full rights in land for the purposes of transfer, mortgage and sale.[9] Thus, the peasants of Bengal did not rent land on short lease from the *zamindars*, but continuously occupied them.[10] However, serious restrictions were imposed upon peasant mobility by the denial of the right of free alienation. Given the fact that there were fewer peasants than the land available for cultivation, the peasant could not leave the land or refuse to cultivate it unless he could find a successor.[11] It was in view of this situation that Currie argued that for the Mughal peasants, 'cultivation was both a right and duty'.[12] The system thus represented the feudal mode of surplus extraction through the use of force.[13] The use of force for the purpose of surplus extraction is also exemplified by the fact that the Mughal army was stationed at important places to assist the lower-level bureaucrats in revenue collection from the reluctant peasants.[14] The repressive nature of the revenue collection resulted in a number of peasant revolts throughout India during the seventeenth and the eighteenth centuries.

These revolts exemplify the different levels of peasants' consciousness and the expression of the same in different forms of movement, given the situation under which the peasants were living. Some of the movements took the shape of 'social banditry',[15] such as the Thugee movement of the eighteenth century, whereas others remained passive, taking the form of mass escape from oppression. The abundant availability of land made the latter kind of resistance 'peasants' first answer to famine or man's oppression'.[16] Thus, pre-colonial Bengal not only embodied private property in land and the existence of different classes of property holders, but also the conflicts based on social contradictions.

A characteristic feature of the Mughal revenue collection was that it was demanded in cash. The cash revenue demand, in turn, was a major contributory factor to the rural monetisation. Therefore, to meet the cash revenue demand, the peasants of pre-colonial Bengal not only cultivated major food crops like rice, but also commercial crops like tobacco, opium, sugar-cane and indigo.[17] Unlike his counterpart in the colonial era, the pre-colonial peasant was free to decide about the type of crop to be produced. The same factor also contributed to the peasant's close association with the market for the realisation of the necessary cash for revenue payment through the disposal of his own produce. There were a number of markets scattered through rural Bengal.[18] These markets were and are still known as *hats*. The existence of numerous rural markets and the peasant's close association with them indicates that 'the primary producer was not only concerned with exchange merely as a form of economic activity required to secure the wherewithal for the payment of revenue, but also that the process of production itself had become partly dependent on the exchange relations'.[19] An important aspect of rural monetisation was the total dependence of the urban area on the villages for the supply of essential raw materials for urban industries and other necessities for the urban population. The rural markets were therefore frequented by urban merchants and their agents. In addition, to facilitate the cultivation of commercial crops, money-lending also developed to a significant extent to supplement the peasant's inadequate capital. The existence of a separate category of money-lenders, locally known as *mahajans*, is evidence of this fact.[20] In many cases money-lending and trading were incorporated in the same person. Consequently, the peasant was not only subject to the rigid revenue demand of the state, but also to exploitation by the merchants and money-lenders. The combination of these factors inhibited the extension of rural monetisation. These three social groups (the *zamindars*, merchants and money-lenders) had a claim on the produce of the peasant, leaving him with little surplus to create a rural market for consumer goods. The villager sold his produce in order to pay the 'revenue, now demanded in cash, and maybe to pay the moneylender unless he preferred payment in kind. For the rest, his life was geared to a tradition based on distribution of the rural produce among agriculturist, craftsmen and village servants.'[21]

The restriction on rural monetisation was reinforced by the nature of urban production. In pre-colonial Bengal, urban manufacturing developed to a significant extent. Bengali cotton textiles, especially the famous Bengal muslin, enjoyed a world-wide market. The manufacture of these textiles was carried out in the cottages of independent workers as well as in the factories owned by local merchants, Mughal nobles and European companies.[22] Of the three, the European companies could claim credit for introducing the manufacture system and wage-labour for the production of commodities in pre-colonial Bengal.[23] However, as production remained restricted mainly to the consumption requirements of the nobility and the international market, there was nothing that the urban areas could send to the villages. The village economy continued to produce everything that the villagers needed.[24] The characteristic feature of the manufacturing sector failed to undermine the self-sufficient nature of the rural economy. Therefore, the pre-colonial Indian economy in general, and the Bengali economy in particular, presented a unique picture of the coexistence of the conditions of money-economy and village self-sufficiency:

> It was the presence of these two contradictory economic elements that probably accounted for the social contradiction manifest in the existence of an individualistic mode of production in agriculture, on the one hand, and the organization of the village community, on the other.[25]

With this background, Bengal was integrated to world capitalism through the colonisation of the country by the British in 1757.

Given these conditions, was India ready for an autonomous capitalist transformation prior to British colonialism? To answer this question one must remember that commodity production (that is, production for the market) was intertwined with the organisation of production in agriculture, which was clearly non-capitalist in nature, and capital remained confined mainly to the sphere of commerce. Under the circumstances, it could follow a different economic logic from that which governs exchanges between commodities or the accumulation of capital;[26] or given merchant capital's failure to achieve any independent development, it could disintegrate with the collapse of the ruling class.[27] Whatever the case may be, to argue that eighteenth-century India in general was ready for the rise of capitalism in the 'really revolutionary way' will simply be an overstatement of the actual fact.[28]

The initial years of British occupation were marked by outright plunder, which illustrated the characteristic form of mercantile appropriation. The plunder resulted in a disastrous famine in 1770, which removed about one-third of the population of the country.[29] It was this famine which made the British East-India Company realise the importance of a more permanent method of government. With that aim in view, the Company began to reorganise the rural economy. In order to bring the pre-capitalist mode of production to the service of British capitalism, the colonial rulers initiated certain basic changes in the concepts of property ownership. The new concepts of property relations were to have far-reaching consequences and marked the beginning of the process of underdevelopment. In reorganising production relations, the British East India Company entered into a permanent settlement with the former *zamindars*, known as the Permanent Settlement of 1793. The salient features of the new land-tenure policy were:

(1) Permanent Settlement of the land revenue with the *zamindars*;

(2) fixation of the revenue demand at excessively high rates, only 10 per cent of which was allowed to be retained by the *zamindars*;

(3) transformation of all 'waste' land into 'Crown Land';

(4) dispossession of the *zamindars* for non-payment of revenue at a stipulated time and the sale in auction of the estate to realise the arrears.[30]

In conferring proprietary rights over land to the *zamindars*, the colonial rulers dispossessed the former land-owning *ryots* from ownership of the land and transformed them into mere tenants-at-will of their former lords. However, as the Company rulers insisted on excessive and rigid revenue demands to ensure an uninterrupted transfer of resources from the colony, the new relations of production did not generate a transformation of the existing social formation. Instead, the new relations of production remained essentially based on the old mode, and 'took their point of departure from it'.[31]

The pressure of revenue demands and the threat of eviction for non-payment encouraged the *zamindars* to create, in turn, a hierarchy of intermediate landowners and increase the rent on land by combining many illegal cesses. They used the same right against the defaulting peasants and dislodged them from the land as the Company did against the *zamindars* for defaulting on revenue payment. Thus the land-owning classes ensured their own continuity by passing on the burden of the revenue demand in the form of increased rent to the peasants, and the dispossessed peasants were made to compete for small plots of land at excessive rents for their own survival. According to one report, within the first twenty-five years of the operation of the Permanent Settlement about 45 per cent of landed property in Bengal in terms of the public revenue demand changed hands. Of this 45 per cent, not less than one-third of all genuine transfers were purchased by the members of the established landed classes. The *zamindars* and their trusty agents were closely followed by native revenue officers and traders.[32]

Commercialisation of tenurial rights introduced new forces into the agrarian class structure. The process led to an enormous increase in the number of non-cultivating interests in land. By the end of the colonial rule, there were 73,000 separate estates in Bengal (West Bengal and Bangladesh) paying revenue to the Crown.[33] Urban professionals, such as government servants, lawyers, merchants and traders, began to acquire land and perpetrated a system based on exploitation and extraction of surplus from the peasants. None of them ventured to invest in agricultural development. The cheap supply of labour from among the dispossessed peasants and intense competition amongst them to rent land on a crop-sharing basis gave plenty of scope for the land-owning classes to obtain a large profit from underdeveloped productive forces, in addition to exorbitant rent and usurious interest. Various other means of production necessary for agriculture remained at the same level as before colonial occupation. The Census of Agricultural Implements in Bengal conducted in 1940 showed that improved agricultural implements were scarcely available in Bengal. The area under artificial irrigation, whether organised or encouraged by the government, was negligible.[34]

Against this general background of stagnation, the rapid expansion of commodity production under colonial control led to the emergence of a large rural proletariat. The peasant was caught in a dual process of proletarianisation. First, his rent obligation was increasing with the expansion of rent-receiving intermediaries, and secondly, he was forced to produce commercial crops, such as indigo, much against his will. The peasant was thus made increasingly vulnerable to fluctuations in world prices of commercial crops. Under these circumstances, the peasant could ensure regular production only at the expense of his own subsistence. He had to take recourse to borrowing at an increasing rate or cut down his own consumption. According to one estimate, during the first three decades of the present century, rural indebtedness in Bengal rose to 100 crores of rupees (one crore is equal to 10 million).[35]. Thus, rack-renting and usury became the two most profitable means of investment for the rural rich, pointing ultimately to the emergence of 'antediluvian' forms of capital, rather than capital in the sphere of production. It was an inevitable outcome in the economic climate of a country subjected to imperialist exploitation.[36]

These emerging relations of production were reinforced by the destruction of indigenous industries. In order to create an international division of labour, the colonial rulers destroyed the indigenous industries, but restricted the growth of modern industrial manufacturing industries. The Bengali cotton textile industry had always existed as a challenge to the nascent British textile industry. Therefore, the prior destruction of the Bengali textile industry through determined colonial state intervention, was a pre-condition for the rise of British industry.[37] The process of destruction began with the withdrawal of the export market through the high tariff wall against imports from India. The most decisive blow, however, came from the collapse of the urban upper classes and of agriculture.[38] Whereas the urban upper classes, together with the nobility, patronised the finer quality of cloth, the poorer section of the population consumed the coarse cloth produced by the handloom weavers. The growing impoverishment of the agricultural population had an adverse effect on the traditional handloom industry.[39] As the old industries were not replaced by the establishment of new industries, the dispossessed artisans were forced into agricultural occupations as their only source of employment. The new situation aggravated the already depressed condition created by the colonial land-tenure system. The extra demand for land and employment created by the dispossessed artisans made rack-renting, usury and petty leasing all the more profitable for the land-owning classes.

In the context of colonial domination, the realisation of the necessary conditions for the development of a capitalist most of production remained incomplete. For example, a large rural proletariat was created, but these workers had to subsist on the land. They did not emerge as free labour alienated from the means of production. Similarly, generalised commodity production was imposed from outside, and the circuit of production was not completed within an integrated and balanced economy, but only by way of the linkage with the metropolitan economy, through dependence on exports and imports.[40] More importantly, however, the dominant classes which emerged in the rural area consequent to the introduction of bourgeois property relations remained parasitic on the system. They emerged more as indigenous allies of the metropolitan bourgeoisie, to facilitate both upward and outward extraction of surplus, than as an independent rural bourgeoisie in their own right.

Within this enforced reproduction of distorted capitalist relations of production, a contradiction between classes was also developing. Exorbitant rent, usurious interest and the coercion of the foreign planters to cultivate commercial crops like indigo generated conflicts among the peasants against both indigenous and foreign exploitation. During the middle of the nineteenth century, there were violent peasant uprisings throughout Bengal. In organising these revolts, the peasants not only brought into sharp contrast the contradictions of a 'deformed' capitalist mode of production, but also demonstrated their capacity to initiate changes in the structure of the society in their own interest. The indigo revolt of 1860 and the rent strike by the peasants of the districts of Pabna in 1873 exemplify the peasants' resolution to resist this system of economic exploitation.

Against this background of increasing peasant violence, the colonial government was obliged to introduce some major changes in the land-tenure system. These changes included confirmation of the proprietary right on certain categories of *ryots* and imposition of rent control. However, it will not be correct to attribute the changes in the tenurial system solely to the peasant uprisings. They nevertheless provided ostensible reasons for the colonial rulers to undermine an organisation of production developed for exploitation by the merchant's capital in the interest of the latest stage of capitalist development in Britain. Since the middle of the nineteenth century, when the country was brought directly under the rule of the Crown, the colonial regime was shifting the source of income from land revenue to greater capitalist extraction of surplus value by the subordination of the peasant economy to capital.[41] However, the process was greatly undermined by the forms of property and of production created earlier by the merchant's capital. The hierarchy of landowners created under the Permanent Settlement appropriated a greater portion of the surplus produced by the peasants. For example, in the 1940s the *ryots* and under-*ryots* paid between 120 and 200 million rupees to ensure only 26.8 million rupees to the Crown.[42] Therefore, even though industrial capital had no intention of building up its own counterpart in India, the disruptions caused earlier in the organisation of production undermined the surety of a regular supply of the necessary means of production.[43] Under these circumstances, important changes in the production relations in agriculture became absolutely essential.

These new changes in bringing the direct producer under the control of the market through the transfer of ownership and the curtailment of the *zamindars*' power over rent increases marked the beginning of a new phase in imperialist exploitation. Therefore, land legislation after the Permanent Settlement such as the Rent Acts of 1859, 1868 and 1885 sought to integrate progressively the colonial peasants to metropolitan industrial capitalism. In doing so, the new legislations did not undermine the power and position of the existing dominant classes, such as the *zamindars* and the subordinate tenurial holders called *jotedars*, as these laws ensured a regular marketable surplus through the mechanism of rent and debt. Instead, to accommodate the interest of the British indigo planters, the Rent Act of 1859 defined 'cultivator' in such a manner that non-cultivating classes continued to grow, undermining the productivity of the poor peasants. In the context of the reproduction of underdevelopment, it is worth noting that, even after the formal abolition of the *zamindari* system with the end of the colonial domination, the actual tiller of the soil is still denied access to the ownership of the means of production. 'The dichotomy between the ownership of land and the labour on it'[44] continues to pervade the rural area even today much to the detriment of agricultural development.

At the end of colonial rule, the rural class structure was characterised by the *zamindars*, and *jotedars*, the rich farmers, merchants, money-lenders, the self-sufficient *ryots*, the poor peasants, including the share-croppers (*bargadars*) and agricultural labourers.[45] After the departure of the British, the Pakistani colonial regime abolished the *zamindari* system and conferred the proprietary right to the former *ryots*. However, by failing to remove the inadequacies of the earlier Rent Acts, such as the recognition of the actual tiller as the owner of the land, the Land Reform Act of 1950 failed to remove all non-cultivating interests in land. Thus, the land reform of the Pakistani period benefited those categories of the rural population, such as the Muslim *jotedars* (large tenurial holders) and the rich peasants, who had hoped to benefit from the communal basis of creation of the state of Pakistan. Since the last days of British colonialism, Muslim peasants came to be significantly represented in the upper and the middle-category peasants in the districts of Bengal that now constitute Bangladesh, but their independent development was frustrated by the overwhelming presence of the Hindu *zamindars* and merchant money-lenders.

It was from the Muslim *jotedars* and rich peasants that a Bengali Muslim urban middle class was gradually emerging whose frustrating experiences with British and Hindu domination brought them to the fold of the Muslim League – the political party of the Indian Muslims dominated by the big landlords of the Punjab and the trading communities of north India. It was therefore not surprising that the land reform of 1950 remained limited to the legalisation of the illegal usurption of land by the Muslim *jotedars* and rich peasants from the departing Hindu *zamindars*. However, by confiscating the surplus generated by the commercial crop for the development of an industrial bourgeoisie from amongst the immigrant non-Bengali trading communities from north India, the colonial regime of Pakistan contributed to the continuity of the 'antediluvian' forms of capital (usury, rack-renting and purchase of land for petty leasing).[46]

In the post-colonial situation, therefore, the whole rural class structure has remained intact with the omission of the *zamindars*. The present rural class structure is composed of the following categories of rural population. The *jotedar*, who own land (ranging from twelve to more than fifteen acres of land), control about 16 per cent of the total cultivable land, but represent only 1.23 per cent of the rural households. They mainly live on rent from tenants and the exploitation of wage-labour. The *jotedars* extract usurious interest from money-lending and invest mainly in speculative trade and land purchase.

The *rich peasants* own between five and twelve acres of land. The total amount of land under their control is in excess of 26 per cent of the total cultivable land, but they represent only 5 per cent of the rural households. Most of the rich peasants are owner–managers and employ wage-labour. Some of them also lease out land on a crop-sharing basis to the *bargadars* (share-croppers). The rich peasants are directly involved with the market, but also indulge in money-lending. They dominate the rural areas and, through their linkage with the national power structure, misappropriate state-provided agricultural inputs.

The *upper-middle peasants* are the next category: approximately 8 per cent of the rural households belong to this category and control about 21 per cent of the total area. Their holding size varies from 3.01 acres to 5 acres of land. They are the self-sufficient owner–cultivators and are also able to produce marketable surplus. A part of their economic surplus is diverted to money-lending instead of productive investment. However, given the capitalist transformation of agriculture, they represent the potential 'kulaks' along with the rich peasants.

The *lower-middle peasant* is the category into which a little more than 7.5 per cent of the rural households belong, but they own less than 13 per cent of the total area. They own land between 2.01 acres and 3 acres. The inadequate amount of land under their control compels them to take land on a share-cropping basis and pursue petty trade. The lower-middle peasants are the potential victims of the capitalist transformation of agriculture, since they are unable to cope with the operation of the market forces. After the poor peasants, they are the largest sellers of land in Bangladesh. Therefore, in the event of a struggle between classes the lower-middle peasants tend to side with the poor and the landless peasants.

The *poor peasant* is the category into which the largest number of rural households belong; about 45 per cent of the rural households in Bangladesh are poor peasants. Only 25 per cent of the total area of land belongs to the poor peasants, whose size of holding varies from 0.01 acres to 2 acres of land. Most of the poor peasants take to share-cropping and also hire themselves out as wage-labourers. They are chronically indebted to the rural money-lenders and are therefore subjected to oppression and exploitation by rural upper classes.

The *landless workers* inevitably do not own any land. About 33 per cent of the rural households in Bangladesh are absolutely landless; they earn their livelihood as agricultural workers. The fortunate few amongst the landless population who own some other means of production, such as a pair of bullocks or a plough, also share-crop land. The average income of an agricultural worker is *Taka* 9.00 only,[47] which is barely adequate for the reproduction of labour, let alone the maintenance of a family of four.[48]

The process of pauperisation and polarisation, which followed from the increasing involvement with the market forces in the post-colonial situation, resulted in significant variations in the size of the classes. Following Lenin, we observe a process of 'depeasantising' in rural Bangladesh, where the relationship between the two classes placed at extreme points is polarised and the self-sufficient independent middle peasants face the prospect of disintegration. The Land Occupancy Survey of 1977 clearly indicates the extent of differentiation and polarisation of relations between classes. According to this survey, 10 per cent of rural households own half the country's cultivable land; the other 50 per cent of the cultivable land is shared between 60 per cent of the rural households; and a third of the rural households own no land at all. However, the survey concludes that for all practical purposes a little less than half of the rural households are landless in Bangladesh.[49] Various development projects of the post-colonial government, such as agricultural co-operatives, village government and the introduction of modern technology, have reinforced the existing class distinction.

Thus Bangladesh is not an exception to the general process of poverty and underdevelopment experienced in other Third World countries. In all these countries, the process of capitalist development under colonial and neo-colonial conditions has generated class differentiation and engendered class conflict by deepening impoverishment. What, however, distinguishes Bangladesh is the increasing poverty of 80 per cent of its population and the accumulation of wealth by the rich, despite the fall in the average national income.[50] The accumulation of wealth by such a miniscule stratum can hardly be justified in terms of the wealth generated by the country as a whole. The country's narrow industrial base and the virtual absence of an internal market cannot justify the increasing wealth of the Bengali upper classes. The manufacturing sector of the country's economy contributes only 10 per cent of the gross domestic product. Moreover, most of the heavy industry (shipbuilding, iron and steel, and the petro-chemical industry) is owned by the state. Under these circumstances, the accumulation of wealth by the miniscule upper classes can only be explained either in terms of the expansion of trade and commercial activities or the persistence of such dubious activities as smuggling, black marketing, hoarding and bribery. In both cases, the process of capital accumulation implies a specific situation where an underdeveloped bourgeoisie is enmeshed in a neo-colonial metropolitan economy. This specific form of relationship illustrates the various levels of integration of the local interests with foreign capital, such as incorporation of local personnel into executive jobs in foreign firms, the financing of local politicians and the provision of custom and agencies for local businessmen.[51] In view of its inherent weakness, the Bengali bourgeoisie is incapable of performing the role expected of it in the country's capitalist development.

Meanwhile, the Bengali *petite bourgeoisie*, who represent the majority of the urban population, abdicated any pretension to a revolutionary role and remained parasitic on the political system. The fact that the *petit-bourgeois* party, the Bangladesh Awami League, was in power facilitiated the 'primitive capital accumulation' by *petite bourgeoisie*. Such a parasitic existence was made all the more desirable since, by nationalising private enterprises, the state enhanced its capacity to distribute patronage.[52] The rural origin of the *petite bourgeoisie* contributed to the strengthening of the ties between the rich and the upper-middle peasants, who, by taking advantage of the rural-development policies of the post-colonial government, stabilised their class position in the rural area. The *petit-bourgeois* elements developed a vested interest in the maintenance of the status quo.

The great majority of the poor peasants and workers are locked in a constant battle for survival. The political situation is extremely tense in the rural area, where, with the intensification of the process of capital accumulation, the poor and marginal peasants are increasingly proletarianised. Increasing poverty generates social tension and discontent in the rural areas. To suppress the growing discontent that arises from the intensification of the process of pauperisation and polarisation, the state augments its repressive power, but ignores the causes of poverty and underdevelopment. In fact, the existing state structure is incapable of resolving the problems of poverty, since the causes lie within the existing relations of production and the underdevelopment of the productive forces. The changes in the existing relations of production would be tantamount to changes in the nature of the state. The whole process will seriously undermine the very basis of the classes whose alliance supports the state.

Meanwhile, growing impoverishment generates tension and intensifies class conflicts, but fails to contribute to the solidarity of the masses against exploitation and domination. The extreme poverty inhibits the growth of an organisational unity, as the rural proletariat competes for scarce commodities like land or employment. Under these circumstances, the struggles remain localised and ephemeral. This will continue to be the nature of the class struggle in Bangladesh so long as these classes are not transformed from 'classes-in-themselves' to 'classes-for-themselves'.

In order to examine the impact of colonialism on the social structure of Egypt, in comparison with Bangladesh, it is important to have some general understanding of the development of landownership in the Middle East after the Arab conquests of the seventh century. Pre-colonial land rights were in fact complex.[53] The Arabic conquests of Egypt, North Africa,

Spain, Syria and Iraq took place principally between 632 and 750 in the context of the decline of the Byzantine and Sassanid empires. The early period of Islam was dominated by two great dynasties – the Umayyads (661–750) and the Abbasids (754–945). In 1258 Baghdad was occupied by the Mongols, bringing the Buwayhid dynasty to a close. From that time onwards, Islamdom was characterised by a series of imperial states which never exercised total hegemony over the cultural Islamic region. The three great empires of the later period were the Safavi empire (Shiah) (1503–1722), the Indian Timuri empire (1526–1707) and the Ottoman empire (1517–1718). Of these, the Ottoman empire is of particular interest, since its land system provided the context for the apparent revolution brought about by capitalist colonialism in the Middle East.

Initially, the Muslim conquest did not involve a radical restructuring of the conquered society; it involved, so to speak, the insertion of a thin layer of foreign political/ideological hegemony over the existing ruling class, which was partly conserved. This also had its impact on land control, giving rise to a classic distinction between *mulk* and *miri* land tenure. *Mulk* tenure involved absolute ownership, but was normally confined to houses and land in towns. *Mulk* conferred two rights: (i) *racaba* or absolute ownership, and (ii) *tasarruf* or the right of usufruct. All other land was *miri* land, that is, the formal property of the state as the spoils of war. In practice, the distinction between these two types of ownership did not amount to much, since the new rulers were not necessarily interested in the cultivation of this land, which was left in the possession of its original owners. The state's right of ownership meant the right to tax its effective owners or to extract labour from them. It did not involve control over the use of land.

There are three other distinctions in the nature of land rights which have to be considered. First, there was *waqf* land, which was property dedicated to some pious purpose. This form of land possession was relatively free from secular interference by the state, since it was protected by holy law. Secondly, there was *matruka* land. This was not an important category in terms of the extent of *matruka* ownership. It referred to land reserved for some public purpose, such as a village threshing floor. Thirdly, there was *mawat* land, which was simply an area of unreclaimed land. Anyone who brought *mawat* land under cultivation could acquire *miri* ownership, that is, the right of usufructuary possession. Although these distinctions have a formal significance, in practice the distinction between them became unimportant. The right of *tasarruf* became equivalent to full ownership, that is, the right of sale, inheritance and mortgage. The state retained the conditional right that *miri* land left uncultivated could be resumed by the state.

There was a rudimentary class structure corresponding to these forms of land control and possession. Throughout the Middle East, there developed an Arab ruling class of governors and military leaders, which remained distinct from the local ruling élite. There was also a class of persons with client status (*mawali*) or newly converted Muslims who formally had equality of rights with their Arab co-religionists, but who were, in practice, second-class citizens. This class played a significant part in social protest against their Arab overlords, particularly in opposition to the Umayyads. Furthermore, there were the so-called *millets*, who were protected minorities such as Jews and Christians (the 'People of the Book'). These minorities were an important source of taxation, especially for the poll tax. There was also a substantial class of slaves employed in domestic and public service. Under certain conditions, such as those that existed in Ottoman times, slaves represented an important component of the administrative and military wing of the dominant class. This fact bears out the observations of recent analyses of slavery that it refers to a form of property right rather than to personal subordination.[54] Finally, nomadic pastoralism remained a form of subsistence, largely outside the control of the centralised state.

Anthropologists normally distinguish between three basic types of nomadism. These are true nomadism (camel husbandry), semi-nomadism (sheep and goat husbandry, normally coupled with some form of temporary land cultivation) and transhumance – the seasonal shifting of whole villages around a determinant pastural region. True nomadism is characteristic of Saudi Arabia; semi-nomadism in the Fertile Crescent; transhumance, Morocco. The nomads existed on the fringe of governed, settled, agricultural communities. When the central state is strong, the nomads are brought within the sphere of taxation. When it is weak, they normally take over the state. The relationship between settled/nomadic society was obviously very fluid. Nomads who managed to accumulate enough wealth often became sedentary cultivators.[55] Nomads themselves were differentiated into 'classes'. Tribal sheikhs often owned fertile tracts of land, palm-tree groves and sometimes whole oases. These lands were cultivated by the sheikh's Negro slaves, emancipated slaves, tenant *fellahin* or the poorer members of nomadic tribes. Such property could either be the personal property of individual sheikhs or it might be regarded as communal tribal property. In the latter case, effective control remained in the hands of the sheikhs. In addition to sedentarisation, there is 'bedouinisation', that is, the unsettling of cultivators under severe economic pressure (such as repressive taxation). When whole tribes settled, they created a land-tenure system known as the *Musha*.

In order to understand the background to land reform in colonial Egypt, it is important to understand the social structure of the Ottoman Middle East. First, the state bureaucracy was controlled by the imperial household and the higher strata of the royal administrative class, forming a typical patrimonial bureaucracy. Secondly, there were the feudal *sipahi* who traditionally formed a noble cavalry. The *sipahis* received a benefice for military service. Weber distinguishes between the European fief and the Islamic benefice (which he sometimes called prebendal feudalism), by claiming that the benefice was a lifelong, not hereditary, remuneration for its holder in exchange for his real or presumed services; the remuneration is an attribute of the office, not of the incumbent. These fiefs which supported the *sipahi* were called Timar or Ziamet. *Sipahi* farmed their own estates and collected taxes from the peasantry. *Sipahi* were not a particularly mobile or efficient force, since it was difficult to keep them on long military campaigns; they had strong economic reasons for wishing to return to or stay on their estates. The sultan came to rely more on his Janissary troops (*Yeni-ceris* or New Troops).

The Ottoman empire secured slaves in Europe by what is called the *devsirme* conscription. Young boys recruited by this means were either allocated to the royal household as 'pages' (in fact senior 'civil servants') – these were the Ic Oglans. The others, Acemi Oglans, went into the imperial slave army, the Janissaries. These slave troops were prohibited from engaging in trade or any craft. They were deprived of family or kinship connection. The Janissaries and household slaves were by no means powerless – they performed key functions of government; they dominated the army. When the imperial household was unable to pay off its troops because of financial crises, the Janissaries promptly took over political control, nominating their own provincial governors. The Janissary troops were eventually destroyed in 1826. It is surely not possible in this situation to talk of an overlap between state functionaries and the ruling class or that the state machine and the ruling class are coterminous. The *sipahi* look like a prebendal feudal ruling class, often in opposition to the paradoxical ruling/slave class.

In the seventeenth century there was a profound crisis within the Ottoman empire. At the same time, the *sipahi* went into decline. When a *sipahi* died, his lands were appropriated by the state and let out to tax-farmers. A decree of 1692 created the life farm (*malikane*) which was in practice a private property that could be bought and sold and transferred to heirs in return for a fee to the state. In 1831, the *timars* were taken over completely by the state. These were then farmed out to *multezin*. In practice, this was not state (*miri*) land, since the tax-farmer came to enjoy what was equivalent to freehold possession (*mulk*). This situation gave rise to powerful *derebeys*, who had virtual control of the countryside. It led to much greater exploitation of the peasantry than had been the case under the *timar* system. The nineteenth century was the great epoch of the *eskiya* in protest against the new exploiting class of tax-farmers turned landlord.

In the period of Ottoman reform, an attempt was made to improve the situation of land tenure. The land code recognised five types of land (that is, the system we have already referred to – *mulk, miri, waqf, matruka, mawat*). This looks curious at first, since we have already seen that the distinction between *miri* and *mulk* is not especially significant. The real point of these formal categories was to tax every piece of land and to establish the title to it by registering its legal owner. The state's claim to ownership meant that the state did not recognise ownership without a title of registration. Politically, the intention was to centralise the power of the administration against the feudal or tribal forms of existence.

As tribes settled on the land, they allotted the arable land to clans on an equal basis. To maintain equality between tribes and their members, the land was periodically re-allotted between tribal subgroups and their members (the *Musha* or shared system). The *Musha* system represents a transition stage between the communal property of the semi-nomadic tribe and the completely divided property of the more settled zones (such as those along the coastal region of the Fertile Crescent). The *Musha* quota can be sold. As the original families or tribal groups broke up into individual households and shares were subdivided by inheritance, inequality arose and shares held by individual cultivators varied considerably.

The land law of 1858 was an attempt to destroy the *Musha* system by introducing registration of divided private ownership. The villagers apparently feared that the new system of registration was the first move in enforcing a new exploitative set of taxes or military conscription, and they falsified their returns. In practice, they disregarded the new ownership titles and continued to farm the old *Musha* system. The result was complete confusion at the village level between legal ownership and customary ownership.

In the nineteenth century there were various attempts both in Turkey and Egypt to bring about social reforms and changes in the nature of landownership. Muhammad Ali (1805–49) sought to transform the Egyptian social structure in a number of important directions. In particular, tax-farming was abolished and peasants paid their taxes direct to the state. Many large estates were granted to relatives or followers of Muhammad Ali. Communal ownership was replaced by one in which peasants enjoyed *de facto* rights of ownership. New irrigation works greatly extended the area of land under cultivation. Planting of long staple cotton was started on a commercial scale in 1821. The amount of cotton exported to Europe doubled between 1824 and 1845. Communications (mainly shipping facilities) were developed to cope with the new export drive. A new system of monopoly was created whereby Muhammad Ali bought crops from farmers at low fixed prices and resold them to foreign exporters at great profits. Land became a commodity. In 1858 collective responsibility for land taxes was abolished. The right of inheritance of men and women was fully affirmed, along with the right to sell or mortgage land. Foreigners were authorised to purchase land. Vast areas of cotton-producing land fell under foreign control. Foreign investment found its way into the big banks, property, industry. Egypt was fully integrated into the external requirements of the world market.

Although Marx's views of the stationary nature of property ownership were empirically unreliable in relation to many Oriental societies, they do have some bearing on the analysis of traditional Egyptian social structure. Although Egypt had a long succession of ruling classes – Pharaohs, Arabs, Mamelukes – it was not until Napoleon's expedition in 1798–1801 and British occupation in 1882 that private property rights in land began to emerge.[56] Before British occupation,[57] it was not uncommon for individual members of the ruling class to gain *de facto* rights to land (including rights of transfer and inheritance), but these rights were recoverable by the state, which retained centralised ownership of land. The exploitation of the peasantry occurred through a variety of mechanisms – tribute, *corvée* or cash. It was the village rather than the individual peasant that was the unit of taxation, and land was allocated on a village rather than individual basis. Under Ottoman rule, the state raised money through a system based on *iltizam* or tax-farming.[58] Under these arrangements, the *multazamin* were obliged to raise a certain level of taxation from districts allocated to them by the state. As Weber recognised, this system was precarious because, in periods when the state was relatively weak, the tax-farmers acquired considerable political autonomy and were able to redirect tax funds into their own pockets.[59] During the French occupation, Napoleon set about breaking the power of the *multazamin* by creating peasant rights to the land, but it was under the land reforms of Muhammad Ali that the *fellahin* were given usufruct rights. At the same time, these reforms created a land-owning class, recruited from Turco-Egyptian state officials, who acquired vast family estates. British occupation completed the process whereby the land came under the control of an agrarian capitalist class producing a cash-crop (raw cotton) for the market on the basis of wage-labour.

The position of the *fellahin* in nineteenth-century Egypt was particularly precarious. The amount of available land was limited by the availability of water, and invididual plots were continuously reduced by inheritance and indebtedness. While the *corvée* was replaced by wage-labour, there was insufficient demand from either agriculture or industry to guarantee anything but seasonal employment. While there was a considerable increase in land cultivation in the late nineteenth and early twentieth century, this improvement never kept pace with population increase. Given these economic constraints, the *fellahin* were increasingly forced to rent or sharecrop additional plots of land or to lease their own land in the hope of finding additional employment. The plight of the peasantry has to be seen in the context of Egypt's location within the world economy. From 1870 onwards, there was a marked downward trend in world prices for cotton. At the same time, repayment of debts drained Egypt of any surplus for reinvestment. In these conditions, the agrarian capitalist class adhered to traditional attitudes towards economic growth, remaining content with existing profits from exports. Cheap labour was a disincentive with regard to technical improvements. Eventually, cotton cultivation for export accounted for one-third of the available land; the production of wheat correspondingly declined. With the growth of commodity production, the previous system of village control of production and communal cultivation was replaced by private ownership of land and a shift in emphasis towards the nuclear family as the major production/consumption unit. There was a corresponding growth in the number of large estates combined with growing peasant poverty and fragmentation of peasant land to pay off mortgages and other debts. Moneylending and peasant exploitation of small plots of land had the effect of limiting the development of full-scale capitalism, permitting a continuation of the old tribute system. Foreign investments went simply to extend land for cotton cultivation, not to develop an industrial base in Egypt.

British textile interests encouraged the development of textile-cotton production, not industrialisation, and Egyptian merchants were mainly interested in import–export control. Similarly, Egyptian landlords wanted irrigation development, not industrial development. Various British governments blocked the development of Egyptian industry, where this threatened British interests. Much has been written of the 'stunting effect' of capitalism in the periphery. Although Marx and Engels thought that British capitalism would inevitably develop the periphery, they had a 'minority view' that, as in Ireland, foreign investment could hold up industrialisation. The majority of writers hold this view with respect to Egypt – for example, Baran, Amin, and Frank.[60] A different position is taken by Clawson.[61] With the growing dominance of finance capital in Europe in the 1930s, there was more investment in Egypt to create local industry; the Egyptian industrial sector thus came under very heavy control of foreign companies. Since the local manufacturing industry had been knocked out by foreign imports, the only source of skill and investment was from overseas. With the decline in cotton prices, attempts to build up local industry were, however, hampered by foreign-exchange problems and inequality in import/export balance of payments. Nevertheless, Egypt shifted towards a policy of import-substitution industrialisation before the Second World War.

The growth of nationalist politics strongly supported a policy against foreign domination of the industrial sector. The development of nationalism split the dominant class between the traditional agrarian capitalist and the new alliance of state officials and industrial bourgeoisie. Since traditional forms of land cultivation, production and ownership were backward looking, it became clear that land reform was a necessary step towards capitalist industrialisation, if peasants were to be converted into full wage-labourers. The land reforms of 1952 created a system of state capitalism in which political and economic control of the *fellahin* was achieved by the agents in charge of the village co-operatives. There has been much debate about the socialist character of Nasser's Egypt.[62] In general, Nasser's revolution had the effect of removing the top stratum of the bureaucracy, which was replaced by officials from the petty bourgeoisie, and of removing the top sections of the land-owning class. Although the very large estates have disappeared, the middle class (15–20 *feddans*) and the upper-middle class (20–100 *feddans*) were not seriously influenced by land reform. Many landowners avoided expropriation by redistributing their land among relatives. These reforms appear to have benefited a relatively small section (approximately 8 per cent) of the *fellahin*, but have done very little for the landless and uprooted peasant. The system of supervised co-operatives may have increased production, but they have also extended government control of village life. Nasser's reforms did not solve Egypt's traditional problems; indebtedness and dependence on foreign finance increased considerably, and the trade deficit reached staggering proportions in the 1970s. The attempt by President Sadat to reduce dependence on state-directed industrialisation through an 'open-door' policy increased production and consumption of consumer goods and luxuries, but did not stimulate basic industries or increase agricultural productivity.[63]

Both Bangladesh and Egypt have been transformed by a long process of capitalist penetration and incorporation into the global capitalist economy, but their dependence on this external economic order has produced an internal situation of social and economic stagnation. Capitalist incorporation created an agrarian capitalist class which was rewarded by the export of raw materials, but this class did not fulfil a progressive social role because there was little incentive to invest in industrial forces of production.

In both societies, as a result of changes in the nature of land rights, the peasants were largely dispossessed and were converted into landless wage-labourers. However, in the absence of industrial employment, they have experienced increasing pauperisation without developing any coherent class consciousness in respect to their social alienation. Periodic peasant uprisings have remained local and episodic; peasant alliances with urban workers have been fragile and transitory. Peasants in both societies also find themselves opposed by an extensive militarised state and an army, which has inherited the apparatus of the old colonial powers. The peasantry is thus caught in a vicious circle of poverty, in societies which are potentially rich in natural resources. The explanation of their dilemma, as we have sought to demonstrate, is to be found in the complex interaction of internal class relationships and the external constraints of global capitalism. The effect of the dynamic of internal and external structures is to reproduce a situation of social stagnation, political repression and economic underdevelopment.

Notes

1 Hamza Alavi, 'India and the colonial mode of production', in *Socialist Register*, London, 1975, p. 176.
2 Irfan Habib, 'Problems of Marxist historical analysis in India', in S. A. Shah (ed.), *Towards National Liberation: Essays on Political Economy of India*, Montreal, Canada, 1973, p. 9.
3 M. S. Islam, 'Permanent settlement and the landed interest in Bengal, 1793–1819', unpublished Ph.D. thesis, School of Oriental and African Studies, London, 1972, p. 113.
4 Anjali Chatterjee, *Bengal in the Reign of Aurangzib*, Calcutta, 1967, p. 254.
5 P. B. Calkins, 'Stability and change in landholding and revenue systems in Bengal', in R. D. Stevens, H. Alavi and P. J. Bertocci (eds), *Rural Development in Bangladesh and Pakistan*, Honolulu, Hawaii, 1976, pp. 12–13.
6 ibid., p. 23.
7 Chatterjee, *Bengal in the Reign of Aurangzib*.
8 ibid.
9 B. R. Grover, 'Nature of land-rights in Mughal India', in *The Indian Economic and Social History Review*, vol. 1, no. 1 (1963), pp. 1–23.
10 B. B. Chaudhuri, 'Agrarian economy and agrarian relations in Bengal, 1859–1885', unpublished Ph.D. thesis, Oxford University, Oxford, 1968, p. 257.
11 I. Habib, *The Agrarian System of Mughal India (1556–1707)*, London, 1963, p. 115.
12 K. Currie, 'Problematic modes and the Mughal social formation', University of Lancaster (mimeo), 1979, p. 13.
13 H. Alavi, 'India and the colonial mode of production', *Socialist Register*, London, 1975, p. 186.
14 W. C. Smith, 'Lower-class uprisings in the Mughal empire', *Islamic Culture* (January 1946), p. 24.
15 E. J. Hobsbawm, 'Social bandits: a reply', in *Comparative Studies in Society and History*, vol. 14, no. 4 (September 1972).
16 I. Habib, *The Agrarian System of Mughal India*, p. 117.
17 M. Martin, *The History, Antiquities, Topography and Statistics of Eastern India*, London, 1838, pp. 710–11.
18 A. Chatterjee, *Bengal in the Reign of Aurangzib*, pp. 94–5.
19 T. Raychaudhuri, 'The agrarian system of Mughal India', in *Enquiry*, n.s. vol. 2, no. 1 (Spring 1965), p. 117.
20 Rajat Ray and Ratna Ray, 'The dynamics of continuity in rural Bengal

under the British imperialism: a study of quasi-stable equilibrium in underdeveloped societies in a changing world', in *The Indian Economic and Social History Review*, vol. X, no. 2 (June 1973), p. 112.
21 Raychaudhuri, 'The agrarian system of Mughal India', p. 119.
22 H. R. Ghosal, 'Changes in the organization of industrial production in the Bengal presidency in the early nineteenth century', in B. N. Ganguli (ed.), *Readings in Indian Economic History*, London, 1964.
23 T. Raychaudhuri, 'European commercial activity and the organization of India's commerce and industrial production', in B. N. Ganguli (ed.), *Readings in Indian Economic History*, London, 1964, p. 72.
24 Habib, *The Agrarian System of Mughal India*, p. 112.
25 ibid., p. 119.
26 Ernest Mandel, Introduction to *Capital*, Vol. I, Harmondsworth, 1976, pp. 14–15.
27 Irfan Habib, 'Potentialities of capitalistic development in the economy of Mughal India', in *Journal of Economic History*, vol. 29, no. 1 (1969), pp. 77–8.
28 S. C. Jha, *Studies in the Development of Capitalism in India*, New Delhi, 1963, pp. 36–8.
29 W. W. Hunter, *The Annals of Rural Bengal*, London, 1868, pp. 20–34.
30 N. K. Sinha, *The Economic History of Bengal*, Vol. II, Calcutta, 1962, pp. 147–81.
31 Utsa Patnaik, 'On the mode of production in Indian agriculture – a reply', in *Economic and Political Weekly* (Review of Agriculture), vol. VII, no. 40 (September 1972), p. A–146.
32 Islam, 'Permanent Settlement and the Landed Interest in Bengal, 1793–1819', p. 237.
33 J. F. Stepanek, *Bangladesh – Equitable Growth?*, New York, 1979, p. 94.
34 R. K. Mukherjee, 'Economic structure of rural Bengal', in *American Sociological Review*, vol. 13 (1948), p. 660.
35 M. M. Islam, *Bengal Agriculture, 1920–1946: A Quantitative Study*, Cambridge, 1972, p. 115.
36 Patnaik, 'On the mode of production in Indian agriculture', p. A–146.
37 Hamza Alavi, 'The colonial transformation in India', in *Journal of Social Studies*, no. 8 (April 1980), p. 46.
38 A. Maddison, *Class Structure and Economic Growth, India and Pakistan since the Moghols*, London, 1971, pp. 54–5.
39 D. R. Gadgil, *The Industrial Evolution of India in Recent Times*, London, 1954, p. 99.
40 Alavi, 'The colonial transformation in India', p. 61.
41 ibid, p. 60.
42 Stepanek, *Bangladesh – Equitable Growth?*, p. 93.

43 Geoffrey Kay, *Development and Underdevelopment: A Marxist Analysis*, London, 1975, p. 100.
44 F.T. Jannuzi and J.T. Peach, *Report on the Hierarchy of Interests in Land in Bangladesh*, The United States Agency for International Development (USAID), Washington, 1977.
45 R.K. Mukherjee, *The Dynamics of a Rural Society: A Study of the Economic Structure in Bengal Villages*, Berlin, 1957.
46 G.D. Wood, 'The nature of rural class differentiation in Bangladesh', Paper presented at the Peasants Seminar held at the Centre of International and Area Studies, Unversity of London, 1977.
47 *Taka* is the unit of Bangladesh's currency. Officially, 41 *takas* are equivalent to one pound (sterling).
48 Data regarding the size of holding, percentage of the total area and percentage of households are taken from the Land Occupancy Survey of 1977. For details see, Jannuzi and Peach, *Report on the Hierarchy of Interests in Land in Bangladesh.*
49 ibid.
50 K. Griffin and A. R. Khan, 'Poverty in the Third World: ugly facts and fancy models', in *World Development*, vol. 6, no. 3, 1978, p. 299.
51 C. Leys, *Underdevelopment in Kenya: The Political Economy of Neo-Colonialism*, London, 1978, p. 17.
52 M. Hossain, 'Nature of state power in Bangladesh', in *Journal of Social Studies*, no. 5 (October 1979), Dacca, Bangladesh, p. 28.
53 D. Warriner, *Land and Poverty in the Middle East*, London, 1962; and D. Warriner, *Land Reform and Development in the Middle East*, London, 1962.
54 B. Hindess and P.Q. Hirst, *Pre-Capitalist Modes of Production*, London, 1975.
55 F. Barth, *The Nomads of South Persia*, Oslo, 1964.
56 N. Tomiche, *L'Egypte Moderne*, Paris, 1966; X. Yacono, *Histoire de la colonisation francaise*, Paris, 1969.
57 P. Mansfield, *The Ottoman Empire and its Successors*, London, 1973.
58 B. Lewis, *The Emergence of Modern Turkey*, Oxford, 1961.
59 M. Weber, *Economy and Society*, Berkeley, 1978, Vol. 2.
60 For a critical review of recent writing on Egypt, see E. Davis, 'Political development or political economy? Political theory and the study of social change in Egypt and the Third World', *Review of Middle East Studies*, vol. 1 (1975), pp. 41–61.
61 P. Clawson, 'The development of capitalism in Egypt', *Khamsin*, vol. 9 (1981), pp. 41–61.
62 A. Abdel-Malek, *Egypt, Military Society*, New York, 1968; P. Mansfield, *Nasser's Egypt*, Penguin, Harmondsworth, 1969; R.

Stephens, *Nasser*, London, 1971; P.J. Vatikiotis, *Egypt since the Revolution*, London, 1968.

63 M.-C. Aulas, 'Sadat's Egypt', *New Left Review*, no. 98 (1976), pp. 84–97.

11 Social Structure of Middle East Societies

The texts of classical Marxism do not provide a substantial guide to the analysis of Middle East societies. The work of Marx and Engels on this region was slight and can be considered briefly under two headings – Asiatic society and Islam. In early Marxism, 'Asiatic society' had a problematic status. The specificity of Asiatic society and the Asiatic mode of production meant that the teleological assumptions of the conventional list of historical transitions (slave, feudal, capitalist and socialism) did not obtain. However, accepting the theoretical validity of the Asiatic mode led Marxists into accepting the privileged position of Occidental over Oriental history. The contrast of a dynamic West and a stagnant East meant that it was difficult to separate Marxist categories from the theory of Oriental Despotism in political philosophy. Furthermore, the implication of the Asiatic mode was that social change had to be located in exogenous causes, specifically in western imperialism and colonialism.

As we have seen, Marx and Engels based their original analysis of Asiatic society in 1853 on the works of James Mill, François Bernier and Richard Jones.[1] On the basis of these studies, Marx and Engels claimed that the key to Asiatic society was the absence of private property and the dominance of the state over civil society in the supervision of public works. It has, however, proved difficult to sustain the argument that private ownership of property in Asia was unknown prior to British colonial legislation. The great majority of Islamic societies, for example, had a complex system of landownership before colonialism; the land system included tribal land, land associated with the royal household, prebendal land and property enjoyed by individuals as legal owners. Contemporary historical research into pre-colonial India has shown the existence of a hierarchy of land rights in which peasants had private and continuous individual ownership of small plots of land.[2] Class relations were not simply a creation of British land registration. Marx and Engels came, however, to emphasise a rather different set of features of Asiatic society in their later commentaries on India and China. The crucial feature of Asiatic stagnation was the self-sufficiency of village life. These self-sufficing villages persistently reproduced themselves without any change in their social form. Under these conditions, the towns dominated the countryside, while the despotic state ruled over a stationary civil society.

Although there has been considerable debate over the main features of Asiatic society, the point of Marx's analysis was to identify the stationariness of Asia and, by contrast, to specify those features of European society which were conducive to the development of the capitalist economy in the West. Despite the evolution of the concept of the Asiatic mode in Marx's own theory of social change, Marx never abandoned the assumption about Oriental stagnation. The ambiguity of the concept in Marx continues to be reflected in Marxist debate. Although Engels abandoned the notion of the Asiatic mode representing a distinct historical epoch in *The Origin of the Family, Private Property and the State* in 1884, the problem of the specificity of Asia came back into political debate in the context of revolutionary Russia. While Marx and Engels had referred to tsarist Russia as 'semi-Asiatic' in 1853, Engels elaborated the idea of the isolated Russian commune as the basis of Oriental Despotism in *Anti-Duhring* in 1877. While the Russian populists attempted to argue that the Russian commune was one possible basis for socialist developments, Plekhanov affirmed the idea that the commune tended to coincide with political absolutism. Eventually, the relevance of the Asiatic mode was rejected by the Leningrad conference of 1931 and this position was reinforced by Stalin, who committed orthodox communism to a unilinear view of history. Pre-capitalist societies in Asia were now seen as unambiguously feudal.

In the post-war period, the analysis of Asiatic societies was focused on arguments relating to Karl Wittfogel's *Oriental Despotism*.[3] Wittfogel was primarily concerned with China and took much of the theoretical inspiration for his work from Max Weber's study of patrimonial bureaucracy. Wittfogel's study of hydraulic society was concerned with the issue of whether it was possible to have a dominant class which did not necessarily own the means of production, but exercised crucial political and administrative functions. The polemical importance of *Oriental Despotism* was the suggestion that the Communist leadership had suppressed the theory of the Asiatic mode, because it implied that the centralisation of power and administration in Russia had preserved the essential features of despotic power. However, although the concept of feudalism has been criticised for being too imprecise in relation to Asia, Wittfogel's 'hydraulic society' is equally vague and general. For example, Wittfogel included a great variety of societies – tsarist Russia, China, Egypt, Islamic Spain and Persia – under the same heading. Wittfogel's theory of centralised hydraulic empires was not free from problems relating to technological determinism. There are additional theoretical problems relating to Wittfogel's analysis of the state and social classes.[4] Although the concept of the Asiatic mode of production did not play a central part in the development of Marxist theories of dependency and unequal exchange in the 1970s, the implications of the concept for political practice and theoretical development in Marxism have never been entirely resolved.[5]

Although Marx and Engels made few systematic statements about comparative religion, Engels's commentaries on religion are of some interest. Engels noted that any analysis of Islam would have to be concerned with the peculiar oscillation between nomadic and sedentarised cultures, because Islam was a religion well adapted to both Arab townsmen and nomadic Bedouin:

> Therein lies, however, the embryo of a periodically recurring collision. The townspeople grow rich, luxurious and lax in the observation of the 'law'. The Bedouins, poor and hence of strict morals, contemplate with envy and covetousness these riches and pleasures.[6]

Periodically the nomadic tribes unite behind a Mahdi to remove the corrupt culture of the towns and to restore the true religion. One dynamic political process of pre-capitalist Islamic societies was therefore the struggle between the towns and the tribal confederations. Engels's analysis of Islam is almost wholly cribbed from Ibn Khaldun and, before examining contemporary Marxist views of the social structure of the Middle East, it is worth pausing to examine in more detail Ibn Khaldun's classical perspective on Arabic society.

Ibn Khaldun (1332—1406) is often identified as a founding father of sociology.[7] The central feature of his social theory is the explanation of social co-operation and conflict. Because people as individuals cannot achieve self-sufficiency, they need to specialise at certain tasks, exchange goods and create a division of labour:

> differences of condition among people are the result of the different ways in which they make their living. Social organization enables them to co-operate toward that end and to start with the simple necessities of life, before they get to conveniences and luxuries.[8]

The two principal environments within which social organisation takes place are 'desert, desert life' and 'town, sedentary environment'. The Bedouin, because of their dependence on camel herding, were not able to sustain a settled or cultivated life. The Bedouin, however, possess a powerful 'group feeling' (*asabiyya*), which is important in helping nomads to face the harshness of desert conditions. Urban dwellers, on the other hand, lack *asabiyya* and have to depend on law, specialised troops and fortifications to maintain social order. *Asabiyya* has three components – kinship ties, companionship and religion. Genuine *asabiyya*, based on Islam, is the source of social superiority, authority and leadership. For Ibn Khaldun, then, Islam provides the main basis of social cement in human societies threatened by human passions and social conflicts. The nomads, despite their superior social solidarity, need the cities in order to supply certain necessities. The relationship between settled and sedentary peoples was thus complex. When the political unity of the towns collapsed, the nomadic hinterland was able to assert its military dominance. When urban life was relatively coherent, the economic dominance of towns over desert ensured the political hegemony of the urban merchants and political élites. Any analysis of the Middle East from a historical perspective cannot, therefore, simply rest on a set of notions derived from the traditional concepts of the Asiatic mode; it will have to take into account the importance of nomadic pastoralism in relation to sedentarised communities.[9]

There are important regional differences within the Middle East which much conventional analysis has ignored by accepting over-generalised notions about Oriental, Asiatic or Islamic society. In particular, it is necessary to distinguish between the social structures of the Maghreb (the Arabic societies west of the Nile), the Mashraq (greater Syria, Arabia and Iraq), and finally Egypt itself. The importance of this distinction is that it was only in the Nile valley that a ruling class existed on the basis of an economic surplus extracted from peasant cultivators. The dominant classes of the Maghreb and the Mashraq were mercantile and urban, securing their surplus from adjacent societies through the medium of international trade. It was this merchant culture which dominated the court life, piety and social relations and it is this centrality of intercontinental trade which is the key to the class structure of classical Arabic society.[10] This analysis of the 'tributary mode of production' has been closely associated with the study of the pre-colonial Arab world and with the characteristics of peripheral capitalist social formations by Samir Amin.[11]

In Roman times, the trade routes that crossed the Middle East played an important part in the economy of the classical world, giving rise to major trading stations in Arabia, such as Mecca. With the rapid expansion of Islam in the seventh and eighth centuries, a large trading area was created among societies linked together by language, religion and culture. Although Weber argued that the bearers of the new faith were warriors, the real integration of Arabic culture was brought about by merchants involved in intercontinental trade. With this expansion of trade, Tripoli, Alexandria, Aleppo and Baghdad became the great entrepôts of world trade.[12] During this period of economic growth, the Muslim courts became great centres of learning, science and poetry. A refined culture of the élite (the *adib* culture) developed amongst the administrative class, but was eagerly acquired by prosperous merchants who became great patrons of scientists and intellectuals.[13] When the main centres of this *adib* culture declined in the Mashraq, it re-emerged in Islamic Spain, which became the main Occidental scholarship and the cradle of European intellectual revival.[14] This culture and the dominance of merchants and administrators as a class were raised on an economic surplus that was largely based on intercontinental trade. Apart from Egypt, the scarcity of arable land and the inadequacy of rainfall meant that the scope of peasant cultivation was limited. As a result, long-distance trade played an essential part in the nature of class relationships in the Middle East, because it 'makes possible, through the monopoly of profit it permits, the transfer of part of the surplus from one society to another'.[15]

Two important consequences follow from this dependence on a transferred surplus. First, there is little incentive on the part of the dominant class to develop the productive forces of the social formation in order to increase a surplus. While banking and transportation facilities become highly developed, there is little expansion of basic technology. Accountancy and arithmetic flourished, but basic technological developments stagnated, apart from the development of clocks and waterwheels.[16] Secondly, a civilisation based on global trade is vulnerable to the disruption of trade routes brought about by nomadic dissidence or by the rise of competitors. Both the Maghreb and Mashraq were thus based on an unstable alliance between town and nomadic tribe, the relationship between the two being subject to what we might term 'the Khaldun effect'. In the Mashraq, this was further complicated by the periodic intrusion of Mongol invaders, Turks and other militarised tribes, most of whom, however, were quickly acculturated to Islamic practice. In summary, pre-modern Arabic culture was held together by the culture of urban clerics, merchants and courtiers whose economic dominance depended on long-distance trade:

> The latter was the basis for this class's alliance with the nomad tribes (its caravaneers) and for the isolation of the agricultural areas, which retained a distinct personality – linguistically (Berber) or in religion (Shiite) – but which did not play an important role in the system.[17]

This culture and economic system were sharply contrasted with the nature of the Egyptian social structure, in which an economic surplus extracted from peasants was the basis of the class structure.

In Egypt the state was directly involved in the organisation of the economy and the repression of the *fellahin*, because of the need for centralised regulation of irrigation, political control and the extraction of tributes from villages. Although Samir Amin argues that the exploitation of *fellahin* was on an individual basis, the weight of the evidence points to a system of communal production and taxation of villages, rather than individuals.[18] The state extracted both goods and services from these self-sufficient production units by means of extra-economic coercion. Villages rather than individuals were responsible for providing labour for irrigation, canals and other public works. The incorporation of Egypt into the world economy as a supplier of raw-cotton exports resulted in the dissolution of the village community, the development of private land rights, the concentration of land by agrarian capitalists, production by the nuclear family for the market, and the growth of peasant indebtedness with the introduction of mechanised production and modern fertilisers. Access to the land for peasants was now based on their ability to raise cash for the purchase of seeds and fertilisers, which in turn extended the social control of money-lenders and merchants. The control of peasants by the state now shifted from political-ideological coercion to direct economic subordination. At the same time, the economic functions of village craftsmen declined, as their occupational skills became increasingly redundant with the importation of modern technology.

The Egyptian economy has thus been transformed by two processes. In the nineteenth century, raw-material exports and manufactured imports made the economy exposed to the downward trend of cotton prices on the world market as the use of man-made fibres increased. In the twentieth century, import-substituting industrialisation has made the economy increasingly dependent on foreign investment, both Russian and European.[19] The effect of these transformations on the Egyptian class structure has been complex.[20] The traditional tax-farming estate-holders of pre-colonial Egypt were able to transform themselves into private owners of large estates, producing for the market and employing wage-labour. In short, incorporation into the world market created a class of agrarian capitalists, but this rural class did not develop the forces of production, because it was able to secure a surplus through the employment of cheap, abundant labour. The Egyptian rural capitalists invested their profits in land and personal consumption, rather than in industrial production. With the development of an urban, industrial capitalist class under Nasser and Sadat, a gap developed between the traditional ruling élite and the modern bourgeoisie in alliance with the civil service, army and political leadership. The creation of private ownership of land and the dissolution of the village commune as a productive unit alienated the majority of the peasantry from the soil without providing them with employment in urban industries. The landless peasantry, which constitutes three-quarters of the rural population, are forced to work irregularly either as agricultural workers or as migrant rural labourers. The peasants who have smallholdings find these continuously reduced by the need to purchase seeds, fertilisers and stock, and they are consequently forced to sell their labour power alongside the migrant worker. The consequence is that these 'masses are caught up in a process of proletarianization without being able to become proletarians'.[21] The result is a vicious circle. The inability of the peasant labour force to achieve complete subsistence and self-sufficient reproduction of the domestic unit compels peasants to secure irregular employment as wage-labourers. The abundant supply of cheap labour, however, compensates for the absence of modern technology and production processes. The gap is met by the state, which supplies limited technology in return for a surplus derived from the rural co-operatives, thereby sustaining the existing social relationships.[22] Clearly, the Lewis model of development on the basis of unlimited labour supplies does not operate in Egypt, not because of assumptions about the seasonality of employment, but because of the structure of relations of production.[23]

While rather similar patterns have developed in the Maghreb and Mashraq with their incorporation into the world economy, the situation in North Africa and the Fertile Crescent was complicated by the historical nature of global trade and the alliance of town and nomad. Although the decay of Islam and the arrival of a 'static society' are identified in the eleventh century by some authors,[24] more decisive changes took place between 1600 and 1800, coinciding with what Marshall Hodgson called the 'transmutation of the West' and with the disruption of traditional intercontinental trade roots.[25] The development of sea routes to Asia via India, the exploration of Africa, the growth of Atlantic trade and the establishment of European colonies were features of the increasing dominance of European naval power from the sixteenth century onwards. Intercontinental trade passed from Arab merchants to the British, Portuguese and Dutch merchant class. With the decline in the trade surplus, the merchant and urban civilisation of Islam went into decline. The consequences of this reversal were manifold: Islam broke down into a collection of competitive dynasties which possessed only a local unity; the great trading cities, especially in Persia, declined in size and importance; the *adib* culture of the courts became formal and imitative; the military capacity of Islam in eastern Europe was undermined; and finally, unequal trading arrangements through concessionary arrangements opened up Islamic markets to manufactured European commodities. The effects of colonial penetration via merchant capital between 1827 and 1862 were to undermine local manufacturing industry and petty commodity production, especially the textile enterprises of Lebanon, Syria and Egypt. Attempts at economic and social reform in Turkey and Egypt tended to increase national indebtedness on foreign bankers, which could only be solved through further loans and increased taxation.

European penetration of North Africa and the Middle East had a profound effect on the traditional relationship between urban populations, peasants and nomads. We have seen that in Egypt the creation of private property in land and the development of cotton production for the market by capitalist farming pushed the peasantry off the land without providing alternative employment in urban occupations. In Algeria, colonisation forced peasant farmers off the cultivated land of the plains and coastal regions, changing the precarious relationship between nomads and peasants. Demographic changes intensified the problem of population distribution, as Algeria's population increased from 3 to 6 million between the middle and the end of the nineteenth century. Rural over-population, urban unemployment and political disruption were the classic ingredients of the Algerian peasant revolution.[26] Throughout the Middle East, a combination of social changes have brought about the demise of pastoral nomadism.

Nomadic pastoral society refers to a form of economic subsistence that can be 'defined as the exploitation of a set of spatially dispersed vegetal resources, water, etc., by mobile herbivorous herds in search of their food'.[27] In nomadic societies, the herd is privately owned by family units, but access to the land and water is a communal right.[28] A nomadic economy presupposes secure access to pasture across traditional migration routes, and this security, in turn, requires some political relationship with adjacent sedentarised societies. Camel nomadism was characteristic of pastoral societies in the Sahara, Syrian and Arabian deserts, whereas transhumance was more common in Iran, Afghanistan and Baluchistan.[29] In the twentieth century, these nomadic communities have been subject to strong political and economic pressures, which have brought about a general process of sedentarisation. Nomads are regarded as an anachronism within the modern nation-state and as a vehicle for political opposition.[30] With the development of modern transport, the traditional camel market has collapsed. Alternative employment for nomads has been found in certain societies, such as Saudi Arabia with the development of oil fields.[31] The conversion of traditional tribal land into private property or the acquisition of such land by the state, as in the Egyptian Desert Law, has also had a profound impact on the movement of pastoral nomads.[32] The sedentarisation of pastoral nomads has, however, to be seen in the context of nationalist revivals and Islamic reform, namely, as part of a process of political unification in the face of western penetration.

The cultural response of Islam to the disruption and decline of traditional society can be seen in three stages. In the late nineteenth century, Islamic reformers attempted to come to terms with western capitalist culture by asserting that pure Islam was compatible with modern rational society. Islamic decadence was caused by foreign accretions and folk religiosity, which had corrupted the original message of the Prophet. This message was an active, ascetic call to humankind to face the challenge of social existence in a responsible this-worldly ethic. Mystical Sufism was seen as one significant medium of cultural decay. Paradoxically, the way forward was a return to scriptural, authentic and original koranic orthodoxy.[33] This cultural response to westernisation did in fact involve a thorough reinterpretation of Islam, which was, in principle, transformed into a democratic, active and modern ideology. In the second stage, Islamic reformism was overshadowed by more overtly national, secular creeds that regarded Islam as a personal faith and not the civil religion of an industrialising civilisation. The failure of nationalist ideology and politics has resulted in a third stage, in which populist Islam has come to prominence as a radical critique of both western secularism and authoritarian nationalism.[34] Although in societies like Iran, popular opposition to pro-western regimes was often inspired by the progressive doctrines of intellectuals like Ali Shariati, post-revolutionary Iran has witnessed a determined repression of workers, students and peasants by a regime which is unable to solve the economic and political problems of the current crisis.[35] The unity of Arab culture, based on urban merchants in alliance with nomadic tribes, was broken by the growth of western capitalism, based on the autonomy of the nation-state:

> the Arab world, because it was tributary and commercial, had to keep a more unified character despite the vicissitudes of history – and could not orient itself towards capitalism until it was integrated, by outside aggression, into the imperialist system dominated by Europe.[36]

No social class exists today which has such transnational loyalties and which can transcend the numerous regional, religious and ethnic interests dividing the Middle East.

In the context of the modern Middle East, it would be impossible to write as Warburton did over a century ago of the 'immutability' of the East. The region has been galvanised by capitalist development, revolution, cultural revival and war. Capitalism, as Marx predicted, has created a world in its own image, but Marx could not have foreseen how diverse and complex that global image would become. The traditional divisions of East/West, traditional/modern and backward/advanced make little sense in a world economy dominated by production of exchange values by capitalist enterprises for the market.

Marx also said that the present was subject to the dead hand of the past, and this is perhaps nowhere more true than in the Middle East, where the legacy of colonialism is oppressive. A new social stationariness may be developing which is characteristic of the post-colonial state. Colonial administrations developed extensive state bureaucracies to achieve political control and internal security. The post-colonial state provides patronage and employment in societies where traditional capitalist roles are underdeveloped. In Algeria and Iraq, the planned development of industrialisation has been blocked by the absence of foreign markets for its commodities. In the under-populated oil kingdoms of the desert, there is no local capacity to absorb the revenues from oil exports. In Pakistan and Bangladesh, chronic underdevelopment has been accompanied by a rigid military, bureaucratic alliance. In addition to Shiite and Sunni conflicts, the Islamic cultural region is deeply divided by national rivalry and competition. Internal class divisions are thus constantly reinforced by the external constraints of inequalities in the global economy. The class dynamic of peripheral regions within the global economy is now closely tuned to the dynamic processes of capital growth and decline.

Notes

1 For a comprehensive discussion, A. M. Bailey and J. R. Llobera (eds), *The Asiatic Mode of Production, Science and Politics*, London, 1981, Part one.
2 B. Chowdhury, 'A sociological study of the development of social classes and social structure of Bangladesh', unpublished doctoral thesis, University of Aberdeen, 1982.
3 K. Wittfogel, *Oriental Despotism, a Comparative Study of Total Power*, New Haven, 1957.
4 B. Hindess and P. Q. Hirst, *Pre-Capitalist Modes of Production*, London, 1975.
5 E. Mandel, *The Formation of the Economic Thought of Karl Marx*, London, 1977; U. Melotti, *Marx and the Third World*, London, 1977; G. Sofri, *Il Modo di Produzione asiatico: storia di una controversia marxista*, Turin, 1969.
6 F. Engels, 'On the history of early Christianity', in K. Marx and F. Engels, *On Religion*, Moscow, n.d., p. 317.
7 F. Baali and A. Wardi, *Ibn Khaldun and Islamic Thought-Styles, a social perspective*, London, 1981.
8 Ibn Khaldun, *The Muqaddimah, an introduction to history*, London, 1958, vol. 1, p. lxxiii.
9 J. S. Kahn and S. Llobera (eds), *The Anthropology of Pre-Capitalist Societies*, London, 1981.
10 E. Ashtor, *A Social and Economic History of the Near East in the Middle Ages*, London, 1976; E. W. Bovill, *The Golden Trade of the Moors*, Oxford, 1958; A. E. Kodsy and E. Lobel, *The Arab World and Israel*, New York and London, 1970; M. Lombard, *The Golden Age of Islam*, Amsterdam and Oxford, 1975.
11 S. Amin, *The Maghreb in the Modern World*, Harmondsworth, 1970; S. Amin, *Accumulation on a World Scale*, Hassocks, Sussex, 1974; S. Amin, *Unequal Development*, Hassocks, Sussex, 1976; S. Amin, *The Arab Nation*, London, 1978.
12 V. F. Costello, *Urbanization in the Middle East*, Cambridge, 1977.
13 M. G. S. Hodgson, *The Venture of Islam*, Chicago and London, vol. 1, 1974.
14 H. Corbin, *Histoire de la Philosophie Islamique*, Paris, 1964; T. F. Glick, *Islamic and Christian Spain in the Early Middle Ages*, Princeton, 1979; M. Fakhry, *A History of Islamic Philosophy*, New York, 1970; D. L. O'Leary, *How Greek Science Passed to the Arabs*, London, 1951.
15 Amin, *Unequal Development*, p. 17.

16 A. C. Littleton and B. S. Yarney (eds), *Studies in the History of Accounting*, London, 1956; R. W. Bulliet, *The Camel and the Wheel*, Harvard, 1975; J. Needham, L. Wang and D. Price, *Heavenly Clockwork*, Cambridge, 1960.
17 Amin, *The Arab Nation*, p. 21.
18 G. Baer, *A History of Landownership in Modern Egypt 1800–1950*, Oxford, 1962; G. Baer, *Studies in the Social History of Modern Egypt*, Chicago, 1965; G. Baer, 'The dissolution of the Egyptian village community', *Die Welt des Islams*, vol. 6 (1959), pp. 56–70; A. N. Poliak, *Feudalism in Egypt, Syria, Palestine and the Lebanon 1250–1900*, London, 1939.
19 P. Clawson, 'The development of capitalism in Egypt', *Khamsin*, vol. 9 (1981), pp. 77–116.
20 M. Hussein, *Class Conflict in Egypt 1945–1970*, New York and London, 1973.
21 ibid., p. 39.
22 G. Stauth, 'Subsistence production in rural Egypt', unpublished paper from Louvain-la-Neuve, Conference on Strategies of Development in the Arab World, 1978.
23 W. A. Lewis, *Theory of Economic Growth*, London, 1955. For a commentary, W. Elkan, *An Introduction to Development Economics*, Harmondsworth, 1973.
24 B. Lewis, 'The Arabs in eclipse', in C. M. Cipolla (ed.), *The Economic Decline of Empires*, London, 1970, pp. 104–20.
25 Hodgson, *The Venture of Islam*, vol. 3, pp. 179 ff.
26 E. R. Wolf, *Peasants*, Englewood Cliffs, NJ, 1966; E. R. Wolf, *Peasant Wars of the Twentieth Century*, London, 1971.
27 P. Bonte, 'Marxist theory and anthropological analysis: the study of nomadic pastoral societies', in Kahn and Llobera, *The Anthropology of Pre-Capitalist Societies*, p. 22.
28 F. Barth, *Models of Social Organization*, London, 1966.
29 R. Patai, 'Nomadism: Middle Eastern and central Asian', *Southwestern Journal of Anthropology*, vol. 7 (1951), pp. 401–14.
30 A. R. George, 'The nomads of Syria, end of a culture?' *Middle East International*, no. 22 (1973), pp. 21–2; H. V. Muhsam, 'Sedentarization of the Bedouin in Israel', *International Social Science Bulletin*, vol. 11 (1959), pp. 539–49.
31 A. R. George, 'Bedouin settlement in Saudi Arabia', *Middle East International*, no. 51 (1975), pp. 27–9.
32 A. R. George, 'Egypt's remaining nomads', *Middle East International*, no. 37 (1974) pp. 26–8.
33 B. S. Turner, *Weber and Islam, a critical study*, London, 1974.
34 G. H. Jansen, *Militant Islam*, London and Sydney, 1979.

35 M. M. J. Fischer, *Iran, from religious dispute to revolution*, Cambridge and London, 1980.

36 Amin, *The Arab Nation*, p. 23.

Name Index

Subject Index